SPINOZA'S ETHICS

PART I AND II

SPINOZA'S ETHICS

PART I AND II

A Platonic Commentary

BY

ALAN HART

LEIDEN
E. J. BRILL
1983

171
S75e-xh

88-2748

ISBN 90 04 06915 1

PRINTED IN THE NETHERLANDS BY E. J. BRILL

*To my family
and
my friends
here and there*

CONTENTS

COMMENTARY

PREFACE

Spinoza's philosophy is designed to be clear, precise, luminous, and convincing. It is all of these, yet, for some, it still presents difficulties. I believe that an aid to the perplexed can be found by comparing Spinoza's work with themes and insights found in Plato's later dialogues.

It is not my intention to prove that Spinoza studied Plato, adopted his dialectic, or accepted his philosophy. This is simply an attempt to clarify his metaphysics and epistemology by comparing his work to that of Plato as interpreted by modern commentators. This is not an exercise in tracing roots; it seeks only to improve comprehension and appreciation of Spinoza's genius by noting similarities with some of Plato's themes. In many ways, this is an old-fashioned book, one that seeks reverberations rather than analyses or proofs. If it serves to illuminate Spinoza's work to any extent whatsoever, that will be sufficient.

In the summer of 1974, The Council for Philosophic Studies and the National Endowment for the Humanities offered an Institute on Modern Philosophy. Professor Margaret D. Wilson directed the Institute, Professor E. M. Curley was one of the lecturers, and Professor T. C. Mark was a fellow participant. Each of these scholars graciously offered suggestions for revisions which resulted in an improvement of the manuscript. I am indebted to them not only for their advice and their wisdom in connection with this work, but for their own philosophical writings. The manuscript itself was initiated by the chiding of my brother, Bruce, who charged that I believed only in the oral tradition of philosophy. Professor Amelie O. Rorty saw the earliest version. Her gentle, yet incisive, comments on it, together with her consistent support and friendship through the calamities and the years, have been extraordinarily generous and sustaining.

Professor Milton H. Williams, Syracuse University, was the advisor for my thesis on Spinoza's theory of the attributes. He and Professor Glenn R. Morrow, The University of Pennsylvania, guided me into philosophy and remain my paradigms of gentlemen and scholars. They were what professors should be.

The University of Akron granted me a Summer Research Fellowship in 1975 which enabled me to devote an entire Summer to Spinoza. It would have been impossible to have completed the manuscript without that assistance. Mrs. Marianne Hall Brown suffered through many drafts in my handwriting and managed to produce a legible typescript without losing either her patience or her pleasant disposition.

Time devoted to scholarship and writing is time well-spent, but it is irreplaceable and is stolen from one's family. Lost forever are the moments I should have spent with Daniel and Jason, two very understanding persons who let me be a scholar when I should have been a father. Similarly, the necessary solitude removed me from the presence of Judith, who holds my universe together. Her unswerving belief that I am better than I am has been the basis for whatever I have accomplished that has been worthwhile.

INTRODUCTION

One of the persisting tasks of philosophy is to discover an interpretation of Spinoza that will improve our understanding of his philosophy and yet not produce more difficulties than it resolves. There have been a number of attempts at interpretation and analysis of Spinoza's works, but many of these more clearly indicate the philosophical commitment of the writer, or of the times, than they reflect Spinoza's thought. Thus, depending upon the scholar, one can find a Cartesian, Aristotelian, neo-Platonic, Maimonidean, Hegelian, or positivistic Spinoza. It is extraordinarily difficult to "see" Spinoza through his own lenses, to discover what he meant to say. With the hope that I may avoid some of the difficulties encountered by my philosophical predecessors, I shall argue that a Platonic interpretation, based primarily on the metaphysics and epistemology of the later dialogues, provides an interpretation that does resolve some problems in Spinoza scholarship. I believe that this will aid our understanding of Spinoza more thoroughly than do other views. I hope to escape an over-emphasis on Spinoza's debt to prior philosophers as well as avoid the claim that Spinoza's philosophy was absolutely innovative. The interpretation which I offer will indicate the genius of Spinoza himself insofar as he molds Plato's philosophy to accord with the philosophy and science of his time.

Some philosophers have found it difficult to identify the Spinozistic theme in the philosophy of Spinoza. That is to say, some commentators can find only echoes of others' philosophies in Spinoza's works to the exclusion of any innovations by Spinoza himself. In his excellent account of different interpretations of Spinoza, in Chapter I of his *Spinoza's Metaphysics: An Essay in Interpretation,* E. M. Curley says, "Wolfson takes us on an exciting philosophical journey, beyond Descartes and the rest of Spinoza's contemporaries back through the medievals to Aristotle, in an attempt to reconstruct the *Ethica More Scholastica Rabbinicoque Demonstrata* which must have preceded, in Spinoza's mind, the *Ethica Ordine Geometrico Demonstrata* which was left us at Spinoza's death."[1] Haserot says of Wolfson's interpretation: "In this account the supposition that Spinoza might have exercised any independence of judgement seems to be taken as unthinkable. *Ethics* I is considered a restatement, scarcely more than a summary of the conceptions of his medieval predecessors. ... In view of the explicit character of Spinoza's statements, this interpretation must appear doubtful."[2]

There are four major problems in Spinoza's *Ethics*, Part I which must be addressed. First, what is his notion of substance? Second, how is substance related to its attributes? Third, how are the attributes related to each other? Fourth, what is the relation of attributes to modes? These are the problems which have bedeviled commentators. Each of the former attempts to clarify Spinoza's philosophy has failed to deal with one or more of these problems successfully.

As noted above, Wolfson interprets Spinoza on an Aristotelian model. "He was, many views to the contrary not withstanding, a hard headed, clear minded empiricist, like most of the medievals and like Aristotle."[3] This view of Spinoza leads Wolfson to identify substance with the *summum genus* of Aristotle and to see the finite modes as individuals which are related in the Aristotelian manner to the highest genus. Curley notes that Wolfson's view that all knowledge is to be found in a species-genus relation entails that "Spinoza's substance is inconceivable, and its essence undefinable, and hence unknowable."[4] However, Spinoza states that we do have adequate knowledge of God, or substance, and the attributes. Brehier notes that the Aristotelian doctrine of substance as underlying qualities or attributes also is not to be found in Spinoza. He says, "Spinoza's God or substance is not Aristotelian substance, the hidden essence of things beyond the reach of mind, which is limited to apprehending properties and accidents."[5] So the Aristotelian views of substance—either as *summum genus* or as unknownable substratum—is at odds with Spinoza's account of substance.

The only commonality between Spinoza and Aristotle to be found in their definitions of substance is that of independence. Aristotle tells us that only substance can "exist apart"; all the other categories depend on it.[6] He also notes that there is a substance which is eternal, immovable, and separate from sensible things.[7] Many commentators believe that "existing apart" means "separate from". Spinoza, however, believes that substance is independent but is not separate from the other things. For Spinoza, God is the immanent cause of the universe, of *natura naturata*, not transcendent, or separate from the world of nature.[8] Thus, here is another significant difference between Spinoza and Aristotelian interpretations.

A further difference between Aristotle and Spinoza is to be found in their views of extension. Aristotle tells us that extension is a continuum, and Spinoza would agree with this view if a continuum is seen to be indivisible. For Spinoza, extension is indivisible as are all the attributes of substance.[9] If one identifies extension with matter, as Descartes does on occasion, one will then assert that extension is divisible. Aristotle says "everything which has not matter is indivisible", and this entails that material things are divisible.[10] For Spinoza, extended objects, finite modes, are perceived to be divisible, but really extension *per se* is indivisible. This, too, is a difference from Aristotle which must be accommodated by the Aristotelian interpretators of Spinoza.

Wolfson is correct in noting that finite modes are individuals for Spinoza. However, the relation of individual to species to genus to *summum genus* in Aristotle is not that of finite mode to substance in Spinoza. Indeed, Spinoza denies the existence of species and *genera* which he calls universals. These are, for Spinoza, terms which "signify ideas in the highest degree confused".[11] There is, of course, a relation between substance and mode for Spinoza, but it is not the relation of part to whole nor of particular to universal. Thus, Wolfson's view does not serve to clarify Spinoza, nor does it appear to coincide with Spinoza's own account.

Still, there is an empirical or Aristotelian influence to be found in Spinoza's work. Nowhere does Spinoza deny the reality of finite modes, or individuals, for example. Nowhere does he assert that the *only* reality is God, substance, or nature. Copleston agrees with Wolfson's emphasis on Spinoza's empiricism. Copleston says, "... it seems to the present writer that however non-Aristotelian Spinoza may be in some respects, he has more affinity with Aristotle's intellectualist view of human perception than with Plotinus' sublime concept of the flight of the alone to the Alone. ... Knowledge of God does not seem to mean for him a state of ecstatic union in which the subject and object distinction is transcended."[12] Thus, the Aristotelian interpretation of Spinoza does coincide with Spinoza's view of the reality of particular modes, but it conflicts with Spinoza's view of substance and its relation to attributes and modes as well as with his view of knowledge.

For some commentators, there appears to be a striking analogy between Spinoza's philosophy and neo-Platonism. They see Spinoza's God as similar to the One. His attributes, immediate infinite modes, mediate infinite mode, and finite modes appear to be similar to emanations of the One. The progress of the mind in its journey to unification with the One in an "intellectual love of God" has been seen as similar to Spinoza's description of the intellectual love of God in his *Ethics*. Brehier notes that "Spinozism bears an external resemblance to the Neo-Platonic theosophies that have flourished throughout history."[13]

Carl Gebhardt noted the Platonic and neo-Platonic influences in Spinoza. He observed that *The Dialogues of Love* by Leone Ebreo (Leo Hebraeus, Judah Abrabanel, or Judah Abravenel) were found in Spinoza's library after his death.[14] However, the Platonism of Ebreo, while it is based upon the *Symposium*, was really infused with neo-Platonic doctrines. According to Nelson, the *Dialogues* argued that Plato's theory of *Eros* in the *Symposium* indicates that sort of true love which brings happiness to man.[15] In Plato, the love of Beauty was the true goal of the lover. The Form ''Beauty'' is eternal and thus in some sense ''divine''. In neo-Platonism, there is a move to identify Beauty with the Good and with Being. The goal of the lover, then, is transformed into a search for unification of the soul with the source of Beauty, Truth, and Goodness-God or the One. Ebreo uses the term *amore intellectuale* to describe the highest goal of the soul—the intellectual love of God. Gebhardt notes that the *amor intellectualis* is also the highest goal of Spinoza's *Ethics* and proceeds with his argument.

The unification of the soul with God is accomplished by means of an ecstatic, direct, inexpressible experience for the neo-Platonists. Gebhardt argues that Spinoza's third sort of knowledge—intuition—is identical to this ecstacy. Intuition is not ''supernatural'' for Gebhardt, it is rather ''super-rational''—over reason, but not contrary to reason.[16] The gradation of experience, rational thought, and intuition (in Spinoza) is in agreement with Plotinus' gradation in his mystical theory of knowledge. Plotinus has placed intuition, the beholding of God, the *Geniessen der Dinge*, as the source of knowledge of the mystics.[17] Gebhardt claims that Spinoza asserted this mystical doctrine of intuition because of the ''perceived and admitted impossibility of mastering reality by reason.''[18] Thus, for Gebhardt one of the main indications of Spinoza's neo-Platonism is demonstrated by his intuitively achieved intellectual love of God.

While it is clear that Spinoza does value intuition more highly than reason, and while it is true that the ethical goal of Spinoza is an intellectual love of God, there are a number of difficulties with Gebhardt's interpretation. First, the One of neo-Platonism differs from God or Nature of Spinoza insofar as the One is distinct from Nature or its emanations, while God is identical to Nature and is constituted by its attributes for Spinoza. Second, the object of the *intellectual* love is eminently knowable for Spinoza, while the object of the intellectual *love* of Ebreo and the neo-Platonists is unknowable but awful and adorable. Third, there is no doctrine of emanation in Spinoza. The attributes are not effects, products, or emanations of God; rather, they constitute the essence of God. Fourth, extension is one of the constituent attributes of God, and this doctrine is equally abhorrent to neo-Platonism, Scholasticism, Cartesianism, and Judaism. Fifth, the intuition of Spinoza is immediate, direct awareness, similar to Descartes' definition of intuition and to Plato's *noesis*. There is no mention of rapture or ecstasy in Spinoza, Descartes or Plato. The difference between reason and intuition is not an emotional difference, for

Spinoza, but rather a difference between mediate and immediate, discursive and direct knowledge.

The primary criticism of Gebhardt's interpretation is that he bases the relation between Spinoza and neo-Platonism on emotional, mystical similarity. That is to say, he stresses the *amor* of *amor intellectualis*. While neo-Platonism and Ebreo stress the emotional aspect of intuition, neither Plato, Descartes, nor Spinoza do so. After all, it is *scientia intuitiva*, intuitive *knowledge*, which Spinoza values as true and adequate knowledge. To affirm that Spinoza is a mystic because he employs intuition is mistaken. It seems to me that mysticism is defined as a direct, mysterious, ineffable emotive experience which is inexpressible and extremely private. The only similarity which I can perceive between the intuition of the mystic and that of Spinoza is to be found in the fact that both experiences are direct and simple (unanalyzable) immediate experiences. However, it should be noted that Spinoza's examples of intuition are mathematical, not inspirational or poetical. The goal of Spinoza is a mathematical intuition of Nature, not a unification of the individual with an unknowable One in a moment of rapture.

While it is doubtless true that Spinoza knew the writings of Plotinus, neo-Platonists, and Ebreo, there is no necessary ground for inferring that either Spinoza's metaphysics or his ethics is neo-Platonic. Wolfson says, "On the whole, Leo Hebraeus' (Ebreo) influence upon Spinoza has been unduly exaggerated. The passages from the *Dialoghi d'Amore* examined by us in connection with Spinoza have all proved to be philosophic commonplaces. Nor has it been possible to establish any direct *literary* relationship between these passages and Spinoza."[19] As Brehier says, "... Spinoza is far removed from the atmosphere of vague experiences, devotion, asceticism, and enthusiasm traditionally associated with divine love...."[20] Indeed, in spite of Gebhardt's efforts, the relation of Ebreo to Spinoza is not demonstrated but is rather tenuous.

The philosopher with whom Spinoza is most often compared and contrasted is Descartes. Some view Spinoza as a Cartesian, while others view Descartes as a secret Spinozist. Spinoza was well-versed in the Cartesian philosophy, wrote a work explaining it, and taught it. He appropriated the Cartesian terminology of substance, attribute, mode, intuition, and notion, but he clarified these terms. He pursued the implications of their definitions and, generally, emphasized the reason to be found in Cartesian philosophy as opposed to the voluntarism.[21] "On the one hand, Spinozism is defined as a revised and systematized Cartesianism. ... Spinoza ... employed Cartesianism in order to facilitate the expression of a radically different vision."[22] Copleston,[23] Curley,[24] and Wolf[25] also write of the agreements and antagonisms between Spinoza and Cartesianism. Still, one can initiate an understanding of Spinoza by contrasting him with Descartes.

Perhaps the most fundamental difference between Spinoza and Descartes is to be found in their concepts of God, nature, and substance. Descartes maintains that there is a separation, distinction, and difference between God and nature. He sees God as Creator of nature, as infinite whereas nature is indefinite, as independent whereas nature is dependent. For Spinoza, God is not only *natura naturans* but also *natura naturata.* There is no separation between the active, creating, independent God or Nature and the dependent, less active individuals for Spinoza. "Whatever is, is in God, and nothing can either be or be conceived without God."[26]

Descartes is not always clear about his definition of substance, sometimes arguing that it is that in which properties inhere[27] and sometimes defining it as that which is independent.[28] Descartes and Spinoza agree that in the univocal sense of the term there is only one substance, God.[29]

Descartes also states that thought and extension are two relative substances which depend only on God. He notes that extension taken generally, or *per se*, is a substance; particular bodies are not substances but are only "certain configuration(s) of members and of other similar accidents."[30] There is no substance of thought taken generally. Each individual mind is a relative substance. Speaking of the two relative substances, Descartes says that "not only are their natures different but even in some respects contrary to one another."[31] Still, though independent and "contrary", there is a causal relation between the modes "mind" and "body".

> ...I declare that the whole of the perplexity involved in these questions arises entirely from a false supposition that can by no manner of means be proved, viz. that if the soul and the body are two substances of diverse nature, that prevents them from being capable of acting on one another; for on the contrary, those who admit the existence of real accidents, like heat, weight, and so forth, do not doubt that these accidents have the power of acting on the body, and nevertheless there is more difference between them and it, i.e. between accidents and a substance, than there is between two substances.[32]

Spinoza agrees that the mind and body are two different modes of two distinct attributes, but seen *sub specie aeternitatis*, mind and body are "one and the same thing expressed in two different ways."[33] There is *no* causal relation between mind and body, because mind and body are modes of different attributes. Spinoza says there can be no connection between them on a modal level because "if two things have nothing in common with one another, one cannot be the cause of the other."[34] Thus, causation requires commonality or similarity for Spinoza, but not for Descartes.[35] For Spinoza, thought and extension cannot affect one another, so neither can their modes affect one another.

There are no relative substances for Spinoza. There is only one independent substance which is absolutely infinite. There are an infinite number of attributes, two of which are thought and extension. There is a significant difference between relative substances in Descartes and the attributes in Spinoza. The attributes do not depend for their existence upon God, substance, or Nature. The attributes are not caused by substance. The attributes *are* God; they constitute the essence of God.[36]

Both Spinoza and Descartes would agree that mind and body, modes of thought and extension, are dependent upon God. Although Descartes states that minds are substances, and Spinoza would disagree, both would agree mind and body depend on God. Spinoza says that these modes are "in" God or Nature.

Descartes and Spinoza share a methodology that values mathematical certainty, intuition, a reliance upon simple and common notions and clear definitions. For all the Continental Rationalists, the concept of God, or Being, is simple, adequate, innate and *a priori*. All the rationalists value intuition and reason, but they also find perception is necessary for one's existence.

While Spinoza and Descartes share problems in philosophy, they greatly differ in their solutions to the problems. It is true that a comparison of Spinoza with Descartes is one method of attempting to understand Spinoza, but it gives us a Spinoza who is reacting to Descartes rather than an active Spinoza who was developing his own philosophy.

H. H. Joachim has written two extended studies of Spinoza's philosophy, one concerned with the *Tractatus*[37] and one concerned with the *Ethics*.[38] Joachim presents a view of Spinoza wherein Spinoza struggles with an absolute idealism which cannot account for diversity. Joachim says, "There is a fatal trend in Spinoza's philosophy towards abstraction, in spite of all his struggles towards the conception of a concrete unity. Thus, things in their temporal being—the actual world of the perceptive consciousness—either turn into illusions, or slip back into the world of eternal timeless necessity, the world of science."[39] The disappearance of finite modes into "mere illusions" due to an "illusory apprehension of a mind" is a result of Spinoza's conception of God or Nature as an abstract unity, according to Joachim.[40] "From an ultimate point of view there are no parts, no things, no persons."[41]

For Joachim, if God is a One, it cannot be a Many. If God is constituted by infinite attributes or infinite numbers of finite modes, then

God cannot be conceived of as a unity. If God is Extension "he would not be Thought, in being Thought he would *not* be Extension. Extension and Thought would lie together in his being and his nature would hold them conjoined, but not intelligibly as one."[42] "The fact seems to be that Spinoza, while struggling to express the conception of God as concretely One, constantly lapses into language which implies God's unity is abstract. So far as the latter tendency controls his expositions, differences are dismissed as illusions, and his theory becomes hopelessly unintelligible and inconsistent."[43] There are then, for Joachim, two competing and contradictory "tendencies" in Spinoza: the concrete unity of God and the reality of differing attributes and their finite modes is inconsistent with the abstract unity of God and the illusion of differing attributes and their finite modes.

I shall argue that Spinoza's God is not the God of an idealistic abstract unity nor is it the "concrete unity" of a God which differs from the attributes and finite modes. It is true that there is an apparent difficulty of One and Many on two levels in Spinoza's philosophy. On the level of God or Nature and the many attributes, one can resolve the difficulty by an appeal to Plato's account of the relation between the Five Great Kinds in the *Sophist*. The problem of negation (Thought is *not* Extension, and Extension is *not* Thought) can be resolved by Plato's account of "other" in the *Sophist*. Plato's accounts do not entail either an abstract unity or a unity composed of conjoined parts, nor does Spinoza's God fit into the nineteenth century views of "abstract" or "concrete" entities.

The problem of the One and the Many on the level of Nature and finite modes is also not a problem for Spinoza himself. It's true that finite modes are dependent effects of Nature and that they are apprehended by imagination or perception.[44] It is not true, however, that Spinoza refers to them as "illusions". Finite modes are real, but of a different sort of reality than God or Nature, the attributes, and the infinite modes. The latter kinds of beings are infinite and causal while finite modes are expressions of Nature. While our knowledge of them *may* be a source of error, it is not necessary that such knowledge be erroneous or illusory. Spinoza does not assert that finite modes are not real, nor does he assert that one cannot have true knowledge of them.

I shall argue that the resolution of the "difficulty" between God or Nature and finite modes can be found in terms analogous to Allen's treatment of the relation between Plato's Forms and particulars.

This brief review of some prior interpretations of Spinoza has indicated some inadequacies. Contemporary philosophers also see Spinoza as a philosopher of science and naturalism.[45] Curley says, "Just as Joachim saw Spinoza through lenses ground by Hegel and Bradley, so I have seen him through those ground by Russell, Moore, and Wittgenstein."[46] While contemporary interpretations of Spinoza are interesting, one may wonder if these do not sacrifice Spinoza's own conception of his work for a relevance or intelligibility peculiar to our own modern understanding of what philosophy is and should be. At least the Aristotelian, neo-Platonic, and Cartesian views of Spinoza are concepts that Spinoza himself might have been comfortable with.

It is my argument that a proper model for interpreting Spinoza is to be found in Plato's philosophy, not in neo-Platonism, not in Aristotelian philosophy, but in the philosophy of Plato's later dialogues. There have been scattered allusions to Plato in other commentators, but none, so far as I know, has attempted a Platonic interpretation.

F. S. Haserot says:

> Spinoza is not a William of Occam nor is he a modern semantic positivist. The philosopher to whom he is closest both in his method and in his ontology is Plato. Certain features of Platonism he would not have accepted, e.g., Plato's cosmology, but so far as the eternity and immutability of the elements of rational universality are concerned, the two philosophers are one. Spinoza did not refer to these elements in the same language, or always with the same special applications, as did Plato but that they are present in his conceptions is a consequence implied in the rational character of the conceptions themselves.[47]

Curley also refers to the Platonism of Spinoza in his works,[48] and notes the "Platonic overtones" in his response to Williamson.[49] Of course, Gebhardt in his work on Platonism and Spinoza also refers to Plato, but this is the Plato of neo-Platonism.

There are some difficulties in offering a Platonic interpretation. In the list of books found in Spinoza's library after his death, we find none which have been written by Plato.[50] This does not mean, however, that Spinoza never read any of Plato's works. We know that there are books that he did read and to which he refers in his works which were not found in his library. There is a persistent rumor that several of the books owned by Spinoza were given to Dr. Schuller prior to his death in partial payment for his medical bills. This rumor is mentioned by Bowne,[51] Wolfson,[52] Wolf.[53] J. G. Van der Bend[54] also mentions a rumor that friends of Spinoza obtained some of his books either before or after his death. These rumors are founded upon Freudenthal's comment that Spinoza's "friends probably took a part of his philosophical library because ... they had a greater claim on his estate than his legal heirs who were strangers who had hostilely opposed him during his life time."[55] It is not necessary to assert that Spinoza did in fact have those books in his library in order for us to argue that a Platonic commentary is a useful explanatory device for Spinoza's work. It would be sufficient simply to point out the consistency of this interpretation and its aid in understanding Spinoza. The fact that one finds no text of Plato in Spinoza's library does not prove that Spinoza was unaware or had not read Plato's works.

An argument against a Platonic interpretation might better be based on the evaluation of Plato found in Spinoza's letter of October, 1674 to Hugo Boxel:

> The authority of Plato, Aristotle, and Socrates has not much weight with me. I should have been surprised had you mentioned Epicurus, Democritus, Lucretius, or any one of the Atomists, or defenders of the atoms. It is not surprising that those who invented occult qualities, Intentional Species, substantial Forms, and a thousand other trifles, should have devised spectres and ghosts, and put their faith in old women, in order to weaken the authority of Democritus.[56]

This letter can be interpreted in a number of ways. First, one might stress that this is a letter opposed to accepting the *authority* of any philosopher. Spinoza is, perhaps, emphasizing the independence of his philosophy from that of any prior philosopher. That is to say, he does not wish to garner acceptance for his philosophy by appealing to the philosophy of either Plato or Aristotle, as was the wont of some of the medieval philosophers. Secondly, it should be noted that this letter is directed to Boxel who had inquired concerning the existence of disembodied spirits, and Spinoza maintains in his philosophy that the human mind and body are one and the same thing. Spinoza, then, is merely casting doubt upon these superstitions. Third, the "occult qualities", "intentional species", "substantial forms", are things to which Spinoza owes no allegiance. With the exception of substantial forms, Plato himself does not owe allegiance to these strange philosophical entities. It is my belief that the doctrine of substantial forms to which Spinoza is taking exception is a doctrine of forms as used in the Aristotelian sense to explain scientific phenomena. Here, too, I believe Spinoza and Plato would be in agreement. That forms exist, are eternal, and are immutable is something which Plato, of course, maintains. However, Spinoza himself asserts the eternity and immutability of his substance, attributes, and immediate infinite modes.

Furthermore, Spinoza does not accept the teleological causation that is to be found in the philosophy of the seventeenth century. Both Plato and Aristotle, of course, did accept final causation, but Spinoza and Descartes eschew such explanations of natural phenomena. Spinoza's acceptance of only efficient causation may be one reason why this letter is one of approval for the atomists.

At any rate, whether or not Spinoza had Plato's books in his library, and whether or not Spinoza had any respect for Plato's philosophy, are not the issues in providing an interpretation of Spinoza. An interpretation of a philosopher requires only that the interpretation improves our understanding, is consistent, and does not violate any of the tenets of the philosophy in question. That is to say, if a Platonic commentary of Spinoza aids our understanding of his work without forcing Spinoza into inconsistencies, or producing more difficulties than it resolves, then it can be argued that the interpretation is successful, and, perhaps, even interesting and enlightening.

To understand Spinoza's philosophy in itself one must carefully read and analyze his works. Only then should one attempt a comparison with other philosophers or philosophical systems. In the following pages, I shall be providing a careful analysis of the following topics of Spinoza: Substance and its relation to the Attributes, and Attribute to Mode Relations. After each of these topics, I shall provide a Platonic commentary in the hope that it may elucidate Spinoza's work. At the conclusion of this part of the book, I shall attempt to summarize the Platonic themes in Spinoza and Spinoza's innovative use of them.

NOTES

[1] E. M. Curley, *Spinoza's Metaphysics: An Essay in Interpretation* (Cambridge: Harvard University Press, 1969), p. 28; hereafter cited as Curley, *Spinoza*.

[2] F. S. Haserot, "Spinoza's Definition of Attribute," *Philosophical Review*, 62 (1953), 508n.; hereafter cited as Haserot, "Attribute."

[3] H. A. Wolfson, "Spinoza's Definition of Substance and Mode," *Chronicon Spinozanum* [The Hague], 1 (1921), 110. Wolfson's early view here is not significantly altered in his later work, *The Philosophy of Spinoza*.

[4] Curley, *Spinoza*, p. 30.

[5] E. Brehier, *The History of Philosophy: The Seventeenth Century*, trans. W. Baskin (Chicago: University of Chicago Press, 1966), p. 167; hereafter cited as Brehier.

[6] Aristotle, *Introduction to Aristotle*, ed. R. McKeon (New York: Modern Library, 1947), p. 274; hereafter cited as *Aristotle*.

[7] *Aristotle*, p. 286.

[8] B. Spinoza, *Spinoza: Selections*, ed. J. Wild (New York: Charles Scribner's Sons, 1930), p. 117, El, Prop. 18; hereafter cited as Wild.

[9] Wild, p. 106, El, Prop. 12.

[10] *Aristotle*, p. 292.

[11] Wild, p. 185, E2, Prop. 40, Schol. 1.

[12] F. C. Copleston, "Spinoza as Metaphysician," in *Spinoza: Essays in Interpretation*, ed. M. Mandelbaum and E. Freeman (La Salle, Illinois: Open Court, 1975), p. 219; hereafter cited as Copleston.

[13] Brehier, p. 160.

[14] Carl Gebhardt, "Spinoza und der Platonismus," *Chronicon Spinozanum* [The Hague], 1 (1921), 179; hereafter cited as Gebhardt, "Spinoza."

[15] J. C. Nelson, *Renaissance Theory of Love—The Context of Giordano Bruno's Ennoia Furori* (New York: Columbia University Press, 1958).

[16] Gebhardt, "Spinoza," p. 228.

[17] *Ibid.*

[18] Gebhardt, "Spinoza," p. 229.

[19] H. A. Wolfson, *The Philosophy of Spinoza* (Cambridge: Harvard University Press, 1934), II, 277; hereafter cited as Wolfson.

[20] Brehier, p. 161.

[21] I argue in the second part that Spinoza adopted the representative epistemology of Descartes, including his concepts of objective Reality and formal Reality.

[22] A. G. A. Balz, *Cartesian Studies* (New York: Columbia University Press, 1951), p. 218. I argue that in a similar manner, Spinoza used and transmuted Plato's metaphysics and epistemology.

[23] Copleston, pp. 229-231.

[24] Curley, *Spinoza*, pp. 156-157.

[25] B. Spinoza, *The Correspondence of Spinoza*, trans. A. Wolf, (New York: Lincoln MacVeagh, Dial Press, 1927), pp. 31-32; hereafter cited as Wolf, *Correspondence*.

[26] Wild, p. 108, E1, Prop. 15.

[27] R. Descartes, *Philosophical Works of Descartes*, trans. E. S. Haldane and G. R. T. Ross (New York: Dover Publications, Inc., 1955), II, 53, 98; hereafter cited as H. R.

[28] H. R., I, 239; H. R., II, 101.

[29] H. R., I, 239.

[30] H. R., I, 141.

[31] H. R., I, 141; R. Descartes, *Œuvres Philosophique*, ed. F. Alquie, II (Paris: Editions Garnier Frères, 1967), 400: "... en sorte que leurs natures ne sont pas seulement reconnues diverses, mais même en quelques façons contraires." Hereafter cited as Alquie.

[32] H. R., II, 132; Alquie, II, 848: "Mais je vous dirai à vous que toute la difficulté qu'elles contiennent ne procède que d'une supposition qui est fausse, et qui ne peut aucunement etre prouvée, à savoir que si l'ame et les corps sont deux substances de diverse nature, cela les empêche de pouvoir agir l'une contre l'autre; car au contraire ceux qui admettent des accidents reels, comme la chaleur, la pesanteur, et semblables, ne doutent point que ces accidents ne puissent agir contre le corps; et toute-fois il y a plus de différence entre eux et lui, c'est-a-dire entre des accidents et une substance, qu'il n'y a entre deux substances."

[33] Wild, p. 149, E2, Prop. 7.

[34] Wild, p. 96, E1, Prop. 3.

[35] This difference harks back to the difference between the pre-Socratic Empedocles, who said "like affects like" and the pre-Socratic Anaxagoras who argued that "unlikes affect unlikes."

[36] Wild, p. 94, E1, Def. 4.

[37] H. H. Joachim, *Spinoza's Tractatus de Intellectus Emendatione* (Oxford: Clarendon Press, 1940); hereafter cited as Joachim, *TdIE*.

[38] H. H. Joachim, *A Study of the Ethics of Spinoza* (New York: Russell & Russell, 1964; rpt. 1901); hereafter cited as Joachim, *Ethics*.

[39] Joachim, *Ethics*, p. 96.

[40] Joachim, *Ethics*, p. 113.

[41] Joachim, *Ethics*, p. 124.

[42] Joachim, *Ethics*, p. 106.

[43] Joachim, *Ethics*, p. 115.

[44] It should be noted that "imagination" is not "fantasy" for Spinoza. A misinterpretation of "imagination" might lead one to assert that objects of imagination are phantasms or illusions, but that is not true for Spinoza. An account of imagination in Spinoza is offered in Part II.

[45] S. Alexander, *Philosophical and Literary Pieces* (London: MacMillan & Co., 1939), pp. 334-335.

[46] Curley, *Spinoza*, p. 78.

[47] F. S. Haserot, "Spinoza and the Status of Universals," *The Philosophical Review*, 59 (1950), 492; hereafter cited as Haserot, "Spinoza and Universals."

[48] Curley, *Spinoza*, p. 156.

[49] E. M. Curley, "Reply to Williamson," *Australasian Journal of Philosophy*, 51 (1973), 162.

[50] J. Freudenthal, *Die Lebensgeschichte Spinoza's in Quellenschriften, Urkunden und Nichtamtlichen Nachrichten* (Leipzig: 1899), pp. 160-164; hereafter cited as Freudenthal.

[51] L. Bowne, *Blessed Spinoza* (New York: MacMillan Company, 1932), p. 317.

[52] A. Wolfson, *Spinoza—A life of Reason* (New York: Philosophical Library, 1969), p. 294.

[53] A. Wolf, *Spinoza's Short Treatise on God, Man, and His Well-Being* (London: Adam & Charles Black, 1910), p. xcvi.

[54] Herman De Dijn, "Historical Remarks on Spinoza's Theory of Definitions," in *Spinoza on Knowing, Being and Freedom*, ed. J. G. van der Bend (Assen, The Netherlands: Van Gorcum & Co. B. V., 1974), p. 48.

[55] Freudenthal, p. 287.

[56] Wild, "To Mr. Hugo Boxel," October 1674, Letter 56, p. 457.

CHAPTER ONE

ETHICS: PART I

METAPHYSICS

In presenting his philosophy by means of the "geometrical order" in the *Ethics*, Spinoza quite properly begins each book with a list of definitions of terms to be examined or used therein. In common with his rationalistic contemporaries, Spinoza accepted the concept of real, or formal, definitions. These definitions describe, or analyze, the essence or nature of the definiendum; they are meant to reveal the real nature of the object being defined.[1]

Spinoza says there are two sorts of definitions:

> You do not distinguish between a definition which serves to explain a thing whose essence only is sought, and concerning whose essence alone there is doubt, and a definition which is put forward only to be examined. For the former, since it has a determinate object ought to be true; the latter need not be. Therefore, a definition either explains a thing as it exists outside the understanding, and then it ought to be true, and does not differ from a proposition, or an axiom, except insofar as it deals only with the essence of things or states, whereas an axiom is wider since it extends to eternal truths. Or else a definition explains a thing as it is conceived or can be conceived by us: and then, indeed, it differs from an axiom and a proposition because all that is required of it is merely that it should be conceived, and not, like an axiom, that it should be conceived as true. Therefore that definition which is not conceivable is bad.[2]

In Letter IV to Oldenburg, Spinoza notes that "the existence of a thing defined does not follow from the definition of every kind of thing; but follows only ... from the definition or idea of some attribute, that is, ... of a thing which is conceived through itself and in itself.... Every definition, or clear and distinct idea, is true."[3] Furthermore, in Letter X to De Vries he says:

> You ask me whether we need experience to know whether the definition of some attribute is true.... We only need Experience in the case of whatever cannot be deduced from the definition of a thing, as, for instance, the existence of Modes: for this cannot be deduced from the definition of a thing. But we do not need experience in the case of those things whose existence is not distinguished from their essence and therefore follow from their definition. Indeed, no experience will ever be able to teach us this: for experience does not teach us the essence of things....[4]

Spinoza also discussed definitions in his *Treatise on the Improvement of the Understanding* and notes that "everything should be conceived, either SOLELY THROUGH ITS ESSENCE OR THROUGH ITS PROXIMATE CAUSE."[5] So the definition of a created thing must include its proximate cause; if the definition is of an uncreated thing, it must include the idea of a cause—that is, the thing must not need explanation by anything outside itself.[6]

These doctrines of definition are retained in the *Ethics*. There, Spinoza notes that definitions are concerned exclusively with the essence or nature of the thing to be defined; that everything requires a cause; and that the cause is either to be found in the essence of the thing defined or outside the thing.[7] Here, too, one must note the relation between deduction, causation, and existence. What can be deduced from a definition can be asserted actually to be a property of the thing and can be said to be "caused" by the thing.

Some important points are entailed by Spinoza's view of definition. First, all "good" definitions are non-contradictory; they can be conceived, but this consistency, or compossibility, of properties or attributes does not necessarily entail existence. Only those non-contradictory definitions which "explain things outside of our understanding" need be true, or refer to existing beings. Some definitions are merely proposed for the sake of an argument, or as a hypothesis, and these need only be consistent. Second, if one offers a definition which purports to be true, or to refer to some existing thing, that definition should either contain in its list of essences its own sufficient cause, or it must contain a reference to its proximate cause. Third, although definitions reveal the essences of things, only definitions of self-caused things are sufficient to prove to us the existence of things. Definitions of finite modes give us the essence of things, and their proximate cause, but experience is required for us to conclude that they exist. That is to say, the *essence* of a finite mode does not include its own proximate cause from which its existence can be deduced. So, we can only be certain of the existence of things whose definition, or whose essence, is such that one can deduce their existence. Only those things whose essence contains their own sufficient cause, only necessary things, can be known to exist without experience. Definitions are true if they are distinct and clear, non-contradictory, and list essences which contain existence or refer to the proximate cause of the existence of the thing. There is, for Spinoza, a close relation between the *truth* of a definition of a thing, its cause, and its existence. Definitions of things *must* contain a reference to a cause, must be causal and conceivable, if they are to be true and not merely stipulative. Definitions which are *only* conceivable and not causal, may not be true; that is to say, they may not refer to existent things. One can *deduce* the existence of necessary things from their definition.

Deduction and causation are one and the same thing for Spinoza. If one cannot deduce the existence of a thing from its definition, then it is a contingent being. Note that contingency is due to our lack of knowledge of the proximate cause of the thing; it is a result of a defect in our knowledge and is not a modality of existence for things. All existing things exist necessarily for Spinoza, but *we* may not be able to ascertain their cause. For contingent things, one needs not only a definition which provides only non-contradictory essences but one also needs experience. Experience is required to ''prove'' the existence of finite modes or contingent things. For Spinoza, all definitions must be consistent, must provide non-contradictory essences. However, all definitions which are consistent need not correspond to an actually existing thing. Some of these essences contain their own existence; some essences can be demonstrated as existing only with the aid of experience.

Spinoza's definition of substance is similar to that of Descartes insofar as it emphasizes the independence of substance. However, from this similarity, Spinoza draws implications and deduces properties which Descartes and his fellow religionists would find abhorrent. ''By substance, I understand that which is in itself and is conceived through itself; in other words, that, the conception of which does not need the conception of another thing from which it must be formed.''[8] The expression ''that which is in itself'' indicates the independence of substance. The expression ''that which is conceived through itself'', not only indicates independence, but emphasizes that substance is self-sufficient, is its own cause.

Axiom I says, ''Everything which is, is either in itself or in another.''[9] Axiom IV says, ''The knowledge of an effect depends upon and involves the knowledge of the cause.''[10] Anything that can be known or conceived through itself must be something which is caused by itself. That is to say, if a thing is conceived through itself, there is no cause outside of it; nothing upon which it depends. The knowledge or conception of the thing itself is sufficient for one to assert that it exists. Its essence is its existence; it is both in itself and conceived through itself. This view of substance as self-caused and known through itself also indicates that, for Spinoza, knowledge and causation are related. If something is known through itself, it is self-caused. If the knowledge of something depends upon the knowledge of another thing, then it is caused by that other thing and depends upon it.

If substance is in itself and conceived through itself—depends upon no other thing for its cause or for knowledge of it—then it is self-caused.

Spinoza defines cause of itself as "... that, whose essence involves existence; or that whose nature cannot be conceived unless existing."[11] Substance is that whose existence can be deduced from its essence, so it necessarily exists. This appears to be a proof based simply upon the definition of substance alone, an ontological proof. Indeed, Spinoza notes that in Proposition 7: "It pertains to the nature of substance to exist"[12] and "would be considered by all to be axiomatic, and reckoned amongst common notions,"[13] if "men would attend to the nature of substance."[14] The definition of substance "must involve necessary existence, and consequently from its definition alone its existence must be concluded."[15] Instead of relying on perfection as the basis of an ontological argument to prove the existence of God, Spinoza utilizes an argument based upon thought alone, a deduction from a definition. Indeed, deduction and causation are one and the same thing in the attribute of Thought or among ideas.

The causal argument depends upon Spinoza's theory of definition. Proposition 7, Part 1 tells us that because substance is unique, it cannot be caused by anything else. It is conceived in itself and through itself, so it must be its own cause. Every definition of a thing must refer to its cause, and the cause must either be in the thing itself or outside the thing. Being unique, substance has nothing mutually in common with any other thing, so it cannot be understood through any other thing. Therefore, it cannot be caused by any other thing.[16] Anything which is caused by itself, exists necessarily.[17] Spinoza does assert that Proposition 7 is "axiomatic" and should be "reckoned amongst common notions."[18] It is an "eternal truth."[19] In his discussion of substance, Spinoza says that "its definition must involve necessary existence, and consequently from its definition alone its existence must be concluded."[20] I believe that Spinoza chooses to use a causal argument because he wished to emphasize the activity of substance; substance as its own cause is a *natura naturans*, nature naturing, not simply existing but acting, using its power.

In Proposition 8, Spinoza says, "Every substance is necessarily infinite."[21] Because it is conceived in itself and through itself, because it is self-caused, substance is limited by nothing but itself. It is complete, finished, contained within itself. Substance is singular. It has nothing mutually in common with any other thing, so it cannot be understood through anything else nor can it be caused by anything else.[22] That which is in itself and conceived through itself can only be infinite, eternal, and free.[23] Substance, then, is that which is so singular, so unique, that it cannot be caused, compared to, or limited by anything else.

Spinoza says each substance is infinite and singular. There cannot be two substances of the same nature, because there would be no way by

which we could distinguish one from the other.²⁴ Consequently, they
would not be unique and singular. If there is only one substance of each
attribute, then it must be infinite, since there is nothing of its own kind by
which it could be limited. So, *each* substance is infinite; but, at this point,
it has been proved only that there is *a* substance for each attribute. It is
still conceivable that there are infinite numbers of substances each of
which has only one attribute. This possibility seems to be evident to
Spinoza in Proposition 8, because he notes that "Substance which has
only one attribute cannot exist except as one substance."²⁵

Proposition 9 begins the identification of substance with God or
Nature. It states that the more reality or being anything has, the more
attributes it has.²⁶ Definition 4 states, "By attribute, I understand that
which the intellect perceives of substance, as *if*, constituting its
essence."²⁷ The Latin reads: "Per attributum intelligo id, quod intellectus de substantia percipit, *tanquam* ejusdem essentiam constituens."²⁸ In
his excellent article, F. S. Haserot lays to rest the subjectivist interpretation of the attributes which turns upon the translation of *tanquam* in the
definition. "Spinoza employs the word twenty-nine times in the *Ethics*. In
twenty-six of these, the word clearly means 'as'. With respect to three, ...
the contention might be raised (though with some question) that Spinoza
employs the term with counterfactual references."²⁹ The subjectivist
view makes the attributes depend upon our intellects. If there were no
intellect to perceive them, substance would be "simply one ineffable and
undifferentiated essence."³⁰ This view of substance would agree with the
Cusanian, Maimonidean, idealistic interpretation and with the
Aristotelian *summum genus*. Unfortunately, it does not accord with
Spinoza's treatment of the reality of thought, minds, extension, and
bodies. As Haserot says, "This interpretation, though it effaces all
distinction from God's nature, threatens gravely the intelligibility of
Spinoza's philosophy and the rational method it professes to follow. It
makes Spinoza a pure mystic with no available explanations of the
modes, for the modes ... cannot be taken as inventions of the intellect,
since if they were they would be simply modifications of thought."³¹ On
the bases of Haserot's analysis of *tanquam*, Spinoza's theory of definitions as providing the essence of the thing defined, Spinoza's commitment to rationalism, the intelligibility of substance, and the reality of
finite modes of differing attributes, I accept the objectivist view of the
definition of attributes. Thus, attributes do in fact constitute the essence
of substance and differ from substance only insofar as the attributes are
infinite in their own kind and not "absolutely infinite".

If Proposition 8 were the final discussion of substance, if we were left
with a proof that each substance was infinite, there would be no distinc-

tion between a substance of only *one* attribute, which would be a substance infinite in its own kind, and an attribute itself. Indeed, Spinoza himself states this when he says, "There is nothing therefore outside the intellect by which a number of things can be distinguished one from another, *but substances or (which is the same thing by Def. 4) their attributes* and their affections."[32] The Latin is clearer in that it separates the clause "or which is the same thing their attributes", from the "affections". Thus, substance may be taken as identical to the attributes, at least until Proposition 9. An attribute is in itself and conceived through itself, as demonstrated in Proposition 10, is infinite and has the same definition as substance. Attributes being conceived in themselves are known through themselves. They, too, are infinite, self-caused, and self-contained. This is not only an argument for the identification of attributes with substance by means of their coincident characters, essences or definitions, but it is also an argument for the objectivity of the attributes.

However, there is an apparent move from the identification of attributes with substance in Proposition 9 which states, "The more reality or being a thing possesses, the more attributes *belong* to it."[33] The Latin reads: "Quo plus realitatis, aut esse unaquaeque res habet, eo plura attributa ipsi *competunt.*"[34] The Wild translation, that of White-Stirling, can be misleading *if* one views the term "belong" in the sense of the *thing* owning, or having, or underlying the attributes. This would make a substance-quality, or substance-property relation between substance and its constituent attributes. It could mislead one into taking Spinoza's relation of a substance to attribute to be akin to the Aristotelian notion of substance-quality. The Elwes translation is better: "The more reality or being a thing has the greater the number of its attributes."[35] A more accurate translation would be: "The more reality or being anything has, the more attributes coincide with it."

The word *competo* can be translated in various ways. In classical Latin, it can mean "to come together, to meet, to agree, to coincide in point of time, to be equal to, to be capable of."[36] It is of interest that the "to be equal to" translation is from Livius, and Spinoza possessed a book written by him. The Thomas Dictionary of Latin and English published in 1587 defines the term as "to be meete or convenient, to appertain..."[37] A Dictionary of Latin to 600A.D. notes that *competor* with the dative case means "to belong to."[38] While the "belongs to" translation has some basis (*ipsi* is dative case), there is at least some merit to considering "to be equal to" or "to coincide with". Seeing that the translation can shift the relation of substance to attribute from an Aristotelian conception of substance as underlying the attributes to a more Platonic conception of attributes as constituting, or equal to substance, one should at least be made aware of the possibility of other translations.[39] The translation which I have suggested above more clearly indicates the identity of attributes and substance and further supports the objectivist view of the attributes. Although it may raise new difficulties, the translation avoids Aristotelian and subjectivist problems.

Proposition 9, then, prepares us for the possibility of a substance which consists of more than one attribute. The relation between substance and its constituent attributes is construed as the relation between a definition and its constituent essential characters. Substance *is* its attribute in the same sense as a real definition is its *definiens*. The more terms in the *definiens*, the greater the power, reality, of the *definiendum*. Proposition 10 shows us that each attribute is conceived through itself. No attribute produces any other attribute. If, as I have argued, substance *is* its attributes, then substance can not cause or produce the attributes. There may be different, distinct attributes which co-exist in substance, which constitute substance, but which are independent of one another. Spinoza says that this should not lead us to conclude that where there are distinct attributes, there are different substances. That is to say, one should *not* assert that each substance is one attribute, or *vice-versa*, that each attribute is a substance. He says that two different attributes should not lead us to conclude that "they *constitute* two beings or two different substances."[40] Spinoza proceeds to state, "It is very far from being absurd, therefore, to ascribe to one substance a number of attributes, since nothing in nature is clearer than that each being must be conceived under some attribute, and the more reality or being it has, the more attributes it *possesses* expressing necessity, or eternity and infinity."[41] It should be noted that substance "has" the attributes here, but later in the scholium, Spinoza says that the absolutely infinite being *consists* of infinite attributes. It is apparent that if a substance has a number of ways under which we may comprehend it, by which it expresses itself, then it is *more* real, more powerful, richer than a substance which has only one way of being known or expressed.

So, Spinoza argues that the more real a thing is, the more ways it can be known, the more attributes constitute it. Substance consists of attributes; it does not hide under or possess the attributes. Given the identity of substance and attributes, it would follow that an infinite substance would consist of an infinite number of attributes. "By God, I understand *Being* absolutely infinite, that is to say, *substance consisting* of infinite attributes, each one of which expresses eternal and infinite essence."[42] Absolutely infinite substance has an infinite number of attributes which are infinite in their own kind. There are two senses of "infinite" here. One is the extensive sense whereby the infinite substance consists of an infinite *number* of attributes. The other sense is intensive: each attribute is infinite, that is, unlimited, self-contained, in its own kind. It should be noted that Spinoza has here identified an absolutely infinite *Being* with an absolutely infinite substance. Substance and being are identical, but only infinite substance is identical with infinite being. There are finite beings, too. Again, absolutely infinite substance *consists* of infinite numbers of infinite attributes. Substance does not contain, or underly the attributes. Each attribute of substance is *an* expression of substance, but no attribute expresses the totality of substance in itself. Each attribute is infinite in its own kind, but God is constituted by infinite numbers of attributes. The argument of Spinoza flows from the singularity of substance to its self-causation, to its necessary existence (Proposition 7) and to the existence of only one substance (Proposition 10, Scholium). He then shows that this one, singular, self-caused substance is identical to God—an absolutely infinite substance.

There is nothing surprising in the definition of God as an infinite substance or infinite being. What *is* innovative is found in the implications of his definition. He says, "... to the essence of that which is absolutely infinite pertains whatever expresses essence and involves no negation."[43] Every attribute belongs to an absolutely infinite substance. One of the attributes is extension. Thus, God, or absolutely infinite substance, is extended. There is no discussion of "positive" or "negative" attributes in Spinoza. The usual claim is that God cannot be extended because extension entails divisibility, and divisibility indicates passivity. This argument, which finds its roots in Aristotle's metaphysics, is rejected by Spinoza. For him, extension *as attribute, per se*, as conceived in itself, is indivisible. Particular, finite, extended bodies are divisible, it is true; but extension in itself is *not* divisible. Extension does not entail passivity. A passive thing, for Spinoza, is a thing which is determined or limited by something else. Now, a singular, unique substance can be determined by nothing else. So it is free, self-determined, and active. God, or absolutely infinite substance, is *active* even though it is extended. Since extension is an attribute, and since each attribute is conceived in itself and through itself, each attribute is self-determined, active, and free. There are no negative attributes, since no attribute can be determined by any other attribute. Each attribute is *sui generis*, has nothing in common with any other attribute *as an attribute*. Thus, it cannot be affected or limited by any other attribute. There is no negation involved in any attribute. So, God, or absolutely infinite substance, must consist of all attributes including extension.

God is an absolutely infinite substance. It is extremely important that
Spinoza so identifies, or defines God, because he had earlier demonstrated, in Proposition 7, that substance must exist. As it has been proven
that substance—even a substance limited to but *one* attribute—necessarily exists, it is even clearer that substance composed of an infinite
number of attributes must necessarily exist. Indeed, the three proofs for
existence of substance depended upon its singularity, its definition, the
theory of definition as referring to the cause of the thing defined, and the
consequence that singular substance must be self-caused.

The first a priori argument that God exists depends upon the notion
that substance is defined as being self-caused. That is to say, it is the
essence of substance to exist. The argument is a *reductio ad absurdum*. It is
contradictory to assert that a self-caused substance is non-existent
because self-caused includes in its essence existence. Thus, to deny the
existence of a substance would be to assert that the existent is non-
existent. That is to say, one would then be claiming that that whose
essence includes existence is non-existent, and this is absurd.

The second a priori proof depends upon the principle of sufficient
reason or sufficient cause. "For the existence or non-existence of
everything there must be a cause or reason."[44] The reason or cause must
be either within the thing or outside it. This argument depends upon
Spinoza's theory of definition which states that the definition of a thing
must either include the cause in itself or refer to the proximate cause.

Because substance is unique, it cannot be caused by any other thing. It
must be self-caused. So the definition of substance—that which is conceived in itself and through itself—entails the concept of self-causation. Its
essence includes its own cause. Now, there is no cause which could prevent God, or an absolutely infinite substance, from existing. Such a cause
would have to be outside of it or within it. If the cause were external,
there would have to be a substance of the same nature to affect it. But,
there cannot be two substances of the same nature; this would violate the
singularity or "conceived through itself" aspect of the definition of
substance. There could not be a substance of a different nature which
prevented this substance from existing, because that would violate the axiom of mutuality—things must have something "mutually in common"
to be understood through one another or to be causally related to one
another. So, the cause or substance which prevents God from existing
could not be outside of God; it could not be a proximate cause. It would,
then, have to be the essence of God Himself which would entail His own
non-existence. God would be a contradictory substance; the definition
would be inconsistent and self-contradictory. Again, it would be *reductio
ad absurdum* to state that the essence of a thing which includes its own

existence is non-existent. So, neither within nor without God is there a cause which could prevent God's existence. God exists necessarily.

Both a priori proofs depend upon causation. The first proof argues that a self-caused thing must exist because its essence includes existence. The second argument depends upon the singularity of substance and the axiom of mutuality which underly the axiom of sufficient causation or sufficient reason. This proof is similar to the conditional proof in logic. Can one find *any* cause or reason why God does not exist? If there is no such cause or reason which can be assigned, then God must necessarily exist.

The third proof is an a posteriori argument based upon the notion that existence is power. Spinoza asserts that it is self-evident that "ability to exist is power."[45] If every thing which exists is finite, then the finite would be more powerful than the absolutely infinite. This is absurd. So, either nothing exists or God exists. We exist, so something exists. If something finite exists—something which is "in something else", then surely something absolutely infinite—something "in itself" must exist. If anything at all exists, then there must be an absolutely infinite substance which exists.

This third argument depends upon the fact that we exist. We must be either self-caused substances or things which are in something else which necessarily exists.[46] Axiom I states, "Everything which is, is either in itself or in another."[47] The terms "in itself" and "in another" indicate either independence or dependence, infinitude or finitude, *in suo generis* or *in alio generis*. This is a reference to Spinoza's theory of definition wherein the cause of anything must be either the thing itself or some proximate thing external to the thing itself.

If something exists, it must be either infinite itself or in an infinite substance. We exist. If something exists, there must be an absolutely infinite substance which exists—whether it is us or God. But we have defined God as an absolutely infinite substance. So, God must exist.

Spinoza notes in the Scholium to Proposition 11 that he is speaking of substances which are independent and self-caused. For a substance, "existence must follow from its nature alone, and is therefore nothing else than its essence."[48] So, in effect, these proofs are ontological proofs which follow from the definition of God as a *substance*. If there is any existent substance, it must be an absolutely infinite substance. If we exist, we must either be that singular substance, or we must be in that infinite substance. In either case, that substance must exist. We shall discover, of course, that we are not a substance, but merely a mode of substance which depends upon God or Nature.

COMMENTARY

The three proofs of the existence of God or Nature and the identification of God with an absolutely infinite substance determine the whole of Spinoza's philosophy. It is, therefore, most important that we understand correctly Spinoza's conception of God, Nature, or the absolutely infinite substance. One key element in this understanding is found in his view of substance as independent and self-caused. It is from this notion that the necessary existence of substance follows, and it is this notion upon which the a priori proofs depend.

Spinoza's definition of God as an absolutely infinite substance is analogous to Anselm's definition of God as a perfect being. That is to say, absolute infinity corresponds to perfection. One difficulty with the notion of perfection has been that of differentiating the positive and negative attributes so that only positive attributes could be claimed as constituting the essence of God. Traditionally, there have been some attributes, notably extension, which have been excluded from God because of their alleged "passivity". If one excludes extension from God, then one must assert that extension is produced *ex nihilo* in some miraculous fashion by a non-extended Being. Nicholas of Cusa attempted to escape from this difficulty by asserting that God was an absolutely infinite Being and included all attributes. He saw God as a *coincidentia oppositorum*—a coming together or coalescence of attributes, God is a unity of opposites for Cusanus, but such a God is unknowable.

Spinoza's view is similar to that of Cusanus, but it differs because his God is not unknowable, nor is there any coalescence of attributes into some ineffable unity. This view of God is similar to the "abstract unity" in the idealistic interpretation mentioned by Joachim in his *Ethics*. The attributes do not fade away into something else, for Spinoza; they constitute God or Nature. Spinoza is quite clear in this regard, and he states in Proposition 2, Part 2, "Extension is an attribute of God, or God is an extended thing."[49] Thus, Spinoza's definition of God as an absolutely infinite substance commits him to the assertion that God or Nature is constituted by *all* the attributes. No properties or attributes can be excluded from the essence of God or Nature as it is known by either reason or intuition.

UNITY OF GOD OR SUBSTANCE

If God is constituted by an infinity of infinite attributes, this does not entail that God is a *coincidentia oppositorum*. It does not mean that God is an ineffable, indeterminate something which produces all the opposing attributes, nor does it require one to assert that God is a substance constituted of contradictory attributes. God is not indeterminate, and hence unknowable, since we do have an adequate idea of God or Nature.[50]

While some accept the Cartesian notion that thought and extension are "contrary", it is not true that Spinoza did. The attributes are diverse, different, and have nothing mutually in common with one another *as attributes*, or *per se*. But, they are not opposites or contradictory; they are simply something else. That is to say, extension is something other than thought. Color and size are different properties of an extended object, but they are not contradictory or opposite one another. The statement that one attribute is not another attribute should not lead one to commit the Parmenidean error that if something is not-x, then it must contradict or oppose x. It is this sort of reasoning which led to difficulties in relating thought and extension to God and to one another. It is this problem which Plato resolves in the *Sophist* by arguing that not-x may be something other than x or it may be contradictory to x. (It seems as if Joachim interprets 'not extension' as 'contradictory to extension'). I believe that thought is something other than extension, but it is not a contradictory of extension nor does it oppose extension.

Absolutely infinite substance can be known, or can be expressed, in an infinitude of different ways, but this does not entail that God or Nature is an aggregate substance. One must not think of God or Nature as a unity composed of parts, the attributes, or as a compound whole. This sort of spatial or "extensional" thinking is incorrect and manufactures difficulties for understanding Spinoza. Imagination is that sort of thinking which uses part-whole, pieces-compound concepts; it is that type of thinking whereby we form ideas of images of extended bodies. Spinoza is quite clear in warning us against using imagination in an attempt to understand God or Nature.[51] It is spatial thinking and cannot apply to substance, God, or Nature which is something other than an extended finite mode.[52] The part-whole relation will not serve to explicate Spinoza's view of God and the attributes any more successfully than will the substance-property or species-genus relations of Aristotle.

Spinoza insists upon the unity and singularity of substance in order to account for the unity and intelligibility of the universe. As there must be an infinitude of infinite attributes to account for the diversity of existing things, so there must be a unique, simple substance to account for the unity and intelligibility of the universe. Nature is singular, unique, just as substance, being, or existence is unified, although it is manifested in different ways. Substance, God, or Nature is identical to itself and can be known only through itself, not by comparison or relation to anything else. But, God or Nature can be expressed or instantiated in an infinite number of ways. That is to say, all of the attributes as well as their modes are but expressions of a single, unique, active order. So, God can be known by means of its attributes or modes. Spinoza states that God or Nature is a unique entity. He says, "God can only improperly be called one or single. ... A thing can only be said to be one or single in respect of its existence and not of its essence; for we do not conceive things under numbers until they have been subsumed under a common class. ... But since the existence of God is His essence itself, and since we can form no general idea of His essence, it is certain that he who calls God one or single has no true idea of God, or is speaking of Him inappropriately."[53] One sees clearly that God or Nature is a particular, unique, singular being for Spinoza—one that differs from every other being and cannot be compared or related to any other being. Since it is absolutely infinite, God must be all-inclusive, and yet it cannot be included in any other being. It is absolutely independent.

Contrary to the Aristotelian notion of substance, Spinoza's God is not an underlying substance common to all particular things and supporting the attributes from which it differs. It is not a common genus but is a particular, active being. It is not a universal, nor is it an abstract entity. One may observe that the difficulty in explaining the relation of God or Nature to the attributes is akin to the difficulties of relating forms to forms. Plato discusses this in the *Sophist*, and his analysis aids our understanding of Spinoza.

Spinoza was aware of the problem of establishing one absolutely infinite substance instead of having an infinite number of substances constituted by one attribute alone. He says:

> You say your difficulty remains untouched (the difficulty, namely, why there can not be several beings, existing through themselves, but differing in nature, just as thought and extension are different and can perhaps subsist through their own sufficiency). ... I say ... that if we assume that something which is only unlimited and perfect in its own kind exists by its own sufficiency then we must also admit the existence of a being that is absolutely unlimited and perfect; which Being I shall call God. For if, for instance, we wish to assert that extension, or thought (which can be perfect each in its own kind, that is, in a certain kind of being) exist by their sufficiency, we shall also have to admit the existence of God, who is absolutely perfect, that is, the existence of an absolutely unlimited being. ... And since the nature of God does not consist of a certain kind of being but of an absolutely unlimited being, His nature also requires all that perfectly expresses being; otherwise His nature would be limited and deficient. This being so, it follows that there can exist one Being, namely God, which exists by its own force.[54]

In short, Spinoza argues that if there is any substance at all, or even if there is any attribute at all, there must be an absolutely infinite substance or God. There would be no sufficient reason for such a being not to exist. There would be no cause which could prevent it from existing. I believe, as noted above, that this one Being, God or Nature, is necessary to insure the unity of Spinoza's philosophy as well as to avoid the problems of relating absolutely different and perhaps contradictory substances to one another. It is the unique absolutely infinite being which unites the different attributes, bridges the chasm between Creator and created nature, accounts for the existence of different sorts of beings without creation *ex nihilo*. God, or Nature, and the attributes are *natura naturans*, active, free, self-contained.

The unity of God or Nature runs through all of the manifestations of existence. It can be understood as the reification of the principle of causation which, for Spinoza, pervades extension as the laws of mechanics and pervades thought as the laws of logic. It would also run through all the other attributes and their modes. Curley is quite correct to stress the *unity* of Nature when he interprets substance as the unified comprehensive theory expressed by the laws of a particular science.[55]

I should suggest that the view of substance, God or Nature as an active existence is closer to that of Spinoza himself (since each attribute expresses a type of existence or being), although it retains Curley's emphasis on Nature as a causal unifying, cohesive, explanatory notion. Spinoza's Nature runs through, or pervades science. As theories pervade the laws included therein, so does Nature or existence itself pervade all of its expressions. A theory differs from its laws, but it is constituted by them. Similarly, Nature or God differs from the attributes, yet it is constituted by them.

God differs from its attributes insofar as it pervades all of them. It is similar to the attributes insofar as it has the qualities of the attributes: independence, self-causation, infinitude. Nature runs through all of the attributes. It is the causality and existence which all attributes have in common but which is expressed differently by each attribute. This interpretation of substance and its attributes is one which differs from the extensional part-whole relation as well as from the species-genus and substance-property relations. I argue that what I term "pervade" or "pervasion" is the proper interpretation of Spinoza's term "immanent". Spinoza insists that God or Nature is the immanent cause of all things not only in the *Ethics*,[56] but also in Letter 73 to Oldenburg. He says, "I hold an opinion about God and Nature very different from that which Modern Christians are wont to defend. For I maintain that God is, as they say, the immanent cause of all things, but not the transeunt cause."[57] Spinoza differs from the "Modern Christians" and from Descartes insofar as they assert that God is "separate" and "apart from" Nature and His creation, whereas the older Christians and Hebrews might claim that "it is God in whom we live and move and have our being". Spinoza's account of God and Nature is akin to that of the older religionists. It is God, or *natura naturans* in which we *natura naturata* have our being.

How can substance be one and yet pervade many attributes? How can substance exist in itself and yet be constituted by an infinity of attributes? How can Nature be one and many? How can Nature, God or substance be absolutely infinite and pervasive, yet differ from its attributes?

Wolf answers these questions thusly, "For Spinoza Substance was not merely the sum of distinct Attributes, but the organic unity of them. Just as each Attribute is not merely the sum of its modes, but the organic or systematic unity of them, so Substance ... is the interconnected system of Attributes—interconnected just in so far as they are the forces or the expressions of the same and only Substance."[58] This view is correct insofar as it stresses the unity and activity of substance, but it does not quite explain the unity of substance in the diversity of attributes and modes.

Wolfson says that substance is "a whole which exists over and above and beyond the sum of the modes. ..."[59] I should agree that substance is a whole which is different from the modes, but it seems to me that Spinoza's insistence upon the immanence of God would legislate against Wolfson's "over and above and beyond" categorization of substance. Indeed, Wolfson says that "substance is thus a whole transcending the universe ... and the relation of substance to the universe is conceived by (Spinoza) after the manner of the relation of the whole to the part, the whole in this particular being a universal of a special kind, a real universal, as distinguished from the attributes which are only nominal universals."[60] I have argued that the whole-part view is extensional, due to the imagination, and incorrect for Spinoza. Furthermore, Spinoza denies the existence of universals. Indeed, it could be argued that God or Nature is a particular. Spinoza does say that it is a singular being and its essence is a singular essence. Consequently, I believe that Wolfson's view of substance is incorrect.

Rice argues that the definition of substance as self-caused indicates "the primordial emphasis which Spinoza places upon the omnipresence of agency: that essence alone is wholly real which realizes itself wholly in act, subject to no other determining agency."[61] It is true that substance as causal agency is omnipresent in Spinoza's metaphysics, and it is true that the more real a thing is, the more independent and active it is. Furthermore, Rice is quite correct in asserting that essence is keyed to activity or agency. Of course, the more attributes or essence a thing has, the more active it is. So, God, an absolutely infinite substance, is absolutely active.

Curley, too, notes that Spinoza somehow identifies ''the power or essence of God or Nature with the scientific laws which govern phenomena.''[62] I think that Curley and Rice are fundamentally right in their emphasis on the power, activity, casuality, and omnipresence of God or Nature. On the other hand, Curley and I would disagree on the separation of Being from substance. Curley notes that Spinoza says ''the most general genus is the notion of Being'' and that there are ''strong indications'' that Spinoza agrees with his contemporaries that ''Substance is a species of the genus Being.''[63] Since Spinoza defines God as ''Being absolutely infinite, that is to say substance consisting of infinite attributes'',[64] I should argue that substance and being are identical for Spinoza and that both are particulars. Thus, I maintain that substance, being, pure activity, and causation are all identical notions in Spinoza's methaphysics. My view corresponds, I believe, to Plato's notion of Existence as one of the Five Great Kinds in the *Sophist* and clarifies Spinoza's concept of God or Nature. It would reinforce Vlastos' and Allen's view that the Forms are causes in the metaphysical sense.

In the *Sophist*, Plato undertakes the project of discerning the relations between forms. Forms are not only to be interpreted as the meanings of common nouns but, more importantly, Plato believes the forms themselves are entities which constitute reality. These entities are independent objects of human knowledge, eternal, and immutable. They cause particular, perceivable, temporal, mutable objects to have certain qualities, so the forms must be understood as casual agents, too.

To make a judgment is to relate words to correspondent entities. Some words refer to forms, some to particulars. Judgments are ''mental sentences'' wherein unspoken words refer to relations between forms and forms, or the relations between forms and particulars. It should be noted that Plato has a referential theory of meaning: words must refer to real entities of some sort. True speech, correct thinking must correspond with reality. Language (sentences) and thought (judgments) should mirror reality. The true philosopher, or dialectician, attempts to apprehend the relations between forms—those real entities which are the objects of reason and intuition. In order to apprehend reality so that one might speak of it truly, the philosopher must be able to clearly identify (and define) each form as it is in itself, *per se*. He must be able to discern the individuality, or singularity, of each form. Additionally, he must be able to note the similarities and differences between the forms. The philosopher, as a metaphysician, must be able to trace out the nexus of reality and to track down each node of reality.

Both Plato and Spinoza are metaphysicians: both are concerned with apprehending reality, noting its unity and its differentiations. F. M. Cornford, in his commentary on Plato's *Sophist*, notes that "dialectic is 'to divide according to kinds,' not mistaking one Form for another, or 'to separate by kinds.' "[65] "The task of philosophy is regarded in the *Sophist* as mainly analytical—the mapping out of the realm of Forms in all its articulations by Division."[66] In order to do this, one must first collect the forms by noting similarities, and then divide them by differences. The twin methods of collection and division constitute dialectic.[67] The problem of "the one and the many" is one of the difficulties to be resolved in this dialogue. Is "Reality," "Being," "Existence," *one* form or is it many different forms? This problem appears to be analogous to the problem of whether substance is one thing "over, above, and beyond" the attributes or whether it is constituted by the attributes. Is substance one or many?

In order to discuss being, or reality, one must first define it. At 247 E, the Athenian Stranger says:

> I suggest that anything has real being, that is so constituted as to possess any sort of power either to affect anything else, or to be affected, in however small a degree, by the most insignificant agent, though it be only once. I am proposing as a *mark* to distinguish real things that they are nothing but a *power*.[68]

It is interesting that this suggestion corresponds to Spinoza's definition of existence as power in *Ethics* I, Proposition 11—the *a posteriori* proof for the existence of God. It is also to be noted that the Stranger's proposed definition includes both activity and passivity, whereas Spinoza would argue that existence is to be defined as active power, the power to affect other things. Indeed, for seventeenth century philosophers, one can assign degrees of reality on the basis of degrees of activity. An absolutely infinite being has more power, more activity, more reality, than a finite being. So, if a finite being exists, an absolutely infinite being must exist.

While it is true that the Stranger's definition is only a suggestion or hypothesis and amounts to only a nominal definition (a "mark" of reality), it is analogous to Spinoza's definition of existence. Spinoza's definition is one which "serves to explain a thing whose essence is sought ..." and is not one which is "put forward only to be examined".[69] It would constitute a formal definition for Spinoza, not simply a hypothetical definition as it is, or may be, for Plato. Existence is power, for Spinoza. Let us, then, at the outset, note the similarity of Plato's and Spinoza's definitions of existence, being, reality. Both accept the necessity for formal definitions, but it is not clear that Plato accepts the definition of being as power throughout his dialogues. Vlastos and Allen would argue that the Forms are causes and are thus active powers for Plato, but not all commentators agree. I shall concur with Vlastos and Allen. Let us agree that, at least for the *Sophist*, Plato accepts this definition of reality, and let us proceed to note the similitude between Plato and Spinoza *vis a vis* their explanation of reality and its manifestations.

The Stranger then notes that for a study of reality as well as for a study of its analogue, language, one must have a method, a science. He says:

> ... Is not some science needed as a guide on the voyage of discourse, if one is to succeed in pointing out which Kinds are consonant, and which are incompatible with one another; also whether there are certain Kinds that pervade them all and connect them so that they can blend, and again, where there are divisions (separations), whether there are certain others that traverse wholes and are responsible for the divisions?[70]

Proceeding on the assumption that language mirrors reality, if some parts of speech pervade all words then some forms or kinds will pervade all the reality. Cornford says, "Specially important is the analogy drawn in the last clauses between the vowels which 'pervade' (διὰ πάντων κεχώρηκεν) the whole texture of speech and certain Forms which pervade (διὰ πάντων) the texture of discourse and enable Forms to blend. These pervasive Forms are obviously the meanings of certain words used in affirmative statements. They are, in fact, the meanings of the word 'is'...."[71] The "Five Great Kinds" are some of the most pervasive forms for Plato. They are the forms which 'run through' the greatest number of other forms which constitute eternal reality. I believe that Plato's term "pervade" is equivalent to Spinoza's term "immanent". The most pervasive form is that of existence, being, or reality for Plato. It runs through all discourse, all judgments, and all other Forms. Indeed, it even seeps down to particular things, which exist in at least some defective manner, at least as reflections of forms.

The most pervasive form, the greatest 'collection' for Plato, is the form "Being". "In Plato's view the highest Form, whether it be called 'Being' or 'The One' or 'The Good', must not be the poorest but the richest, a universe of real being, a whole containing all that is real in a single order, a One Being that is also many."[72] I suggest that the Spinozistic analogue to Plato's "Being" is Substance, God, or Nature. Substance is the richest entity for Spinoza, insofar as it is an absolutely infinite being. It is immanent in all things; it pervades all the attributes and modes. It is singular, "one" in Plato's terms; and it is also constituted by infinite numbers of attributes, "many" in Plato's terms. Substance is power, existence, causation, activity for Spinoza, and this is analogous to Plato's "Being".

Cornford comments on the relation between a generic form and its constituent species: "The generic Form is said to 'embrace' them, as a whole embraces its parts, and also to 'pervade' them as a single character 'extended throughout them all'."[73] Being is that form which blends together, unifies, all other forms into an orderly whole. Similarly, substance, God, or Nature blends together and unifies the attributes and the modes; it embraces them insofar as all are real existents, and it pervades them insofar as each attribute is an instantiation of the activity or causality of substance. That is to say, each attribute and its modes are expressions of the activity of substance or Nature.

One who apprehends God or Nature, is one who recognizes the unity and the diversity of reality. As the Stranger says at 253 D "And the man who can do that discerns clearly *one* Form everywhere extended throughout many, where each one lies apart, and *many* Forms, different from one another, embraced from without by one Form ...."[74] The relation of substance or Nature to its attributes is akin to the relation of the form Being to some of the other "great kinds." Being is singular, unique, and it pervades "same" and "different". It embraces "same" and "different" even though it differs from them and even though these two forms are different from one another. Similarly, Substance or Nature pervades extension and thought, which differ from substance insofar as they are only infinite in their own kind and differ from one another insofar as they have nothing mutually in common. The maps of reality understood by Plato and Spinoza are analogous.

Cornford's accounts of mis-interpretations of Plato's dialectic and the relations between forms echo the errors in past Spinoza commentaries. Cornford notes that dialectic is not formal logic, and it does not deal with propositional forms or symbols. Plato is concerned with the structure of reality. Spinoza is not a linguistic philosopher, nor is he an Aristotelian logician. Spinoza, too, is concerned with the structure of reality and not simply with the logic of scientific theories. The interpretation which Curley offers of Spinoza is one which stresses the structure of scientific theories and their relation to the structure of reality and in this regard, although it is an illuminating and interesting commentary, it misses the metaphysical concerns of Spinoza. Cornford says Plato is concerned with "the structure of the real world of Forms. ... All through, Plato is speaking of the real nature of the Kinds mentioned and their actual relations in the structure of reality, not about symbolic patterns under which statements can be classified."[75] Russell and Wittgenstein cannot properly provide models for Plato's philosophy nor for that of Spinoza, since they separated logic and language from ontology. Plato and Spinoza, in their use of formal or real definitions and in their belief that language and philosophy are equally concerned with reality, are the antithesis of contemporary philosophers.

An Aristotelian interpretation of Plato's dialectic is incorrect according to Cornford:

> Here it must once more be stated that no satisfactory account of relations of Platonic Forms can be given in terms of Aristotelian logic. We have seen that Plato was not concerned with propositional forms; his Dialectic studies realities, and his conception of these realities was radically different from Aristotle's. (For Aristotle) specific and generic concepts are not primary substances with an independent existence, not full-blooded realities, but abstractions. As a consequence, the higher we ascend in the hierarchy of genus and species, the further we are from full reality.[76]

For Spinoza, as for Plato, the most pervasive entity is the most real. This is contrary to Aristotle's view. For Spinoza, substance is most real, most knowable, while, as noted in the introduction, for Aristotle substance would be least real. Furthermore, I think it should be reiterated that Spinoza's substance or Nature is *not* an abstraction, not a universal. It is a particular, singular, eternal entity. Similarly, I do not believe that Plato's Forms are universals, or abstractions in Aristotle's sense. They, too, are particular, real entities which unify, embrace, pervade other eternal entities.

The twin processes of Collection and Division constitute the science of reality and thought which Plato terms "dialectic". One collects all of the similar forms into one pervasive, all-encompassing form which "blends" with the similar forms. This collection is accomplished by means of intuition. After the collection has been formed, one discerns the differences between the forms and divides them into "natural kinds".

The greatest collection noted by Plato in the *Sophist* is Existence. Existence is "a single Form or character extended everywhere throughout the many diverse Forms which blend with it."[77] The forms, Same, Difference, Motion and Rest, are almost as "great" as Existence. Plato's term "great" indicates the extent of forms with which a particular form "blends", or which that form "pervades". The five forms noted do not constitute a complete list of "great kinds" but only some of the most pervasive kinds.

The form of the collection itself differs from the forms in that collection. That is to say, for Plato, the form which pervades all of the divisions of "natural kinds" is itself a "natural kind". Some argue that the collective form is a common character which runs through all of the forms of the division, and this is correct. However, it would be incorrect to assert that a common character is a "class" or an "abstract universal". It is true that this is the interpretation of Aristotle and his disciples and that this view is the basis for his development of the logic of classes. But, this is not a correct view of Plato's account. Cornford notes that "Plato ... uses 'Kind' (γένος) and 'Form' (εἶδος) indifferently. Both mean, not 'genus' or 'species' or 'class' but 'Form' or 'Nature' (φύσις and ἰδέα) are used synonymously."[78] A form, whether it be the collective form or a divided form, is a natural entity, a singular, unique entity which exists, is similar to and different from other natural entities. "No one of the Kinds is thought of as a class, either of entities or of predicates."[79]

The most pervasive kind or form is the "richest" and "most real" for Plato, whereas the most universal class is "poorest" and "least real" for Aristotle. The "great kinds" are not classes nor are they categories. "In several places, Aristotle says that Being (existence) and Unity are not categories, precisely because they can be predicated of everything...."[80] I believe that the "great kinds" are singular entities which blend with or pervade other singular entities. These great kinds are not classes, and their relations with one another cannot be properly interpreted in terms of class inclusion or exclusion. Cornford's diagram better represents the relations between great kinds than does an Euler diagram:[81]

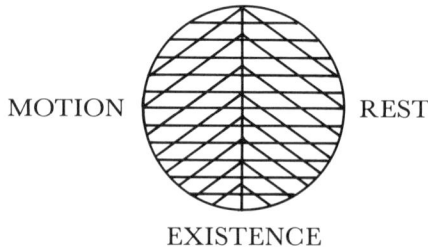

MOTION   REST

EXISTENCE

Each form is an entity or a "natural kind" in itself, even the collective form which pervades the other, similar forms. In a sense, one could say that the forms in that collection, or the forms into which the collection can be divided, constitute the collective form even though they differ from that form in terms of pervasiveness. The collective form is more pervasive than its constituent forms. Motion and Rest constitute Existence, and yet Existence differs from Motion and Rest.

Plato's account of collection and division and the interpretation of forms as "natural kinds", or singular entities, corresponds with Spinoza's epistemology and metaphysics in a manner too apparent to overlook.

Existence is the most pervasive nature for Plato. Spinoza defines God or Nature as "being absolutely infinite" (ens absolute infinitum).[82] God or Nature is the most pervasive entity for Spinoza; it runs through the attributes of thought and extension as well as the other infinite attributes. It is eternal and immutable as are the forms. Substance, God, or Nature is not an abstraction; it is a unique singular entity. Furthermore, one knows God or Nature by intuition for Spinoza as one apprehends Existence for Plato.

Corresponding to the forms of the division, the other "great kinds", are Spinoza's attributes. The attributes differ from God or Nature in much the same way that Existence differs from the other "great kinds": Nature is absolutely infinite (most pervasive), while the attributes are infinite only in their own kind (less pervasive). Each attribute is a unity and not an abstraction, class, or universal. Corresponding to Cornford's diagram of the relation between great kinds would be the following:

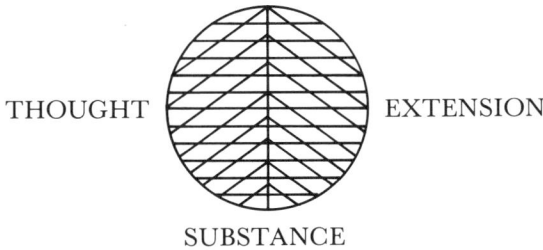

THOUGHT   EXTENSION

SUBSTANCE

One should also note that Plato's view of the relation between the collective form and its constituent divisions corresponds with Spinoza's account of Nature, or Substance, and the attributes. Substance is a unique, singular entity which pervades the infinite number of attributes. It pervades the attributes in terms of existence and causation. That is to say, each attribute exists necessarily and within each attribute there are causal laws. Substance, or Nature, differs from the attributes, but, as Spinoza himself notes in his definition of attribute, they constitute substance. So, analogously to Plato's account of a collective form and its divisions, one can say that Nature differs from Thought and Extension and the other attributes but, in a sense, it is constituted by them. The difference between Nature and the attributes is a difference between absolute infinity and infinity in its own kind, a difference which is similar to differences in pervasiveness between the different sorts of forms or natures for Plato.

For both Plato and Spinoza, collection and division (intuition and reason) provide maps of reality. For both Plato and Spinoza the objects of collection and division do not fit the Aristotelian model of classes or universals. These objects are related in terms of pervasiveness, or immanence, or "blending", but not in terms of inclusion or exclusion.

Plato's dialectic is not Aristotle's logic of subject, copula, and predicate. As Existence is not a class, universal, or abstraction, so Nature is not an abstraction, universal, or class. The attributes and the "great kinds" are also not abstractions, but are "natures". Spinoza's metaphysics and epistemology cannot be interpreted through Aristotelian lenses any more than can Plato's dialectic without producing glaring anomalies. Both Plato and Spinoza are using logics of pervasiveness, or immanence, instead of logics of class inclusion and exclusion. Both Plato and Spinoza are dealing with real natures, real entities not with abstractions.

If one accepts Cornford's statement that forms are natures, one may then more clearly perceive the similarity between Plato and Spinoza. If Existence is the richest nature for Plato, then it is analogous to Nature for Spinoza. Indeed, the Spinozistic account of substance and its constituent attributes as *natura naturans*—nature naturing—seems to accord with Plato's metaphysics of forms or natures. The only exception to the similarity of forms and Spinoza's Nature would be found in Spinoza's stress on the activity, the "naturing", the causation between substance and its modes. If one also notes that the modes are *natura naturata*—nature natured—are similar to the particulars of Plato, then one may conclude that Part I of the *Ethics* and the dialectic of Plato are both to be construed as maps of reality. That is to say, dialectic and *Ethics* I both deal with forms and their relations (God and its attributes and infinite modes) and cease at particulars (finite modes). Dialectic and *Ethics* I are both concerned with eternal entities.

Furthermore, on the basis of the kinship between forms and Spinoza's Nature, Substance, or God, certain relations become more intelligible. It would be odd to claim that Existence causes or creates Same, Difference, Motion and Rest. Similarly, it would be odd, and incorrect, to assert that Substance, or Nature causes or creates Thought and Extension. For Plato, the forms are eternal; for Spinoza, the attributes and Nature are eternal. It would make sense to use the terms "expressions" or "aspects" of Existence or Nature to indicate their relations with the other "great kinds" and attributes. The forms are eternal and immutable, but they are active in "causing" particulars to exist and have their qualities, as Allen argues. It must be admitted, however, that in *Timaeus* and *Philebus* Plato must employ the Demiurge and the Agent to account for activity and creation. For Spinoza, too, substance is active and causal, but only within the sphere of *natura naturata*.

To clearly understand Spinoza, one must abandon Aristotle and note the similarities with Plato. To be sure, there are differences between Spinoza and Plato, but the relation between the philosophies is one of a development from a paradigm. That is to say, Spinoza's philosophy is patterned on the metaphysics and epistemology of Plato. It is true that Spinoza includes in his notion of Nature not only necessary existence but also causation. God or Nature pervades the attributes not only insofar as the attributes exist necessarily, but also insofar as there are analogous causal laws within each of the attributes. As Spinoza says, "The order and connection of ideas is the same as the order and connection of things."[83] Still, I believe that we have demonstrated the high degree of similarity which holds between Plato and Spinoza. And, we have shown that only a Platonistic view of Spinoza's substance and attributes is consistent. Only on this view can God or Nature be One and yet remain constituted by many attributes without incurring inconsistency and paradoxes. Existence is One and pervades the many other Great Kinds and Forms as Nature is One and pervades the attributes and modes. The inclusion/exclusion, part-whole, substance-property relations, which are apparently due to imagination or extensional concepts, fail to capture Spinoza's metaphysics of Nature as unified and as differentiated.

ATTRIBUTES AND MODES

Spinoza has argued that God or Nature is *an* absolutely infinite, self-caused, singular substance, but he has not yet proved that God is *the only* substance. It is true that there can be only one unique, singular God or absolutely infinite substance, but it remains to be demonstrated that there is only *one* substance of any sort. The promise Spinoza made in the Scholium to Proposition 10 that he will show "in nature only one substance exists" must still be redeemed.[84]

Proposition 12 states that "no *attribute* of substance can be truly conceived from which it follows that substance can be divided".[85] Proposition 13 states that "substance absolutely infinite is indivisible."[86] If my argument that attributes constitute substance is correct, then why does Spinoza need two propositions to prove indivisibility, one about attributes and one about substance? The answer to this question is that Proposition 12 is still based upon the supposition that there could be infinite numbers of substances each infinite in its own kind. Spinoza is arguing in Proposition 12 that no infinite substance, even one composed of only one attribute, could be divided because that would require that the parts either "retain the nature of substance" or not.[87] However, the "nature of substance" is to be infinite and self-caused. This is also the nature of any attribute, and attributes constitute the nature of substance by Definition 4. If substance, or an attribute, could be divided, and if each part did retain its nature, then each part of substance would be infinite and self-caused and would be itself an attribute or a substance.

Thus, as Spinoza says, "from one substance more substances could be formed, which is absurd."[88] The Latin more clearly states that each part would be infinite and self-caused and would be "constituted by a diverse (separate) attribute, and so from one substance many would be constituted."[89] Furthermore, the divided parts would have to be different from the substance, so substance could exist and be conceived without its parts, which is equally absurd. If, on the other hand, the parts did not retain the nature of substance, then by means of this division, substance would lose its infinite and self-caused nature. This would be another absurdity. Note that here Spinoza is quite clear that the relation of substance to attribute is not one of whole to parts, nor one of an underlying substratum which differs from its properties. Similarly, he is clear that the attributes are themselves infinite and self-caused, so they are not merely dependent qualities.

Proposition 13 uses similar arguments to prove that absolutely infinite substance is indivisible. If the parts of a divided substance were to retain the nature of absolutely infinite substance, then there would be a number of absolutely infinite substances having the same nature. Proposition 5, which is a form of the principle of the identity of indiscernables, legislates against this alternative. It is interesting to note that in the demonstration to Proposition 12, Spinoza also appeals to Proposition 5 but there he uses it to argue against the possibility of producing different substances of different attributes from one substance. In Proposition 13, Spinoza uses Proposition 5 to argue against having different substances of the same attributes. So, on the basis of the same proposition, we cannot have *different* substances of *differing* attributes produced from one substance, and we cannot have different substances of the same attributes (absolutely infinite substances) produced from one substance. Each substance, then, must be simple and indivisible. In some respects, this treatment of the divisibility of substance recalls the discussion of the "one and the many" aspects of forms in the *Parmenides*, and this will be discussed in the commentary of this section.

Having shown that any substance whatsoever—either infinite in its own kind or absolutely infinite—is indivisible, Spinoza says in the Corollary to Proposition 13 that "no substance, and consequently no bodily substance *insofar as it is substance*, is divisible."[90] Now, the only candidate for "corporeal substance" would be a substance whose only attribute was extension or which included extension among its attributes. So, Spinoza is denying divisibility to extension as an attribute or as constituting a substance. An absolutely infinite substance must include extension as an attribute, and, since God is an absolutely infinite substance, God must be extended *and* indivisible. It is not at all surprising that God is indivisible; but, at least in the seventeenth century, it was extraordinary that extension would be considered indivisible. Indeed, as we have seen, philosophers generally excluded the attribute of extension from God because of its divisibility and implied passivity. There are two points to make concerning Spinoza's denial of the divisibility of "corporeal substance."

The first point is that Spinoza denies divisibility of extension *insofar as it is a substance*.[91] The nature of substance is to be infinite and self-caused. It is in keeping with the seventeenth century view of infinity as self-contained, or accomplished, or finished, that the infinite is considered to be indivisible. So, if one considers extension to be infinite, it would be indivisible. Descartes was aware of the argument that the infinite was indivisible, so he termed extension "indefinite", divisible into innumerable parts.[92] But, indefinite divisibility and the absence of space indicates that extension is a continuum. For Spinoza, a continuum is indivisible. "Infinite" means "indivisible" for him. If one grants that the nature of the infinite is to be indivisible, and each attribute is infinite, then extension, as an attribute constituting the nature of substance (Definition 4), must be infinite and indivisible.

The indivisibility of extension *per se* also follows on epistemological grounds. If one considers extension *insofar as it is substance*, one knows it by intuition or reason. Intuition or reason apprehends things *sub specie aeternitatis*. The amount of extension in the universe is indivisible. A physicist considers extension, or energy, or "matter", as indivisible in amount insofar as it cannot be created or destroyed. That is to say, in the "collective" sense, extension cannot be altered. But, in the "distributive" sense, it can be shifted about. It is true, of course, that one can divide any particular body, or finite mode of extension; but one cannot divide "body itself" or "extension considered as an attribute". A particular body is "known" by imagination or perception. Here, one forms an idea of an image, and one can conceive of that image as divisible. Only finite modes are divisible, and it is only through perception or imagination that one can consider extension as divisible. Only temporal, particular finite modes are divisible; the attribute itself, or Nature as constituted by extension, is indivisible. Spinoza himself discusses this in the Scholium to Proposition 15.

No substance is divisible, and none of its constituent attributes is divisible. Extension is an attribute; so it, too, must be indivisible. This conclusion indicates an immense difference between Spinoza and Descartes not only in their conceptions of extension but also in their conceptions of God.

For Descartes, "... we cannot conceive of body excepting in so far as it
is divisible."[93] "Extension in length, breadth, and depth constitutes the
nature of corporeal substance."[94] Because of its indivisibility, Descartes
excludes extension from the nature of God. He says, "... thus, in corporeal nature since divisibility is included in local extension, and
divisibility indicates imperfection, it is certain that God is not body."[95]

"Since God is Being absolutely infinite of whom no attribute can be
denied which expresses the essence of substance,"[96] and since "extended
substance is one of the infinite attributes of God"[97] and since absolutely
infinite substance is indivisible,[98] it follows that God is an extended
substance for Spinoza. Those who deny that God is extended do so
because they believe extension is divisible. Spinoza says the "sole foundation (of their argument) is the supposition that bodily substance consists of parts".[99] They believe in the divisibility of corporeal substance,
because they confuse imagination with understanding, modes with
substance, finite things with the infinite. When one uses imagination, he
is considering the attribute of extension "abstractly or superficially."[100]
One forms an idea of an image of a finite mode which is apparently
"finite, divisible, and composed of parts."[101] If one understands, or conceives of extension "insofar as it is substance", "as it exists in the intellect", and not in the senses, then "we find it to be infinite, one, and indivisible."[102] In Letter 12, Spinoza says that "if the thing is apprehended
as it is in itself, which is very difficult to do, then ... it will be found to be
infinite, indivisible and unique."[103]

In effect, Spinoza is charging Descartes and his fellows with confusing
imagination and understanding. Indeed, in the Scholium to Proposition
15, Spinoza points out that the conception of extension as divisible is
inconsistent with a Cartesian denial of the void. Spinoza says, "there is
no vacuum in nature ..., but all the parts are united ... it follows that they
cannot be really separated."[104] So, Descartes *should* assert that corporeal
substance *per se* or in general, is indivisible, but particular bodies can be
imagined or perceived as divisible. This is, of course, Spinoza's view.
Spinoza uses the term "substance" more consistently than does
Descartes insofar as all substance is infinite, indivisible, eternal. Modes
are finite, divisible, temporal and are apprehended not by the intellect
but by the imagination or perception. Whatever is known by the
understanding, by reason or intuition, is eternal, immutable, indivisible,
and infinite.[105]

Proposition 14 states that the only substance is the absolutely infinite
substance, God. We have demonstrated that God must exist in Proposition 11, and in Proposition 5 we have proved that one cannot have two
substances of the same nature. So, if there is one absolutely infinite

substance consisting of all the attributes, there cannot be an absolutely infinite substance constituted by any particular number of attributes, because this is inconsistent with *absolute* infinity. There could not be a substance infinite only in its own kind, because it would be indistinguishable from an attribute which constitutes an essence of the absolutely infinite substance. Similarly, there could not be a substance consisting of some number of the attributes constituting the absolutely infinite substance; it would be indistinguishable from a group of attributes constituting God. There could not be an infinite substance which had none of God's infinite number of attributes. So, there is only one substance which is absolutely infinite, singular and unique.

Since everything which is, is either in itself or in another and since a substance is conceived in itself and through itself, then God—the absolutely infinite substance—must be in itself. Everything else must be in it. "Nothing can be or be conceived without God."[106] If everything is "in" the only substance, then everything depends upon that substance. Thus, Spinoza can argue that "everything which takes place takes place by the laws alone of the infinite nature of God."[107] God's nature pervades all attributes and modes.

God or Nature is not a static, eternal entity removed from the world, but it is an active being which is causing, sustaining, and producing its effects. The activity of substance is its "expression." Nature expresses itself insofar as it produces or causes things; and the laws by which things become or occur are the laws of Nature or God itself. Everything which occurs does so in accord with the laws of Nature; they are expressions of the essence of God. God is active thus everything either constitutes the essence of God, or it is an expression of that essence. One cannot too strongly emphasize the active character of God or Nature for Spinoza, since failure to do so would produce an abstract immutable being separate from its effect—the world. For Spinoza, God *is* the world; the world is an expression of an immanent God which is active in that world insofar as all its constituents follow the laws of nature.

Given the account of God as absolutely infinite substance and as absolutely infinite power (since existence is power), one can clearly understand Proposition 16: "From the necessity of the divine nature, infinite numbers of things in infinite ways (that is to say, all things which can be conceived by the infinite intellect) must follow."[108] Because an absolutely infinite substance is constituted by an infinite number of infinite attributes, one of which is Thought, anything which can be conceived by or inferred from that absolutely infinite nature must be. To "come under" the infinite intellect is to be conceivable, or understandable, to "follow from" the nature of the attributes themselves. Anything which "follows from" the absolutely infinite nature of God is an "expression" of God, an effect of God. It is due to the necessary nature of God and occurs in accord with the laws of nature. So, given an absolutely infinite substance constituted by an infinite number of attributes each of which is infinite in its own kind, it seems clear that an infinite number of things follow necessarily from the essence of God.

A number of shocking corollaries follow. First, whatever is conceivable (comes under the infinite intellect) must be. Every non-contradictory essence must exist necessarily, at some time or other, caused by the laws of Nature. God is the efficient cause of everything; he causes things immediately, not through intermediate causes, and He is the "absolutely first cause."[109] So, God is the first cause in the sense that God is eternal and necessarily existent, and He is the efficient cause of everything insofar as there are no intermediate causes, no relative substances, or subsidiary causes. There is no need for angels, and this denial of God's messengers, or subsidiary causes was one of the charges brought against Spinoza. God is that substance which operates from its own necessary laws in accordance with its own nature; and, as efficient cause, it brings other things into existence.

Proposition 17 reaffirms the singular, independent, free and absolutely infinite nature of God, asserting that "God acts from the laws of His own nature only and is compelled by no one."[110] Of course, since God is the only substance, there is nothing outside of God to compel His action, and nothing within God could force Him to act in a manner contrary to His essence. The latter case would require an inconsistent or contradictory nature for God. Thus, everything which occurs does so simply because it follows from God's essence.

If God acts solely because of His own nature and solely in accordance with His own essence, then God is free. Freedom means a lack of external constraint, an ability to act in accordance with one's own essential nature. That substance which acts in accordance with its own laws, as an independent singular substance must, acts freely. This is not to assert, however, that God can act in any willy-nilly manner whatever. God cannot act in a manner contrary to His own Nature, or essence, since that would indicate a contradiction within His nature. So, whatever happens, happens in the only way it could. It happens necessarily. Those things which are contradictory or opposed to God's essence cannot occur; they are impossible. The universe is composed of things which occur necessarily, in accordance with the laws of nature. While these things occur, or follow, necessarily from God's essence and in accordance with natural law, they were not necessary in the sense that their essence contains their existence. There is only one necessarily existent substance:

God or Nature. The things which follow from that Nature follow necessarily, but they depend for their existence upon the essence of God and God's existence. Thus, although it may appear odd to say it, God is the first cause of the existence of things which exist necessarily. The order of Nature is a necessary order in the sense that it is caused and follows from the power of God in the only manner in which it could occur. But, the individual entities of that order depend upon God and His laws for their existence. So, all things other than God, its constituent attributes, the immediate and mediate infinite modes, exist as hypothetical necessities; that is, they depend upon God's laws. These finite modes exist necessarily, that is to say, they must exist as they are, when they are, and in the order in which they occur due to the necessary laws of Nature. However, their existence does not follow from their own essence; rather, it follows from the essence of God.

Nature itself is free, but everything in the order of Nature occurs in accordance with its necessary laws. There are no miracles, no breaches in causality, no contra-causal freedom for God, man or any other sort of entity. All occurs serenely in the only way it could happen: naturally, in accordance with the essence of God or Nature. Things are what they must be, and things happen as they must. As Spinoza says, "... from the supreme power of God (His essence as an absolutely infinite, necessarily existent substance), or from His infinite nature ... all things have necessarily flowed, or continually follow by the same necessity, in the same way as it follows from the nature of a triangle, from eternity to eternity, that its three angles are equal to two right angles."[111] It should be noted that God or Nature does not impose order on a chaotic Nature, it *is* the order of nature. Thus, natural sciences are causal sciences wherein things are explained by necessary, causal relations.

Whereas Descartes on occasion views the laws of mathematics as due to the will of God,[112] for Spinoza the laws of mathematics follow the order of Nature or God Himself. These mathematical entities and relations must be what they are because they, too, constitute the nature of the law of non-contradiction, constitute the nature of God insofar as the attribute of Thought constitutes His essence. The laws of natural science and the laws of thought are equally necessary and causal. "The truth and formal essence of things is what it is, because as such it exists objectively in God's intellect. Therefore, the intellect of God, insofar as it is conceived to constitute His essence, is in truth the cause of things, both of their essence and their existence...."[113] So, everything which exists, and every law obtaining within the universe itself, does so because it follows from the very essence of God. God cannot change, violate, suspend those laws and the order of existence, since to do so would be to contradict His own nature. It would be inconsistent and self-contradictory; it would violate God's essence as Thought itself. Thus, it may well be said that God and laws of reason are identical.

There is no "free will" for either God himself or for the human beings who are simply finite expressions or effects of God's essence. All things act in accordance with God's essential laws, the laws of nature. This is true not only for finite modes of extension but also for the modes of all the attributes. Man's thoughts, images, volitions, and emotions all follow from the nature of God with the same necessity as the nature of the triangle includes 180°. God's actions are in accord with the necessary laws of Thought, because they *are* the laws of thought.

"God's intellect is the sole cause of things."[114] There are no causes other than God. If God is an active substance of absolutely infinite power, and if God is Nature, then Nature must follow its own essential laws and must in accordance therewith produce the universe. God has no choice, no free will, no "freedom" to create or not to create: God must cause everything to be what it is and when it is. Some think that the necessity to create the universe, which follows from God's own essence, detracts from the power of God, but only those who sharply separate God and Nature, the Creator and His creation. Some think that God must not create everything which is in His intellect, lest He lose His power to create more and thereby become something less than omnipotent. Some think that God is indifferent to everything, and He creates only "by a certain absolute will."[115] But none of the above suppositions are true for Spinoza. Spinoza's God is Thought and operates (or acts) necessarily in accordance with the laws of thought insofar as these constitute His essence. These laws are necessary, with conclusions following from premises with the same necessity as effects follow from causes.

As God's activity has been effected in accordance with the laws of Thought and the laws of Extension from eternity, so God's creation has been occurring from eternity. This is not to say that everything which follows from the nature of God, or from Nature itself, has actually occurred. God, being eternal, continually acts. Things occur in time, one after another, because the laws of nature are also laws of efficient causation. The laws themselves are eternal, but what occurs in accordance with them may be temporal. Still, nothing is merely an empty possibility, indeterminate, or fortuitous. What happens, happens necessarily. Only human ignorance of the necessity embodied in the laws of nature accounts for indeterminancy, possibility, chance. Once one understands the inexorable laws of Nature or God, one apprehends the causal order in Nature and in thought, and one understands that all that is, is what it is and when it is in accordance with those laws. One understands, then, that the essential laws of God or Nature are causal, rational laws of necessity. There is no freedom to violate these laws for humans, God or Nature.

Spinoza's argument against attributing free will to God is an argument against irrationality, indeterminism, chance. It is an argument based upon his commitment to an orderly, rational, intelligible universe. The mind of man, as an expression of the infinite intellect of God, can come to understand the laws of nature and can rest assured that things truly are as he conceives them to be and as they must be. Those who believe that both God (Nature) and humans have free wills—in the sense of "freedom" which entails the ability to act contrary to causal laws, contrary to one's character, contra-casually—are those who elevate man's ignorance of the laws of his own nature and of nature itself into a supreme principle governing the universe. These persons see the irrational will as the foundation for nature and man's unstable knowledge, whereas Spinoza accepts the laws of the intellect for a stable nature and knowledge.

Arguments which attribute freedom to God in the sense of an ability to do or not to do what reason demands, or what natural laws cause, are arguments which depend upon an incomplete knowledge of human nature and nature itself. Ignorance of human nature accounts for the false distinction between intellect and will in man and leads one to attribute this separation to God or Nature itself. This argument, founded in ignorance of human nature, then proceeds to compare human intellect and will to that of God. Analogies from finite to infinite are false, because the infinite is the cause of the finite and differs from it. Spinoza says God's intellect is "... sole cause of things, both of their essence and of their existence; for an effect differs from its cause precisely in that which it has from its cause."[116] Spinoza's causal axiom asserts that cause and effect must have something mutually in common; it does not assert that they must be identical. So, if God is the cause of human intellect and will, there is something in common but also something quite different between them.[117] The intellect of God "differs from our intellect both with regard to its essence and its existence, nor can it coincide with our intellect in anything except the name."[118] The difference in essence between man's intellect and God's is a difference between the finite and the infinite; the difference in existence is one between the existence of a dependent, "determined" effect and a necessarily existent, independent, free, self-caused cause. What is common between the human intellect and will and that of God is that the human intellect and will is a mode of God's attribute, Thought.

Thus, one may observe that Spinoza's metaphysics is one of necessity, reason, lawfulness, and it is different and distinct from the metaphysics of his contemporaries who separate God and Nature, will and intellect, freedom and necessity.

God's activity is necessary; it follows from His intellect in accordance with His essence, and it constitutes the laws of His nature. Although everything produced by God is produced necessarily, none of His effects has a necessary existence. That is to say, none of the finite modes, which are effects of the necessary causal activity of God or Nature, has its existence included in its essence. God alone, or Nature itself and its constituent attributes, exists necessarily, in itself, and conceived through itself. Since modes are effects, and since the cause and effect must differ from one another, then God or Nature and its finite modes are different, although they have something mutually in common through which they can be mutually understood. That is to say, the modes are modes of attributes, and it is through these that one can understand the relation between God or Nature and the modes.

DEFINITIONS AND MODES

Some interesting points are contained in an example Spinoza uses to explain God's causal activity. Spinoza notes, in the Scholium to Proposition 17, that man's essence is "an eternal truth."[119] That is to say, the "truth and formal essence" of man "exists objectively in God's intellect."[120] This essence, or formal nature, or real definition, is consistent and is constituted by compossible properties. The attributes of thought and extension constitute the formal essence of man, so these attributes must be non-contradictory, as I have argued earlier in this section. Wolfson says, "In the eternal truths there is only essence; there is no existence in them."[121] The fact that the essence of man is an eternal truth means simply that the essence exists, as an essence, as a definition. It exists formally in God's intellect, but it does not necessarily exist as an entity, independently. The formal essence, or definition of man cannot exist as a universal, as an Idea or Form (independent of Thought) or abstract entity. It cannot be a "substantial form," or existent, reified class or abstraction, because Spinoza denies the existence of these sorts of things. Yet, this example seems to assert that there is, in the intellect of God, an idea of the essence of human nature. This is a puzzle which must be solved in order to understand Spinoza. Perhaps one should consider this as a particular essence; a singular essence which is instantiated by particular existences. In the sense that it is an *eternal* truth, Spinoza means that it is contained within, or follows from, the Nature of God, or the attributes of Nature.

Spinoza's theory of definition, we recall, requires that the definition of an existing thing must contain its cause. God is His own cause; man can be defined *essentially* by reference to the necessarily existent attributes of thought and extension. In *Cogitata Metaphysica* I, 1, Spinoza notes that "real beings are divided ... into those 'whose essence involves existence,' i.e. God or Substance, and those 'whose essence involves only possible existence.' "[122] The *essence of man* exists necessarily in the infinite intellect of God; *a* man's *existence* is only possible. The essence of man is an eternal truth; his own existence does not follow from the necessarily existing attributes, however. Wolfson says:

> Man, being only a mode, or a thing which does not exist through itself, or a thing which is created, must be defined through his proximate or efficient cause, which is God, or through the attributes whose mode he is, and it is these attributes, namely extension and thought, not the universals animality and rationality, that may be considered as the genera through which man is defined or understood....[123]

It should be noted that Wolfson here must be understood as speaking of the formal nature, or real definition, of man in general—of the "eternal essence". It is only through the common notion of man that one can "understand" or "define" him. It is true that God or Nature is the efficient cause of the essence of man, but it is equally true that any particular man must be "understood" through his own proximate cause—his parents. Of course, the individual man can only be "known" through perception; he cannot be known insofar as one cannot deduce his existence from the infinite attributes. One can apprehend finite modes only by sense perception. In a sense, of course, since the infinite number of finite modes follow from the eternal laws of nature and necessarily existent attributes, and since these do constitute Nature or God, the laws, too, are the proximate cause of any particular man. But, if one attempts to "understand" or "apprehend" individual finite modes by means of eternal, infinite attributes and laws, one is doomed to failure. Explanations of particulars must involve their particular proximate causes. Explanations or definitions of essences can and must be in terms of eternal laws and infinite attributes, or Nature alone, or God Himself.

A person's existence depends upon the eternal laws of nature through which the attributes act. That is to say, the existence of any particular mode depends upon its proximate cause, which is another finite mode. The laws of nature are eternal, the essence of man is eternal, but the laws obtain in time and the existence of any man is temporal, of a limited duration. The particular instantiation of an eternal essence follows from eternal natural law and is a temporal existence. The concept or essence of man is necessary and eternal; the existence of any man is dependent upon proximate causes.

Spinoza notes that different particular, individual modes can have the same essence. He notes that a father differs from his son in regard to the son's existence but "… the two will exactly coincide in essence".[124] If the father should die, the son continues to exist, but "if the essence of one could be destroyed and become false, the essence of the other would also be destroyed".[125] So, apparently for Spinoza, essences exist independently of their particular instantiations, independent of their existent modes, but not *vice versa*. An essence, then, seems to be "a common nature" which is separate from any particular finite modes of which it is an essence, because the different individuals can have the same essence. Furthermore, the essences are eternal truths, exist necessarily as essences. The finite modes seem to resemble Plato's particulars in their individuality, finitude, dependence, and temporality.

ESSENCES AND MEDIATE INFINITE MODE

In Scholium 2 to Proposition 8, Spinoza uses the terms "human nature generally"[126] and "human nature itself"[127]. I should suggest that "human nature in general" is the same as the "essence" of man in Proposition 17, Scholium and is the real definition of man. A real definition is a clear and distinct idea which can be apprehended by intuition or reason. Clear and distinct ideas are eternally true. The essence of man exists necessarily in the intellect of God. It seems to me that the totality of "essential natures" or essences, eternal truths and common axioms or definitions, constitutes the mediate infinite mode which Spinoza calls "the face of the whole universe". Included in the mediate infinite mode is also to be found the causal laws (common notions or axioms) which govern the causal relations between finite modes. Thus, essences—common natures and causal laws—common notions—are constituents of the mediate infinite mode. This infinite mode is the final necessarily existent mode of *natura naturans*. Since this is an eternal essence, a "common character", it cannot serve to indicate any particular, finite mode's existence. The existence of a finite mode is not only dependent upon its essence and the eternal laws of nature, but it is determined to existence by some other finite mode. Thus, there are two sorts of proximate causes needed to account for the existence of any finite mode: the eternal proximate causes which follow from *natura naturans* and the temporal proximate causes which, while due to the eternal essences and laws, are needed to bring particular existents into being at some particular moment in time. The determinants of individual existence are both eternal and temporal; apprehended by intuition, or reason, *and* perception.

The relation between the eternal and the temporal, the essence and the existence of finite things, the infinite and the finite, the necessarily exis-tent mediate infinite mode and the finite mode which exists because of other finite modes, is akin to the relation between Forms and particulars in Plato. It seems to me that the Spinozistic essences of finite modes are similar to Plato's Forms insofar as the essence is eternal. They differ from Plato's Forms insofar as Spinoza's essences do not exist independently of God's intellect. They do not exist in themselves, but exist "formally" in the intellect of God. They do not exist independently of God, but, then, nothing exists outside of God or Nature for Spinoza. Forms *are* entities, formal realities which exist independently of the Demiurge. Thus, Spinoza consistently denies substantial forms, universals, and abstrac-tions as existing things, while he retains common natures, or essences, as objective realities in God's intellect. Substantial forms, etc., are fictions invented by men when they abstract from ideas of images. Essences are found in God's *intellect*; they are not at all due to imagination but rather are due to the laws of understanding. The only *entities* which exist for Spinoza are particular, singular things: he is a nominalist. But, there are *ideas* of essences, both in the minds of men and God, and these essences are general, common natures. Yet, because each of these common essences differ from other essences, they are particulars, too; as each of Plato's Forms is a particular one. Perhaps one might view Plato's many Forms and Spinoza's common essences as particulars of reason as opposed to particulars of sense perception. The finite modes seem to resemble Plato's particulars in their individuality, finitude, dependence, temporality, and in their perceptibility.

MODES

As if to emphasize that God and His finite modes are not absolutely separate and distinct but do have common attributes, Spinoza notes in Proposition 18 that God is the immanent and not the transient cause of *all* things (*omnium rerum*). Since everything is in God, God's laws pervade all of the occurrences within the universe. That is to say, natural laws pervade everything; nothing is self-determined, or self-caused, but God or Nature. God, or Nature, pervades the attributes which constitute nature and the infinite modes which follow from the essence of God or Nature.

Propositions 19 and 20 assert that God and His attributes, which con-stitute His essence, are equally eternal and exist necessarily. Thus, the attributes are not subjectively known expressions of God which exist only for human conception, but they do in fact constitute God. God or Nature is constituted by the attributes which are eternal, free, and immutable. The only difference between God and the attributes is that God is absolutely infinite whereas attributes are infinite only in their own kind.

If the nature of God is identical to that of His attributes, and if God acts in accordance with His own nature, then the laws of the attributes are equally the laws of nature or God. The laws of Nature pervade its constituent attributes. What follows necessarily from the laws of nature follows with equal necessity from the attributes of Nature or God. Since the essence of God entails the laws of His activity: that is to say, since God acts in accordance with His essence, through His attributes, the laws of nature indicate the order of His action. When Spinoza uses the expressions "follow" or "flow," he means that things are lawful and occur in accordance with the laws of Nature or God. Those laws, as I said above, are causal laws where effects are caused by or determined by causes. The laws are necessary, in the sense that a given determinate cause produces a given determinate effect. The laws are free in the sense that they are not compelled by forces outside of Nature or outside of any attribute. The laws of nature are expressed within the attributes.

All of the things which "follow from the absolute nature of any attribute of God must forever exist, and must be infinite...."[128] The generally accepted view of those eternal and infinite expressions of each attribute is that they constitute the infinite modes. In Letter 64, Spinoza says the immediate infinite mode of Thought is "absolutely infinite understanding," which I take to be the intellect of God. The immediate infinite mode of extension is motion and rest. The mediate infinite mode is "the face of the whole Universe which, although it varies in infinite modes, yet remains always the same."[129] Although the mediate infinite mode of each attribute is different, seen *sub specie aeternitatis*, it is the same. I should argue that the only eternal and infinite expressions of nature are the infinite modes and these include the specific laws of nature, essences peculiar to each attribute, and eternal truths and axioms which obtain within each attribute.

Propositions 21 through 23 demonstrate that the eternal, infinite, necessarily existent attributes which constitute Nature, God, or Substance are themselves active powers. They produce eternal, infinite modes. While substance and its attributes are equally active and self-caused, modes are their effects. Substance is a free thing, a thing which exists "from the necessity of its own nature alone and is determined to action by itself alone".[130] To be free is to be self-caused and self-determined. To be self-caused is to "exist from the necessity of its own nature." Necessarily existent things are free. However, some things are not free but are necessary. Spinoza says, "That thing ... is called necessary, or rather 'compelled', which by another is determined to existence and action in a fixed or determinate manner".[131] Generally, the things which are caused to exist by something else are termed things which exist necessarily. This confusion between the "necessary existence" of a free thing and the things which are compelled to "exist necessarily" could be clarified if one spoke of "compelled" and "free" things. One could also speak more clearly if one spoke of things whose necessity was in themselves (free) and those whose necessity was due to something other than themselves (compelled or caused by something else). But, to modern ears such talk seems to lack the impact of strict causality for determined things and the necessary existence of things whose essence includes existence. Compelled things are things whose existence is necessitated by the laws of nature, whose existence is that of "hypothetical necessity". Free things exist because of their own essence and their own laws.

Substance and its attributes are free; their essence includes existence. Spinoza, stressing their free activity, calls them *natura naturans*: nature naturing. And they act in accordance with their own laws. Their productions, the infinite modes, are infinite and eternal. But, they are not self-caused. They are eternal because their existence "is conceived necessarily to follow from the definition alone of the eternal thing."[132] These things are "eternal truths".[133] It should be noted that these "eternal truths" or "infinite modes" *follow* from or are "determined by" the eternal thing: God or its attributes. Thus, the modes are *natura naturata*: nature natur*ed*; they are caused or compelled in both their essence and their existence. They are effects of the activity of Nature or its attributes.

If Nature or God is the only self-caused thing, it is the only thing whose essence includes existence. It is the only free, independent thing; everything else exists in God. Thus, God is the immanent cause. Since the modes are not self-caused, they must be caused by God; so, God or Nature pervades everything and His causal laws compel everything. In short, God or Nature is the first cause, because it is self-caused. Because God causes everything else, it is the efficient cause of everything. Furthermore, since the modes are not independent but dependent, God must preserve them. He is the cause "of their continuance in existence".[134] Thus, for the existence of modes, of everything other than substance or the attributes, God's immanent and eternal causation is required. In Scholastic terms, God or Nature is the *causa in fieri* and the *causa in esse*.

In addition to being the "existential cause" of the modes, which follow from His own existence, God or Nature is also their "essential cause". That is to say, God is the cause of the essence of every mode. The eternal essences, or eternal truths are truths which "follow from the definition

alone of the eternal thing'',[135] but they can be conceived as not existing.
So, their essence does not involve existence.[136] Nothing can be conceived
which does not depend upon God—the immanent, absolutely infinite
substance. The knowledge of God, Nature, or Substance is involved in
the knowledge of anything else. Everything else is in Nature; it is dependent upon God or Nature. So, if the conception of anything involves the
knowledge of God, and if the ''conception'' of something constitutes its
real definition or essence, then the essence of everything depends on,
involves, is caused by God. As God or Nature is the cause of Himself, He
is the cause of everything else.

Spinoza refers to Proposition 16 as being the basis for Proposition 25.
Proposition 16 demonstrates that from God's infinite activity an infinite
number of things follows. From Proposition 16 onward, Spinoza has
been stressing that God or Nature is eternal, absolutely infinite, *active*,
and powerful. There is nothing which could limit or restrain God's activity insofar as there is no other existent substance. That is to say, God acts
freely, in accordance with the laws of necessity which constitute his
essence. These causal laws are laws whereby a given determinate cause
produces a given determinate effect necessarily. Given the cause, the
effect is compelled. Thus eternal and infinite modes are caused by God;
they ''follow'' from the nature of the attributes. I should, then, interpret
the phrase ''exists necessarily and infinitely'' as it appears in Propositions 22 and 23[137] as meaning that the existence of infinite modes is
caused by the attributes. Their existence is the result of something other
than their own essence.

Since there are no external limitations for God's activity, it can be expressed in an infinite number of ways. Not only does God cause infinite
modes, He also causes finite modes. There is no reason for the non-
existence of finite modes given the absolutely infinite power of God.
There is no reason which would prohibit the attenuation of God's activity
from the infinite to the finite. There are eternal essences, or eternal
truths, or real definitions of finite things, so they are conceivable, at least
by God's infinite understanding.[138] There is nothing inconsistent or contradictory in the conception of the essences of finite things, so they follow
from God's activity. If they are conceivable, then they exist eternally as
essences in God's intellect. There is nothing within the eternal essences of
finite things to prevent their existence, as essences, and there is nothing
outside God to prevent their existence as essences. But, whether or not
the essences become expressed as particular, finite modes depends upon
other finite modes. So, from the infinite power of God, both essences and
particular existences of finite modes result.

In the Corollary to Proposition 25, we find the first discussion of finite modes. Spinoza says, "Individual things are nothing but the affections or modes of God's attributes, expressing those attributes in a certain and determinate manner."[139] These individual, particular, or finite modes are the expressions of God's activity or power, and they follow from necessary causal laws. Their essence is caused by God and their existence caused by God's causal laws which obtain within each attribute. To account for their existence at this time, or by means of their efficient, proximate cause, one must abandon the eternal and infinite and look to other finite modes. Of course, even the action between finite modes is to be accounted for in terms of necessary causal laws, and these are laws of Nature or God. The laws hold not only within the attributes and eternal and infinite modes, but also between finite modes. Thus, the determination to existence of any finite mode is due to another determined finite mode and the causal laws of God.

As God or Nature is the absolutely infinite power which pervades the universe of infinite and finite things, and as God is the only independent thing, then God necessarily determines, or causes, everything not only insofar as its essence and existence is concerned, but also insofar as its activity is concerned. That is to say, everything follows necessarily from Nature and acts necessarily in accordance with natural laws. Nothing, save Nature Itself, can cause itself to act; nothing derives its power and its existence from itself except the self-caused cause. All things which are so determined or caused cannot, by their own power or by means of their own existence, render themselves "indeterminate," uncaused, free, or chancey. That which has been caused by Nature to be what it is and act as it does, cannot abrogate the causal chain—the laws of nature—which constitute an expression of Nature's, or God's, power. So, Propositions 25 through 27 indicate that God causes the essence, existence, and power, or activity of all modes—infinite and finite. Furthermore, if a mode is part of God's, or Nature's, causal chain, if it follows from God's activity, it cannot escape from causation. There is no contra-causal freedom among infinite modes. They are caused by God or Nature, and they cause things in a causal (fixed and determinate) manner. Thus, causation holds between the attributes and their infinite modes. Causal laws obtain within the eternal things.

Whereas finite modes are mentioned in the Corollary to Proposition 25, Spinoza clearly states the implication of the causal doctrine for finite modes in Proposition 28. This states that "singular or finite things which have determinate existence"[140] are determined to *existence* and *action* by other finite things alone. That is to say, the essence of finite, or particular things is due to the attributes and the infinite modes. However, the existence or action (and we recall that power *is* existence for Spinoza)[141] of any individual finite mode is caused by some other finite existence. Finite existence is due to, caused by, follows from, other finite existence. One cannot account for the existence and causation between finite things by means of eternal and infinite things. One can understand that there are finite things because of the absolutely infinite activity of God which is unlimited in range. However, to account for the activity and existence of any finite thing, one must know the proximate cause of that finite thing. The cause of the existence of a finite thing is another finite thing.

For Spinoza, the existence of any *individual* finite thing requires a knowledge of *its* proximate cause. The existence of *all* of the finite things and their causal laws can be explained by an appeal to infinite and eternal essences and the causal laws therein. Infinite and eternal essences and their laws follow from the attributes. The attributes constitute the "absolute nature" of God. Thus, from the absolute nature of God, the attributes, follows infinite and eternal essences, causal laws, eternal truths. The absolute nature of God is what Spinoza terms *natura naturans*. God is the proximate cause "absolutely" of the infinite and eternal modes. Thus, the real definition, or essence, of man follows "absolutely" and "immediately" from the nature of the infinite modes and their respective attributes. The existence of any particular man, though, cannot be explained by means of the biological laws and the definition of man. To explain the existence of Fred, one needs to know his parents and the particular circumstances at the time of his conception. These particularities are not due to God's absolute nature, but rather to God's nature insofar as it conserves the particulars and the laws of their activity. Finite modes are due to God's pervasive activity within the infinite modes and between the finite modes which are effects of infinite modes. In short, while everything, including particular finite modes, is in God, and while God's laws pervade everything, one cannot explain individuals as immediately following from His absolute nature. One needs individuals, time, and causal laws operating within time, to explain other individuals. So, God is, indeed, the first, efficient and immanent cause of the infinite and finite modes. But, He is the proximate cause of only those things which follow from His "absolute" nature—the infinite and eternal modes and their laws.

Although the cause and effect must have something mutually in common, be pervaded by the same attribute, they must also differ from one another.[142] Infinite modes cause the essence and existence of finite modes. So, the existence of a particular person differs from the eternally existent essence of man. Essences, real definitions are eternal and follow from the nature of the attributes. But a particular person is temporal; his existence follows from his parents. There is no particular, individual essence for each finite mode. He says that "with regard to essence, two men may exactly resemble one another."[143] Individual things differ not in essence but in existence; Spinoza talks about "human nature generally" and "human nature itself."[144] So, there are no essences for each individual, only for finite things "in general." The reason or cause for the existence of numbers of finite things is to be found in other finite existences. The reason, or cause, for finite things being of the same sort is to be found in the eternal essence, real definition, in which they share. Thus, there is an "existential" causation which holds between finite modes and which accounts for their existence. This chain of individual causes is an expression of God and His natural laws. The causal laws constitute God as He acts within the attributes and between finite modes of each attribute. To account for the existence of a finite mode, one must be able to identify *its* finite proximate causes and specify the time and place of the causal laws operating between those finite modes. Insofar as God is Being Itself, all existence, whether eternal or temporal, is pervaded by God.

There is also a causal relation between the essence of finite things in general and a particular finite mode. There is, then, an "essential causation" which obtains between eternal essences and an individual of that sort or type. What makes Fred a man is that eternal essence which is expressed temporally. There is a causal relation between eternal infinite essences and temporal finite things of that sort; a causation between things of different orders of essence and existence. There is also causation between things of the same order of finitude and temporality; finite modes cause the existence of other finite modes but not their essence.[145] Insofar as God's activity is expressed by the causal laws, we can say that God or Nature is the cause of everything which follows from His activity, whether it is infinite and follows from His absolute nature immediately, or whether it is finite and follows from His nature mediately.

Given that there is but one God, Substance, or Nature which exists necessarily and in which everything exists, whatever does exist is a result of God's essence and activity. God is the cause of those things which follow immediately from His attributes: the infinite modes. He is the cause of their essence, their activity, and their existence. The existence of anything is its power, so the modes have their activity determined by God, too. Nothing, except for God Himself, or Nature Itself determines itself to action. Everything else is determined in respect of essence, existence, and activity. This is nothing other than the assertion that everything in the universe is causally related to God and follows from the necessary existence or power of God. This holds not only for infinite modes, but also for finite modes. The finite world is a concatenation of causality amongst the finite modes; the causal laws being the eternal expressions of Nature which are numbered among the constituents of the mediate infinite mode. The infinite modes are necessary expressions of Nature which are caused immediately by *natura naturans*.

There is, then, a "horizontal" causality between finite modes and other finite modes of the same attribute to account for their existence and activity. There is a "vertical" causation between the attributes, their infinite modes, and their finite modes. The vertical causation is in a descending order of perfection, with those things immediately produced by God being more perfect (infinite and eternal) than those following from Him mediately (finite and temporal).[146] Everything is governed, or determined, by necessary causal laws which are either due to their own essence or to the nature of some other thing. This causality holds not only for essences but also for existences; everything which exists does so either because of its own necessity, or because of the necessary activity of something else in accordance with the causal laws of Nature.

Apparently, the mediate infinite mode (the face of the whole universe) is the point at which the infinite and the finite interact. That is to say, it is the point at which vertical causation—from infinite to finite—occurs. The essence of man causes the essence of finite men, for example. It is also the point at which the causal laws which operate or obtain between finite modes are to be found. Those causal laws must be eternal and must hold between finite modes of any particular attribute. There are no causal laws which are limited to relations between only two finite modes. Thus, the mediate infinite mode seems to be the least pervasive, least general of the infinite modes and thus seems to be the locus of those least general scientific laws.

INFINITE INTELLECT

Proposition 30 states that "the actual intellect, whether finite or infinite, must comprehend the attributes of God and its affections, and nothing else".[147] This is so because truth has been defined as the agreement of an idea with its ideatum, and the only ideata which exist are either the attributes of God or modes. If the infinite intellect constitutes the immediate infinite mode of Thought (understanding), it must necessarily follow from the attributes of Thought. If the intellect is finite, it follows from the immediate infinite mode. In either case, the intellect is to be understood as being constituted by adequate ideas. Only adequate ideas, clear and distinct ideas, are things which "necessarily exist in nature".[148] All adequate ideas are true, but a finite intellect can ascertain necessary existence only of ideas which are clear and distinct and not "mutilated and confused". Since the only inadequate ideas are those of imagination and perception, I believe that the ideas "understood" or "comprehended" by the actual intellect are clear and distinct ideas of God, the attributes, and the infinite modes. Thus, the infinite intellect comprehends the attributes of God, and the finite intellect comprehends the attributes and/or the infinite modes. The finite intellect cannot have adequate ideas of finite modes which are known only through imagination and perception.

This view is supported by Proposition 31 wherein Spinoza states that "the actual intellect, whether it be finite or infinite, together with will, desire, love, ..., must be referred to the *natura naturata* ...".[149] All modes of thought depend upon, or are caused by, or are conceived through the attribute of Thought. So, the intellect is a mode and not an attribute. This intellect may be viewed as the infinite mode or as the finite mode of Thought. In the Scholium, Spinoza says that the actual intellect is the understanding itself.[150] If, as Spinoza says, "we can understand nothing through the intellect which does not lead to a more perfect knowledge of the understanding", and this knowledge is of the "utmost clearness",[151] it follows that both the finite and the infinite intellects contemplate the attribute of Thought. The finite intellect contemplates the infinite mode which is either constituted by adequate ideas and their laws or causes the adequate ideas and laws which constitute the mediate infinite mode of thought. In either case, some commentators interpret this as indicating that all knowledge in Spinoza is reflexive. That is to say, the intellect contemplates the intellect, clear and distinct ideas are the objects of the intellect. To say that a mode of thought contemplates ideas, or other modes of thought, is not to claim that Spinoza's epistemology is exclusively a coherence theory, however.[152]

The infinite intellect, being a mode of thought, is caused by the attribute of Thought. If one seeks the causes of the finite intellect, one must turn to the essence of man as contained within the infinite mode of Thought and to other finite modes. Either intellect is composed of clear and distinct ideas and is compelled to existence and action by something else. That is to say, the intellect is necessitated. If the intellect is a mode of thought and is determined to existence and action by something else, then so equally all the other modes of thought are compelled or necessitated. Will, desire, love are other modes of thought, so they, too, are caused or compelled to existence and action. So, there is no free will, either infinite or finite.

God Himself "does not act from freedom of the will".[153] We have seen that God's acts are due to His own essence and follow necessarily from

His nature. God is free only in the sense that He is not compelled by anything outside of Himself, but He is determined, or caused, to act by His own nature. God's essence includes His existence, and His existence is His activity.[154] So, God acts from or because of His own nature, but He must act as He does. Any other action would be inconsistent with His own nature or essence, as Spinoza discusses in the Scholium to Proposition 17.[155]

If one views the intellect and will as being infinite modes, then they are caused, or determined to existence and activity by God as He is constituted by the attribute of Thought. So, the immediate infinite mode of Thought, which Spinoza viewed earlier as "understanding" has been further analyzed into the "intellect" and the "will". In Corollary 2 to Proposition 32, he says that "will and intellect are related to the nature of God as motion and rest, and absolutely all natural things ...".[156] We had seen that the two immediate infinite modes are "in Thought, absolutely infinite understanding, in Extension, motion and rest".[157]

I believe there is no difficulty in understanding that the intellect and will are equally determined, or caused, or compelled, if we accept the position that the intellect is constituted by or comprehends only adequate ideas. All adequate ideas contain or include their own affirmation or denial. The essence of an adequate idea, then, includes its affirmation and denial. The will is simply the affirmation or denial of an idea. So, adequate ideas compel, or necessitate, or determine the will by their very essence alone. Insofar as adequate ideas are caused by, or follow from, or are determined by the attribute of Thought, and insofar as each adequate idea contains its necessary affirmation or denial, then the will is necessitated or determined. As the infinite mode of motion and rest is determined by Extension, so the infinite mode of intellect and will is determined by Thought. Even finite wills are determined insofar as they constitute the adequate ideas or intellect of man. If the finite intellect contains adequate ideas then it is caused, and its constituent will is caused. All things follow causally, necessarily, from God or Nature, in accordance with its laws, and this includes the finite intellect and will.

If Nature is what it is; that is, if Nature has a certain essence or definition, and if that essence includes existence, and existence is power or activity, then God's activity is just what it is and cannot be other than it is. Everything which follows from God follows necessarily in its manner and order. To have been produced in another order or manner would have required a God of another essence and activity. Even then, whatever followed from that other God would have followed necessarily in its order and manner. But there cannot be two absolutely infinite Substances or Gods. There is only one God. Whatever is, is necessarily, occurs necessarily, is produced necessarily, and acts necessarily. God wills necessarily and man's will is necessitated by God.

Spinoza's metaphysics is, then, a metaphysics of necessity. Everything occurs, exists, is determined, necessarily in a necessary manner and order. Everything acts necessarily. Even God exists necessarily, that is, in accordance with His own essence. God cannot not exist. In the Scholium to Proposition 33, Spinoza discusses the terms "necessary", "impossible", and "contingent". He says, "A thing is called necessary either in reference to its essence or cause. For the existence of a thing necessarily follows either from the essence and definition of the thing itself, or from a given efficient cause."[158] The only thing which is necessary by reason of its essence is God. Thus, God is free, because He is not compelled or caused by anything else. But He exists by the necessity of His own essence. Everything other than God and its attributes is necessary, because it is caused by something other than its own essence. Everything other than Nature and the attributes is compelled, determined, to existence and action by an efficient cause other than itself. The ultimate efficient cause, the immanent and first cause, is God or Nature. From this cause, the infinite modes follow. The infinite modes cause the finite modes essentially, and finite modes bring other finite modes into being. So, everything which exists is necessary.

A thing which is not necessary is impossible. Spinoza says a thing is "impossible either because the essence of the thing itself or its definition involves a contradiction, or because no external cause exists determinate to the production of such a thing."[159] If we cannot ascertain the real definition or essence of a thing, its formal nature, then we cannot know with certitude whether it is necessary or impossible. If we cannot comprehend the entire order of causation, we cannot understand whether a particular finite thing is necessary or impossible by means of its causes.

We cannot know the essence of any finite mode, and we cannot comprehend the infinite chain of finite modes involved in the causation of any finite mode. Thus, only in the case of finite modes is the mind not caused to affirm or deny the existence of the ideatum of an idea by the very nature of the idea itself. That is to say, only in ideas of finite modes is one faced with inadequate ideas. Only here can one entertain doubt concerning the existence or non-existence of the object of the idea. Where inadequate ideas are found, one finds contingency or possibility; belief instead of knowledge. The only type of knowledge that contains inadequate ideas is knowledge of the first kind, opinion or imagination. Thus, it is only a "deficiency in our knowledge,"[160] a lack of adequate ideas which accounts for contingency or possibility. In themselves, everything is necessary or impossible by means of its essence or the causal laws of Nature.

In Scholium 2 to Proposition 33, Spinoza argues that "things have been produced by God in the highest degree of perfection, since they have necessarily followed from the existence of a most perfect nature."[161] God is most perfect, because He is absolutely infinite, and because His essence includes His existence and power. Spinoza argues that perfection causes perfection. That is to say, things are perfectly what they are; they could not have been anything other than what they are, given the necessity of God's essence and power. Even "imperfect" things, produced mediately by God, are as perfect as they could be given the necessary cause of their existence and essence. God could not have acted otherwise. Given His perfection, everything produced is perfect.

God's power, will, and intellect are all necessary and follow from His essence. God does not deliberate, decide, and then act because God is eternal and "in eternity there is no when nor before nor after".[162] God's decrees are co-eternal with His acts and His essence. God does not look to the model of the Good, as does Plato's Demiurge, since there is nothing outside of God at all. In particular, there is nothing outside of Him which could determine Him to act. God's acts are in accord with His essence, and He produces everything necessarily. God's essence is Thought, as well as the other infinite attributes. Thought includes Intellect and Will. Those who believe that God wills the world into existence must agree that given God's essence, the world follows necessarily and perfectly.

An argument which accounts for the existence and perfection of finite modes follows from our understanding of God's necessary activity. Spinoza says, "... there is no reasoning which can persuade us to believe that God was unwilling to create all things which are in His intellect with the same perfection as that in which they exist in His intellect".[163] The attribute of Thought constitutes the essence of God, and ideas are modes of Thought. Adequate ideas, then, follow from God's nature. Given that God's essence is His power, and given that His power leads to the production of everything, God causes or produces all the ideas in His intellect necessarily. Since every idea has an ideatum, it follows that God produces the ideata of those ideas with equal necessity whether the ideatum be a mode of thought or a mode of extension.

In Propositions 34 to 36, Spinoza concludes Part I with the proof that the essence of God is identical with His power and that power is exercized necessarily. That is to say, everything is in God, is caused by God, and exists necessarily. Everything which exists does so in a "certain and determinate manner"[164] and is causally related to everything else. Thus, God causes everything, and God's effects cause other things necessarily.

The metaphysics of Spinoza presents us with a causal nexus which ranges in a vertical order from God and His constitutent attributes to infinite and finite modes. It extends horizontally between finite modes *ad infinitum*. The concatenation of finite modes is bound together by causation, and causation is an expression of the activity of God. The activity of God, His power, essence, and existence is itself necessitated by His own nature. Everything is in God, depends upon God and His expressions. Spinoza's metaphysical system is alive, active, causal. Causation constitutes God's activity which causes individuals to exist and constitutes the activity between individuals. Thus, God and His causal activity are the first, immanent, and necessary causes of everything.

COMMENTARY

We have argued that Spinoza's view of the substance-attribute relation is one that asserts that attributes constitute substance, are identical to substance. The relation is not to be construed as subject-predicate, or substance-property. We have also argued that Spinoza could not accept a position which interprets attributes as subjective perceptions of substance. F. S. Haserot had argued for the objectionist view of attributes as constituting substance in his article "Spinoza's Definition of Attributes."[165] E. M. Curley also argues that "Spinoza ... does identify substance with its attribute, or rather, with the totality of its attributes".[166] If one contends that the attributes constitute substance and that the intellect 'perceives' them, then one might be led to ask the following questions: (1) how can a finite intellect 'perceive' the infinite number of attributes which constitute substance; and (2) how can a simple substance be composed of infinite numbers of attributes.

F. S. Haserot argues that the intellect referred to in the definition of attribute, "By attribute I understand that which the intellect perceives of substance as constituting its essence",[167] is the infinite intellect. Haserot says, "No finite intellect ... could perceive all the attributes. Nevertheless all the attributes are attributes of substance. Hence the term 'intellect' in the definition cannot refer to the finite intellect".[168] Curley says that the intellect mentioned in the definition of attribute "is later referred to as an infinite intellect".[169] The later reference is to Proposition 7, Part II of the *Ethics*, in the Scholium, where Spinoza says, "... everything which can be perceived by the infinite intellect as constituting the essence of substance ...".[170] Curley continues, "If it is to perceive all the attributes and there are infinitely many of those attributes, then it must be what Spinoza would call absolutely infinite, and not merely infinite in its own kind. And since an attribute is defined as something which this intellect perceives, there could hardly be an attribute which the intellect failed to perceive''.[171]

In his article which is designed to support the objectivist account of the attributes by references in the *Short Treatise*, W. Kessler stresses the importance of the term 'perceive' in the definition of attribute.[172] He says, ''This explanation recognizes a connotation of passivity in the term 'perception'. If we take Spinoza's definition seriously, we must assume that he chose the term 'percipit' carefully in defining 'attributum' and that he had in mind the distinction he would make in Part II of the *Ethics*''.[173] Because of the passivity implied by 'perception', and because of his remarks in the article, it appears that Kessler infers that the intellect in question is the finite human intellect. Surely, the absolutely infinite intellect would have only adequate ideas and would then 'conceive' the attributes as constituting substance. While Haserot, Curley and Kessler agree that the attributes are the objective essences of substance, they disagree about the intellect which perceives the attributes.

I agree with Kessler that it is the finite intellect of man which perceives the attributes of substance, but I disagree with his reasoning. It is true that Spinoza makes an important distinction in Part II of the *Ethics* between an idea, which is a conception of the mind, and an idea of an image which is a perception of the mind. However, it does not seem plausible that Spinoza would claim that one has an idea of an image of an attribute. Furthermore, Spinoza does say that intuition ''advances from an adequate idea of the essence of certain attributes of God to the adequate knowledge of the essence of things''.[174] In Proposition 47 of Part II, he says, ''The human mind possesses an adequate knowledge of the eternal and infinite essence of God''.[175] So, I should argue that Spinoza was not yet prepared to stress the passivity of 'perception' when he used the term in his definition of attribute, but he was still using *percipit* as a synonym for *concipit* as was common in the seventeenth century. Only later, in Part II of the *Ethics*, does Spinoza stress the difference.

In favor of Kessler's claim that it is the finite intellect which apprehends the attributes, one could refer to Part II Propositions 40 and 47. Here it seems that the Haserot-Curley contention that one requires an infinite intellect to know the infinite attributes of God is inconsistent with Spinoza's account of the powers of the human mind. I believe that one can account for knowledge of the infinite attributes by a finite intellect, if one makes a specific distinction between ''knowing by acquaintance'' and ''knowing by description''. This is akin to the distinction of knowing ''that'' a thing is and knowing ''what'' a thing is. The finite intellect knows the attributes, Thought and Extension, because a human being is a finite mode of thought and extension. Thus, one knows two attributes by acquaintance, or by the old epistemological dictum that like knows like. We know *what* two attributes of substance are. On the other hand, we do possess an adequate idea, a clear and distinct idea, a definition of God as "Being absolutely infinite, that is to say, substance consisting of infinite attributes".[176] We recall that definitions which are conceivable are equivalent to axioms in terms of clarity and distinctness or adequacy. If the finite intellect can have an adequate definition then God must have infinite attributes. What is deducible from an adequate idea is adequate itself. Spinoza says, "Hence we see that the infinite essence and the eternity of God are known to all; and since all things are in God and are conceived through Him, it follows that we can *deduce* from this knowledge many things which we can know adequately, and that we can thus form that third sort of knowledge (intuition) ...".[177]

Further support for the argument that the finite intellect apprehends infinite attributes can be found in Spinoza's letter to DeVries. Spinoza says, "... There is nothing more evident to us than the fact that every entity is conceived *by us* under some attribute, and that the more reality or being an entity has the more attributes there must be attributed to it. So that the absolutely infinite being must be defined etc."[178] It is clear that an absolutely infinite substance must have an infinite number of attributes. This can be deduced by a finite intellect from the definition of God. We can thus know by definition *that* God has an infinite number of attributes; an infinite intellect is not required in order to make this inference. It is true that we cannot know *what* the attributes other than Thought and Extension are, but we can know that there are an infinity of them simply from the apprehension of the idea of God. So, Kessler is quite correct in referring to the *Short Treatise* wherein "Spinoza asks where we get the idea of infinitely many perfect attributes in Substance. ... (And Spinoza answers) 'Whence, then, but from the infinite attributes themselves which tell us *that* they are, without however telling us, at the same time, what they are: for only of two do we know what they are' ".[179]

Thus, in order to guarantee the objectivity of the attributes, one need not appeal to an infinite intellect. One need only appeal to a finite intellect which can apprehend the definition of God. It is true that finite intellects cannot *comprehend*, or know by acquaintance, all the infinite attributes. This sort of knowledge is limited to the attributes of Thought and Extension. However, finite intellects can *apprehend* the fact that infinite attributes must constitute the essence of an absolutely infinite being and can know *that* such attributes must exist without knowing *what* they are.

The second question concerning the simplicity of a substance constituted by infinite attributes has been examined in pages 42 to 66. We
have argued that infinite attributes are real, objective, constituents of
substance, but substance itself is unique, singular, and simple. Kessler
states the problem thusly: "Objectivists are obliged ... to respond to the
subjectivist charge that an objective multiplicity of attributes would be
inconsistent with the simplicity of substance".[180] Propositions 12 and 13
are designed to prove the indivisibility of the attributes and of substance
itself. Clearly, if an attribute is divisible, and if it constitutes substance,
then substance would be divisible. If something is divisible, it is possible
to break it into parts; it would be a compound thing and not something
simple. But, Spinoza's substance is not a whole composed of parts, so it
cannot have an attribute which is composed of parts or which is divisible.

For Spinoza, extension *per se* is indivisible because it is an attribute,
and attributes are infinite. That which is infinite is complete and self-
contained. If extension was divisible, it would have to be constituted by
equally infinite and self-contained parts, or it would have to be constituted by incomplete, dependent parts. The absurdity of either of these
hypotheses leads Spinoza to assert that extension, and all the other
infinitude of attributes, are indivisible.

As a corollary to the metaphysical argument, Spinoza argues that
extension *per se* can be understood only through intuition or reason. It is
only as thus apprehended, as one appreciates the essential nature of
extension, that one can grasp its indivisibility. In an excellent commentary on extension and substance in Spinoza, E. Brehier notes the importance of making a distinction "between extension as an object of the
understanding and extension as an object of the imagination; it is the
imagined extension which is composed of parts, divided into bodies of
which it is the total sum; but for the understanding, extension is infinite
and indivisible."[181] As one imagines, or perceives, extended finite
modes, one may be misled into assenting to the divisibility of extension.
The contradiction between the divisibility of imagined extension (modes)
and indivisibility of understood extension (attribute) is resolved by an
appeal to Proposition 12. It is, of course, the mark of a rationalist to
decide such problems by means of argumentation, or "thought experi-
ment", rather than by empirical experimentation.

Intelligibility for Spinoza, as for Plato, is a function or effect of order
and unity. As the Demiurge organizes chaos as much as possible to produce a cosmos, an order which is intelligible (and, for Plato, good), so
Substance itself is the order, unity and foundation for intelligibility of all
the constituents of nature. As Brehier says, "This clarifies the Spinozist
notion that unique substance and universal intelligibility are one,

provided that the relation of a substance to its attributes is not a simple relation of subject to predicate; an indivisible substance must be the reason that explains the existence of modes in each Attribute. Intelligibility does not depend on the nature of an attribute, for intelligibility is order, and the order according to which modes derive from each other in each attribute can be identical in spite of the distinction between attributes".[182] The proper relation between substance and its attributes is not one of whole to parts, nor is it a relation of subject to predicate. It is, as argued above, a relation of one pervasive, immanent nature running through its constituents.

One might view Spinoza's insistence upon the indivisibility of substance and its attribute of extension as a denial of the usual whole/part, spatial, extensional interpretation of nature. He is arguing, instead, for an intensional view of the relation between nature, its attributes, and its modes. This is a view which requires not only the simplicity of substance, but also its indivisibility, its singularity, and its immanence. Brehier says, "Unity of substance, therefore, signifies universal intelligibility provided that substance is not a subject, but, more than anything else, the root of the unique order displayed in each attribute".[183] It is this immanence of causality which pervades all of the attributes and modes, combined with the unity and simplicity of Substance, God or Nature which accounts for the intelligibility of Nature. The one causal law which is expressed within each attribute and instantiated in the activity of the finite mode is the law of God, Substance, or Nature. There is no separation of God from His attributes and modes; they are in God and are pervaded by the causal laws of His activity. God cannot act in accordance with unknowable laws for unfathomable reasons or purposes. Such a God would not only be inevitably split asunder from its universe and, therefore, be unknowable, but it would also be unintelligible since the effect can only be known through its cause. That is, nature itself would be denied intelligibility if one could not understand the laws of its Creator. Thus, we should have an unknowable God and ignorance of nature and its laws, unless God and Nature and the laws of God and Nature were identical. The only consistent means of representing the plurality of attributes and the unity of God, Substance or Nature, is to be found in the relations between Forms in Plato's *Sophist* and *Statesman*.

The relation between more and less pervasive Forms in the *Sophist* is analogous to the relations between substance and its attributes, between the attributes, and between attributes and infinite modes. Cornford says, "... the generic Form partakes of (blends with) the specific Form no less than the specific partakes of the generic."[184] If one views the generic

Form as analogous to Substance or Nature and the specific Forms as attributes, then one might say that "Substance blends with (coincides with) the attributes no less than the attributes blend with (coincide with) Substance." It is true that Nature is more pervasive than any one of the attributes, and that the attributes can be considered as separate from one another, but the attributes considered as a whole constitute, coincide with, or are identical to Nature or Substance. Nature embraces, pervades, runs through the attributes, and the attributes constitute the essence of Nature or Substance. So, while there is a hierarchical relation between generic and specific Forms, between Substance and its attributes, it is a symmetrical relation and not the relation between a subject and its predicate. Substance coincides with the attributes, and the attributes coincide with Substance.

Nature or Substance is considered to be one thing, a unity, although it is constituted by an infinity of attributes. So, too, each generic Form is a "one and a many."

> This generic Form he now sees as a unity which is complex, 'embracing' a number of different Forms, which will figure in the subsequent Division as specific differences or as specific Forms characterized by their differences. ... The many forms, which after Collection were seen to be embraced by a single generic Form, are now seen 'entirely marked off apart.'[185]

Each attribute is infinite in its own kind and is completely separated from every other attribute insofar as it has "nothing mutually in common with it." There are no causal relations between the attributes, although the causal laws of Nature pervade or obtain within each of the separate attributes.

As each attribute is unaffected by any other attribute, as each has its own infinite and finite modes, no attribute is reducible to any other attribute. The identity of the attributes is achieved by means of their coincidence with Nature; it is not a reductionist identity. Seen *sub specie aeternitatis*, each attribute is identical to Nature and to the other attributes. Each of the separate attributes is an expression of the one, singular, unitary, and only Substance, God, or Nature. This view agrees with Cornford's analysis of the relations between the Five Great Forms. He says, "It is now established that all five Forms are distinct. No one can be reduced to, identified with, any other (nor, we may add, evolved, or deduced from any other)."[186] If one interprets the Five Great Forms as similar to the attributes, then one may say that there is an analogy between Plato and Spinoza in their treatment of the relations between Substance and the attributes (Existence and the other Great Forms) and between the attributes themselves (the Five Great Forms).

The less pervasive Forms, the more specific Forms, found under the Great Forms seem to be analogous to the immediate and mediate infinite modes of Spinoza. Cornford says, "The names Animal, Biped, Rational, are names of parts or constituents of the complex specific Form, Man. This Form too is a One that is also many. So both the generic Form and the specific are complex".[187]

The Platonic system of reality, discovered by Collection and Division, is a system wherein the Forms pervade one another, yet are separate from one another. It is a system which is one, singular, and unitary, but one in which there are distinct, irreducible differences. "We can now see that the whole field of reality, divided up into all the subordinate Forms can be regarded as covered by Forms, every one of which can be negatively described as 'that which is not so-and-so'."[188] This separation of Forms is not a spatial division, it is a distinction among Forms which are pervaded by a common Form. That is to say, those separable, unitary, simple (complex but uncompound) Forms have something mutually in common even though they are different from one another. They "share in," or "blend with," or "coincide with," the common Form which pervades them. Analogously, the attributes, which are totally different from one another, have something mutually in common: God, Substance, or Nature.

The relation between the attributes and their respective infinite modes parallels that of the relation of substance and its attributes, but only in some respects. Understanding has something mutually in common with its attribute, Thought, but it differs from Thought insofar as it is not self-caused. It is infinite and eternal, but it "follows from" Thought. It shares in the attribute of Thought, but it differs insofar as the effect differs from the cause. Similarly, motion and rest has something in common with its attribute, Extension, although it differs from the cause.

There is an important disanalogy between Plato's treatment of Forms and their inter-relations and Spinoza's treatment of Substance-attribute and attribute-attribute relations. For Plato, the Forms are eternal and static with only the relations of pervasiveness, similarity, and difference holding between them. For Plato, the only causal activity of the Forms is to be found in their relation to perceivable particulars. For Spinoza, too, there is no causal relation between Substance and its attributes, nor between the attributes. These entities are all eternal, but they are active. That is to say, for Spinoza, the eternal entities are necessarily existent, and existence is power, activity. The activity is restricted to intra-attribute relations, not inter-attribute relations. There are causal relations only between the attributes and their respective infinite modes which "follow" from them. There is causality between the infinite modes

and the finite modes. Spinoza has added causation to the relation between infinite and eternal entities which is not found in Plato. In effect,
Spinoza does have one sort of Form, the attributes, causing another sort
of Form, the immediate infinite modes. Thus, Propositions 21 and 23
prove that God, or one of God's constituent attributes, causes or determines the infinite and eternal modes to exist. Indeed, God or Nature,
causes everything to exist because it is the active power of nature itself.
Spinoza's God and its constituent attributes are equivalent to causation,
and action, and the laws thereof. Thus, Plato's Form to Form relation
compares to the substance-attribute, attribute-attribute relation in
Spinoza with the important exception of the activity of the attributes *vis-
a-vis* the infinite and eternal modes.

The relation between the Five Great Forms in Plato's *Sophist* seems
more analogous to the relation of Substance and attributes in Spinoza
than it does to the relation of attributes to infinite modes because the latter
relation is a causal relation for Spinoza whereas the former is not. Still,
the relation of "blending", or "coinciding", or "pervasiveness", does
hold between all the entities of Spinoza's system insofar as everything is
in God. Cornford says:

> The method of division exhibits Forms arranged in systematic classifica-
> tion, spreading downwards from a single genus through a definite number
> of specific differences to the indivisible species at the bottom. Below that
> there is nothing but the indefinite number of individual things which may
> or may not partake of indivisible specific Forms. They are below the
> horizon of science; the method considers only the *One* which is divided and
> the definite *Many* which are its parts.[189]

One could say, too, that Nature is a One which is constituted by the
many attributes into which it can be "divided". There is no causal relation here, between substance and its attributes or between the attributes.
One can also say that each of the attributes is a One which is the cause of
its infinite modes. Still, the relation is amenable to Collection and Division, with the mediate infinite mode comparable to the "indivisible
species at the bottom". Below the mediate infinite mode are the
"indefinite number of individual things."

This account of the relation between generic and specific Forms notes
its similarity to Spinoza's account of the relation between Substance and
its attributes, between the attributes themselves, and between the
attributes and their respective infinite modes. The similitude is also to be
noted in the pervasivity of each One in its constituent Many. That is to
say, each Many (each specific Form) is in its respective One (its generic
Form). This parallels Spinoza's Proposition 15 wherein he states that
"whatever is, is in God". Thus, the Many can be understood through

the One which pervades them, just as the attributes can be grasped through knowledge of Nature, God, or Substance itself. As each generic Form is one, unitary, simple, though constituted by its many specific Forms, so is Nature one, unitary, simple though constituted by the attributes. And, furthermore, each attribute is a One which is simple, unitary and constituted by its constituent infinite modes. The requirement for a unifying One or Nature to order the diverse Many or attributes is a requirement for the intelligibility of the real world of Forms or Nature. Each of the Many must be found in some ordering, unifying, intelligible One in order to realize an intelligible reality, as each attribute and its infinite modes must be in Nature to insure an orderly, rational God or Nature.

I should suggest that intuition in Spinoza is comparable to Plato's ''collection''. Reason in Spinoza is concerned with the attributes and their relations to the infinite modes. The realm of finite modes is the realm of perception and imagination for Spinoza as is the realm of particulars for Plato. The infinite number of finite modes can be explained by the causal laws which constitute the infinite modes and by the essences in which modes participate.

In addition to emphasizing the need for organization by placing diversity in a unity in agreement with the Platonic scheme of Collection and Division, Spinoza again does go beyond Plato to stress the causal activity of God in Proposition 15. Not only are the Many in God, but they depend upon God for their existence. Here Spinoza has the infinite modes, the *natura naturata*, in mind rather than the *natura naturans* of the attributes, because the attributes are not caused by God. For Spinoza, God or Nature causes the infinite modes which are unified by their respective attributes. Plato requires a sort of entity different from the Forms (or the Ones) to account for the causal order of his *natura naturata* or cosmos of particulars. Plato appeals to the Agent in the *Philebus* and to the Demiurge in his *Timaeus* to organize ''as far as possible'' the chaotic world of Nature. Still, the Forms themselves are ordered naturally into collections and their respective divisions, and Plato notes in *Statesman* that one's divisions should be in accordance with ''natural kinds'' lest one err. Similarly, Spinoza's attributes are the ordered natural kinds.

Proposition 16 states that infinite things follow from God or Nature due to its necessary causal activity. Spinoza here asserts that each of the infinite number of attributes causes its own infinite mode, and each infinite mode has infinite numbers of essences which produce infinite numbers of finite modes. This is another disanalogy from Plato in two respects. In the first case, while attributes cause eternal infinite modes, Forms do not cause eternal Forms for Plato. In the second case, there is no infinite number of Forms for Plato. Each One has a definite number (though, perhaps, innumerable for us) of Forms in its division. One dips into infinity only when one enters the world of particulars, for Plato.

It should be noted that the infinite things which follow from God or Nature must "follow" necessarily from God because of His very nature as an absolutely infinite being. While there must be an infinitude of infinite modes and finite modes, for Spinoza, it still follows that God or Nature acts freely insofar as He acts in accordance with His own laws alone. The Demiurge, on the other hand, decides, because order is better than disorder, to organize the world on the pattern of the Forms. There is an aura of choice in the activity of the Demiurge in contrast to the necessity of Spinoza's Nature.[190] Spinoza's account of the relation between God and the universe is one in which God is the first, efficient and immanent cause. There is no purpose, no goal, no desire, or will for Spinoza's God. What occurs happens necessarily, lawfully, rationally. Spinoza denies teleological causation and derides teleological explanations as being due to man's ignorance of his own nature as well as ignorance of the nature of God. Plato, on the contrary, does emphasize the need for teleological explanation not only to account for the activity of the Demiurge, but also to account for the activity of man.[191] With the departure of teleology from his account, Spinoza also dismisses a moral tone from his account of God, Nature, or Substance and its relation to the universe. Good and evil are not interwoven into the fabric of Nature for Spinoza as for Plato. For Spinoza, the fabric of the universe is produced on the loom of necessity.

The immanence of God is proved in Proposition 18: "God is the immanent, and not the transient cause of all things".[192] Spinoza argued, in Proposition 15, that everything is in God or Nature; nothing exists in itself or through itself except God, Substance, or Nature. None of the modes is outside of, or independent of, the unifying order of Nature. Similarly, for Plato, none of the specific Forms is separated from a generic Form. No Form is not pervaded by the Five Great Forms. If everything is in God, for Spinoza, then everything either is coincident with God (the attributes) or causally dependent upon God (the modes). That which is coincident or dependent upon Nature or God is pervaded by that nature, those causal laws, that activity. So, God is in everything, too. As the specific Forms are in the generic Form, so the generic Form pervades, or blends with, or coincides with the specific Forms. So, also, everything is in God or Nature, and Nature is in everything. The symmetrical relation between specific and generic Forms is paralleled by the relation of God to *natura naturans* and *naturata*; God pervades all modes, and all modes are in God. Existence pervades all Forms as all Forms are in the collection of Existence. However, Forms and particulars are not related by pervasion for Plato. There is no symmetrical relation between Forms and particulars as there is between Forms and Forms.

For Spinoza, every mode which exists has something mutually in common with every other existing thing: God or Nature is its cause and pervades its essence. This mutuality, or similitude between all modes of all attributes is achieved only *sub specie aeternitatis*, only on the level of God or Nature. Furthermore, insofar as all the modes are effects of God or Nature, they must differ from God as "the effect differs from the cause precisely in that which it has from the cause". Each mode, then, differs from God in both essence and existence.[193] This similarity and difference between God (and its attributes) and the modes is analogous to the pervasiveness of "Same and Difference" in the Collection and Division of Forms. For Plato, too, all Forms are identical to themselves and different from any other Form. Each division within the collection is pervaded by the One and so has "something mutually in common" with the One and with its fellows in the division, even though the specific Form differs from its fellows and from the One.

In Propositions 19 through 26, Spinoza is concerned with the eternity, causality, and necessity of God. He notes therein that God is eternal; His essence includes existence. Since God's existence is necessary, and is equivalent to His power or activity, then God's activity is eternal and necessary. What follows from the necessary, eternal, and infinite activity of God or His constituent attributes is itself eternal and infinite. That is to say, the causal activity of each attribute produces a mode which is itself eternal and infinite and necessary. It is not necessarily existent, however, because the infinite mode does not contain its existence in its essence. It is not a *natura naturans* but is *natura naturata*. Insofar as each infinite mode derives its existence from an attribute, it differs from the attribute in terms of its existence.[194] So, the infinite mode must exist because of the necessary activity of the attribute not because of its own necessity. Each infinite mode is a necessary effect of the causal activity of the attribute and is similar to the attribute in respect to infinity and eternity.

Not only do attributes cause infinite and eternal modes which follow immediately from the nature of the attribute, but these immediate infinite modes (understanding, and motion and rest) also possess a causal action which produces other infinite and eternal modes called mediate infinite modes. Spinoza mentions only one mediate infinite mode—the face of the whole universe. One might infer, if only on the basis of consistency and symmetry, that each attribute must have an immediate and mediate infinite mode. It is at the level of the mediate infinite modes that infinity and eternity cease for Spinoza. So, one might note that the mediate infinite modes are analogous to the *infimae species* of Plato's division. This inference is confirmed in the Scholium to Proposition 17.

In Proposition 17, Spinoza is arguing that God acts freely, but necessarily, in producing *natura naturata* and, insofar as God is the cause, He must differ from *natura naturata* essentially and existentially. It is here that the "essentialism" of Spinoza is evinced. He says, "... the truth and formal essence of things is what it is, because as such it exists objectively in God's intellect".[195] That is to say, God has an idea of the formal essence of all existing things. That idea is eternal, infinite, necessary (because it contains no inconsistency) and is a result of the nature of God or Nature itself. The idea is singular, unitary, indivisible. It is an "essence" of particular things, a common character, analogous to a Platonic Form. As Spinoza says:

> ... For example, one man is the cause of the existence but not of the essence of another, for the essence is an *eternal truth*; and therefore with regard to essence the two men exactly resemble one another, but with regard to existence they must differ. Consequently if the existence of one should perish, that of the other will not therefore perish; but if the essence of one could be destroyed and become false, the essence of the other would be likewise destroyed. Therefore a thing which is the cause both of the essence and of the existence of any effect must differ from that effect both with regard to its essence and with regard to its existence.[196]

The eternal truth, the essential nature of man, is but one of the ideas of God which constitute the formal essence of individual things. This common character is the cause or the essence of the individual thing.

Since the efficient causal activity of God pervades not only the attributes and infinite modes, but also the finite modes themselves, God is the cause of the existence of the finite mode, too. Finite modes, or individual things, or particular things, are "nothing but affections or modes of God's attributes, expressing those attributes in a certain and determinate manner."[197] The determination to existence of a finite mode is the result of the causal activity of another finite mode.[198] Thus, the essence which constitutes the mediate infinite mode of an attribute of God is the finite mode's essence whereas the existence of that finite mode is due to the action of another finite mode—which is an expression of God, too. The production of any particular finite mode, then, requires essential causation following from an attribute to its immediate infinite mode to its mediate infinite mode to its finite modes. It also requires existential causation, whereby one finite mode causes another finite mode to exist. This is, of course, only an instantiation of God's or Nature's pervasive causal activity. Again, if one interprets finite modes as akin to Plato's particulars, and if one views the eternal truths or essences as similar to the Forms of *infimae species*, a striking similitude may be observed.

In Spinoza, there is no doubt whatsoever about the causal relations between an attribute, its infinite modes, and its finite modes. This causal activity is one instance of the unity of God or Nature with *natura naturata*. The same causal laws bind all of the entities which constitute Nature, not only physical causation (within the attribute of Extension and its modes) but also logical causation (within the attribute of Thought and its modes). In his article, "Reason and Causes in the *Phaedo*," G. Vlastos argues that Forms are causes, too.[199] The Forms are related by logical necessity among themselves and between themselves and their respective particulars. A Form is also the physical cause of a character or property in a particular. "The logical relation of a term to a concept under which it falls is at the same time the metaphysical relation of a sensible to an eternal Form".[200] This appears quite similar to the relation between the eternal essence of man in the mediate infinite mode of Thought and its instantiation as a particular idea as well as the relation between the essence of man as a physical entity and a particular human being. The unity of Plato's Forms, particulars, and terms is asserted by Vlastos: "... all intelligible necessity, physical no less than mathematical, must be grounded on logical necessity, since it represents the inter-relations of eternal Forms, be these articulated in discourse or imaged in the physical world."[201] Not only is logical necessity, or intelligible order, the ground of Plato's metaphysics, epistemology, and natural science, it is also the basis for Spinoza's philosophy. Logical necessity is the causal order in the attribute of Thought, identical to the physical necessity in the attribute of Extension. It is the pervasive unity which is expressed by the immanence of God in everything and everything in God.

While one can assert that there is an essential causation between the mediate infinite mode (the eternal essence of man) and its finite mode (a particular instance of that essence), one might still wish for a more complete explication of the relations between the infinite and finite modes. How can one account for the unity of the essence of man and the existential diversity of men? This problem is similar to that of the relation between a Form and its particulars, between the eternal One and the temporal Many, between the rational One and the perceivable Many. It is not the same problem as that of discerning the relations between the One that is a generic Form and the Many that are its specific Forms. That problem was resolved, for Plato, by the notion of Collection and Division. It was a problem resolved by intuition and reason, by dialectic, and it involved only logical necessity, not physical causation.

The problem of the relation between the eternal essence of the mediate infinite mode (a One) and its finite determinations (a Many) is similar to the problem of Forms and particulars which arises in the *Parmenides*. Parmenides, in questioning the young Socrates about the relation between Forms and particulars, seems always to interpret the relation in a spatial, divisible way. He says, "Then each thing that partakes receives as its share either the form as a whole or a part of it?"[202] Parmenides continues, "Do you hold, then, that the form as a *whole*, a single thing, is *in* each of the many, or how?"[203] At 131b, he uses the analogy of a sail. "You might as well spread a sail over a number of people and then say that the one sail as a whole was over them all."[204] At 131c: "In that case, Socrates, the forms themselves must be divisible into parts, and the things which have a share in them will have a *part* for their share. Only a *part* of a given form, and no longer the *whole* of it, will be in each thing. ... Are you, then, prepared to assert that we shall find the single form actually being *divided*? Will it still be one?"[205] Finally, Parmenides says, "Well then, Socrates, how are the other things going to partake of your forms, if they can partake of them neither in part nor as wholes?"[206] To which the bewildered Socrates replies, "Really, ... it seems no easy matter to determine in any way."[207] Clearly, the spatial analogy offered by Parmenides fails to explicate the relation. The part/whole, in/out, divisible relations all fail.

It is interesting that the relations suggested by Parmenides are all relations which are derived from perception, yet Parmenides is one of the most rationalistic of all philosophers. Perhaps this is an example of Plato's irony at work, and this makes even more interesting the selection of the form "Largeness" as an example taken in the *Parmenides*. In a similar failure of reason to divorce itself from perception and its relations, we find the rationalist Descartes arguing that extension has as its principal attribute divisibility, while the rationalistic Spinoza pleads for the indivisibility of extension *per se*.

At any rate, the Forms are not perceivable, spatial, or divisible for Plato any more than attributes or infinite modes (immediate or mediate) are divisible for Spinoza. The relation between Forms and particulars is a causal relation and an intentional relation for Plato as it is for Spinoza. R. E. Allen argues that particulars are images of Forms and consequently are caused by Forms in terms of existence and quality.[208] He says:

> Forms are like originals; particulars are like images or reflections. ... (The analogy) places the One over the Many; there may be many reflections of a single thing, and those reflections gain their community of character from that thing. Second, the analogy expresses degrees of reality. ... Third, the analogy illustrates how particulars may approximate to forms

and yet be categorically distinct: reflections may differ in the degree to which they are true to their original, but no matter how faithful they are to it, they can never become it, for it is of a different order than they. ... But the original, then, is a standard or criterion, by which we judge of images and their adequacy.[209]

The many particulars are unified by the One which is a Form. Particulars are reflections, images of the One and are less real and of lesser quality than the Forms. There is a category distinction between particulars and Forms which can be bridged only metaphorically by "community," "participation," "reflection," "resemblance." We find an analogue in relating the mediate infinite mode to its finite modes.

MEDIATE INFINITE MODES

The mediate infinite mode, for Spinoza, is termed "the face of the whole Universe" (*facies totius universi*) which "although it varies in infinite modes, yet remains always the same."[210] There is some question about the nature of this mode. Wild views it as "consisting of finite modes."[211] R. L. Saw argues that this mode is itself a complex body constituted by other bodies compounded by simple bodies and which provides "the notion of the whole of nature as an individual with an infinite number of changes in its parts, yet itself unchanging."[212] L. C. Rice also considers it to be constituted by a series of individuals "out to infinity (where) we reach the *facies totius universi*, which changes in infinite ways without loss of identity."[213] Some support for this interpretation of the mediate infinite mode as being constituted by particulars may be found in the Scholium to Lemma 7, Part II. There Spinoza says, "Thus, if we advance *ad infinitum*, we may easily conceive the whole of nature to be one individual, whose parts, that is to say, all bodies, differ in infinite ways without any change of the whole individual."[214] However, I believe that this illustration is intended only to indicate that something can vary numerically, in its constituents, yet retain specific identity. It is the same *sort* of thing, even though its parts have changed. The illustration is not intended to indicate that the mediate infinite mode is constituted of individual *parts*, but rather to indicate that parts can change although specific identity remains. "Same" can also mean identical "*sub specie aeternitatis*."

Legislating against the view that the mediate infinite mode is constituted by an infinite number of finite modes are the following points. First, the mediate infinite mode is *infinite*. No amount of finite modes could constitute an infinite mode; no amount of limited things could constitute a complete, finished, infinite mode. Secondly, the mediate infinite

mode is eternal, and the finite modes are temporal. While some may wish
to argue that there is a specific eternity to the infinity of finite modes
although there is no eternal existence for any finite mode itself, I believe
that the most that one could attain from an infinite series of finite things
is an indefinite duration and not an eternal mode. Finally, R. L. Saw
herself seems to be inconsistent insofar as she characterizes the finite
modes as "derived, dissoluble, and in a sense, illusory", then proceeds
to construct an eternal and infinite mode from them.[215] Thus, this view
seems to be inconsistent with Spinoza's claim that the "face of the whole
universe" is eternal and infinite.

H. A. Wolfson argues that this mode is a principle of the constancy of
motion and rest among the particular bodies and a principle of order and
coherence among particular aspects of nature.[216] He suggests that the
mode may be a mode of extension as well as of thought. He says, "... the
mediate infinite mode ..., if taken with reference to the principle of the
preservation of the proportion of motion and rest, will be a mode of
extension only, but if taken with reference to the principle of the order of
the whole of nature, will be a mode of both extension and thought".[217]
There is an echo of Wolfson in E. M. Curley's view of the mediate
infinite mode. After arguing that the immediate infinite mode of extension is constituted by laws of motion and rest, he says that the face of the
whole universe "would refer to the sum of those other general facts which
depend causally on the nature of extension."[218]

I should argue that there are many mediate infinite modes, many
"faces" of the whole universe, one for each of the infinite attributes of
Nature. None of the "faces" is constituted by particular, finite modes,
however. Each mediate infinite mode is constituted by essences of lesser
generality than the immediate infinite mode in that attribute. The
mediate infinite mode of thought is constituted by general natures, common natures, or eternal essences of particular, finite modes—such as the
essence of man. Thus, this "face" will remain eternal, infinite, and identical although the finite modes are temporal, finite, and only specific
identities. The mediate infinite mode of extension is constituted by laws
of motion and rest, causal laws, common notions, of less generality than
those of the immediate infinite modes. For example, they may be laws of
terrestrial mechanics *vis à vis* Newton's laws of mechanics. It is true, furthermore, that the mediate infinite modes themselves vary insofar as each
is an expression of its attribute, but they are identical, the "same" face of
the one universe, *sub specie aeternitatis*.

I have argued that these general natures (common natures) or general
laws (common notions) which are partial causes of the finite modes are
akin to the *infimae species* of Plato's collection and division. In his work

on the *Treatise for the Improvement of the Understanding*, H. H. Joachim argues against this view. He says:

> This body of traditional doctrine, however, is profoundly modified by his (Spinoza's) refusal to recognize that the *genera* and *species* of *Aristotelian and Scholastic Logic* are real in any sense, or in any sense constituents of what is real.

> Thus, he still holds fast to the traditional doctrine that the essence of a thing is really what it is, its form or formal being, and therefore also what it is, truly conceived or known to be. But, ..., *he refuses to identify the essence with the infima species*—with the specific form which, though logically individual or indivisible, *as exemplified in many singulars as a common or universal nature predicable of them all.* The essence, he asserts, reciprocates with the thing, of which it is the essence; and is itself, therefore, a real individual or singular. ... and he assumes, therefore, that essence, and nothing else, is the content *both* of the clear and distinct idea, or the adequate conception, of a thing and of its perfect definition.[219]

This statement is illustrative of the difficulties which assail commentators on Spinoza who have commitments to Aristotelian views. Thus, I should argue that Spinoza does not accept Aristotelian and Scholastic interpretations of *genera* and *species*. They are not real, for Spinoza, and cannot be constituents of reality because such forms are abstracted from sense perceptions and would not be adequately known. They are imaginations for him. For Spinoza, genera and species are known by intuition or reason. They are Platonic entities apprehended by reason, not Aristotelian abstractions from sense. Thus, Spinoza does indeed accept essences, or forms, but as reasonable entities or intuitional entities, which *do* constitute reality, but not the reality of sensed entities. The essences are not independent of Thought but are caused by Thought, whereas Plato's Forms are independent entities. Joachim is correct in asserting that Spinoza does not accept these entities as "the *infima species*" which are "exemplified in many singulars as a common or universal nature *predicable* of them all".[220] But, I have argued that Spinoza does accept them in the Platonic sense of *infima species* which does not at all entail predication, inclusion, or the subject-predicate, substance-quality relation of Aristotle. The Platonic sense of *infima species* is a reciprocal relation, a pervasivity. That is to say, the mediate infinite modes pervade the finite modes and cause the finite modes to have that particular essence. The finite mode is "in" the mediate infinite mode. Indeed, Joachim notes that Spinoza does have a reciprocal relation between the individual and its essence, as I argued above. However, while Joachim found this puzzling and troublesome to explain in terms of the Aristotelian logic and classificatory schema, I find this to be a clear view in accord with a Platonic interpretation of Spinoza. Furthermore, the clear and distinct idea of an existent thing would be its essence or definition, but this cannot be an account of knowledge of a finite mode, but only of eternal and infinite modes. For humans, there are no adequate ideas of finite modes, because they cannot be known by reason or intuition, because they are not only essences but are finite existences caused partially by other finite modes.

In brief, then, Joachim's argument that essences are not *infima species* is true only if one accepts an Aristotelian view of *infima species* as predicates. It is not true if one argues that Spinoza uses a Platonic logic instead of an Aristotelian/Scholastic logic. The *infima species* are entities independent of thought for Plato, but the common natures or essences of Spinoza are dependent upon Thought and are caused by the immediate infinite modes.

FINITE MODES

The mediate infinite modes cause the finite modes in the sense of an eternal essence causing the qualities of a finite mode of a particular sort. Finite modes are akin to the images or particulars of Plato. The finite modes are caused to exist by other finite modes operating in accordance with a particularization of a causal law; that is to say, a causal law which holds at a particular time and place. One cannot explain the existence of finite modes without reference to other finite modes. Curley says, "Finite modes require, as their partial cause, other finite modes and hence do not share the eternal nature of their cause".[221] The "eternal nature of their cause" is the eternal essence, I should argue. Finite modes, then, are less real, or more removed from the immediate activity of God, contain fewer properties than God and the infinite modes, but they still exist. They are qualitatively deficient in the sense that they are not eternal essences and are not infinite. So, they are akin to images in being deficiently real and falling short of their standard.

Allen argues that particulars are "exemplifications" of Forms. The relation between Form and particulars "can be explained by treating exemplifications not as substances in which qualities inhere but as relational entities in which resemblance and dependence so combine as to destroy the possibility of substantiality. Plato's use of the metaphors of imitation and reflection, and his characterization of particulars and Forms, indirectly indicates that he accepted this solution."[222] The finite modes are not substances for Spinoza. They are "modifications" of attributes, finite "determinations" or "expressions" of the attributes from which they "follow". The metaphors used in Spinoza's explanation of the modes' relation to attributes and infinite modes seem akin to the

Platonic metaphors employed in explaining the relation of particulars to Forms. The particulars are dependent for existence and essence upon other categories of entities.

Particulars cannot be deduced from Forms, because knowledge by means of division deals only with Forms. To account for the existence of the infinitude of particulars, one needs to call upon the Demiurge, the elements, the receptacle and the natural, necessary laws that obtain within the receptacle.[223] Plato himself felt the need for explaining the perceivable particulars by reference to something other than the eternal, static Forms. In Spinoza, one cannot deduce the existence of any finite mode, or all the finite modes, from the eternal attributes and infinite modes. "Similarly, there is no problem in Spinoza of deducing the finite from the infinite. ... Deducing the finite solely from the infinite, in his philosophy, is in principle impossible. Even an infinite intellect could not do it."[224] Spinoza himself says, "the understanding cannot descend from universal axioms by themselves to particular things, since axioms are of infinite extent and do not determine the understanding to contemplate one particular thing more than another".[225]

For Spinoza and for Plato, one needs individuals to explain individuals. Wolfson discusses the notion that the attributes can contract themselves to produce finite modes in a manner reminiscent of the Talmudic _Zimzum_.[226] This seems to be contrary to Spinoza's argument that finite modes can only be caused, and thus explained, by at least some reference to other finite modes. Wolfson's discussion calls to mind the difficulty in explaining the relation of the Infinite to particulars by means of contraction or attenuation. It would seem that these attempts have in common the heritage of Plotinus' conception of the One and its exfoliation of the world. However, this is not Plato's doctrine, for Plato has no theory of "emanation" as an explanatory principle.

It is true that Plato's metaphors of participation, imitation, resemblance, sharing, and patterning are not clear, but it is clear that one cannot account for the existence of particulars by deduction from Forms. It is equally clear that reason ceases to be applicable at the level of particulars. Spinoza's position that finite modes "follow from" infinite modes, that they are "expressions", "modifications", "determinations" of attributes is not much clearer than Plato's metaphors. It is true that there is a thread of necessity and causation between the natural essences and the finite modes for Spinoza and that causal laws pervade all the sorts of entities in his metaphysics, but even he cannot deduce finite modes from their infinite modes. He, too, must rely upon finite modes for the explanation of other finite modes. He, too, must rely upon perception for his knowledge of finite things. Thus, reason and intuition are applicable only to the infinite and eternal for Spinoza, as division and collection are applicable only to Forms for Plato. For both philosophers, sense perception and imagination are required for dealing with particular, finite temporal individuals. Certitude ceases when one plunges into the perceptual world of temporal particulars for both philosophers. We have argued that the existence of a finite mode requires the eternal activity of God mediated through the infinite modes and expressed by the finite modes, too. Again, we must note the similitude between Plato and Spinoza in their accounts of the existence of finite, changing things and their relation to the eternal entities of their systems.

While the finite modes are like "images" in Plato, I should not at all advocate the view that they are "mere appearances" or "phenomena" for Spinoza. Nor should one read Plato in this fashion. After all, in the later dialogues, Plato does not dismiss the particulars as unreal shadows. In Spinoza, too, the finite modes are existent things, produced by necessity, determined to their actions by Nature. They are real, but not eternal or self-caused. They are not phantasms but are particular, temporal, transitory things which necessarily express the eternal things. They are not false claimants to existence, not ghostly ephemera, but are rather claimants to existence of a different sort than the infinite modes and attributes. The existence of finite modes is a dependent existence as the existence of the particulars, or "images", is a dependent existence for Plato. So, while finite modes and their correspondent particulars are not eternal, not infinite, they are still existents. It is true that they are not Nature, not Substance, nor attribute, nor infinite modes, but they are pervaded by Nature and existence. They are images of Nature, as particulars are images of Forms, but they are existent.

Thus, the metaphysical foundations of both philosophers lead inexorably to an epistemology that is bifurcated into certitude and fallibility, reason and perception, eternity and time. There are similarities to be found not only between the metaphysics of Plato and Spinoza, but also in the epistemologies of these two philosophers who are committed to a reasonable, intelligible, orderly, unified world which retains a rich diversity of categories of existence. They both have asserted a community, a sharing, between the eternal and the temporal, the infinite and the finite. There is no complete and utter separation for these philosophers, but there is instead a bond between the world and its cause.

I have argued here that the similarities between the metaphysics of Plato and that of Spinoza are too significant to be dismissed as mere happenstance. The "fit" of Platonic Forms to Spinoza's attributes and infinite modes, and the coincidence of relations between Forms and particulars with the relation between mediate infinite modes and finite modes, is remarkable. The character of the Form "Existence" as absolutely pervasive and eternal coincides with Spinoza's notion of God or Nature. I believe that Spinoza's metaphysics can be properly interpreted as Platonic in its intent, unity, and intelligibility. Furthermore, I believe that such an interpretation resolves many of the difficulties entailed in other commentaries on Spinoza.

Upon reaching finite modes, the metaphysical part of the *Ethics* might appear to end. However in *Part II*, of the *Ethics* we shall find a discussion of the finite modes of extension and thought and their relations to one another. The second part is concerned with bodies and ideas and the knowledge thereof. As his metaphysics does not contain "leaps", as his metaphysics is unified by the pervasiveness of Nature, so, too, will Spinoza's epistemology be pervaded by his metaphysics.

NOTES

[1] Curley, *Spinoza*, pp. 108-113; has an excellent account of Spinoza's theory of definitions. Curley notes on p. 36 that Spinoza does *not* use the Aristotelian notion of definition by genus and difference.

[2] B. Spinoza, *The Correspondence of Spinoza*, trans. A. Wolf (New York: Lincoln MacVeagh, Dial Press, 1927), "To Simon DeVries," March 1663, Letter 9, pp. 106-107. Emphasis added. Hereafter cited as Wolf, *Correspondence*.

[3] Wolf, "To Mr. Henry Oldenburg," October 1661, Letter 4, in *Correspondence*, p. 81.

[4] Wolf, "To Simon DeVries," about March 1663, Letter 10, in *Correspondence*, p. 109.

[5] Wild, *On the Improvement of the Understanding*, p. 36.

[6] Wild, *On the Improvement of the Understanding*, pp. 37-38.

[7] Wild, pp. 100-101, E1, Prop. 8, Schol. 2.

[8] Wild, p. 94, E1, Def. 3; B. Spinoza, *Spinoza Opera*, ed. C. Gebhardt (1925; rpt. Heidelberg: Carl Winter, 1972), II, 45: "Per substantiam intelligo id, quod in se est & per se concipitur: hoc est id, cujus conceptus non indiget conceptu alterius rei, a quo formari debeat." Hereafter cited as Gebhardt.

[9] Wild, p. 95, E1, Axiom 1; Gebhardt, II, 46: "Omnia, quae sunt, vel in se, vel in alio sunt."

[10] Wild, p. 95, E1, Axiom 4; Gebhardt, II, 46: "Effectus cognitio a cognitione causae dependet, & eandem involvit."

[11] Wild, p. 94, E1, Def. 1; Gebhardt, II, 45: "... id, cujus essentia involvit existentiam, sive id, cujus natura non potest concipi, nisi existens."

[12] Wild, p. 98, E1, Prop. 7, Schol. 2.

[13] Wild, p. 99, E1, Prop. 7, Schol. 2.

[14] *Ibid.*

[15] Wild, p. 101, E1, Prop. 10, Schol. 2.

[16] Wild, pp. 95-96, E1, Axioms 4 and 5.

[17] Wild, p. 98, E1, Prop. 7, Dem.

[18] Wild, p. 99, E1, Prop. 8, Schol. 2.

[19] Wild, p. 100, E1, Prop. 7, Schol. 2.

[20] Wild, p. 101, E1, Prop. 8, Schol. 2.

[21] Wild, p. 98, E1, Prop. 8; Gebhardt, II, 49: "Omnis substantia est necessario infinita." Perhaps a more felicitous translation would be: "*Each* substance ...." At this point, Spinoza has not yet proven that there is only *one* substance. The possibility of infinite numbers of infinite substances exists.

²² Wild, pp. 95-96, E1, Axioms 4 and 5.

²³ Wild, p. 95, E1, Definitions 7 and 8.

²⁴ This appears to be similar to Leibniz' concept of the identity of indiscernibles.

²⁵ Wild, p. 98, E1, Prop. 8, Dem; Gebhardt, II, 49: "Substantia unius attributi non, nisi unica, existit." "A substance of one attribute does not exist if it is not unique." The White-Sterling translation does not appear to capture Spinoza's stress on the singularity or uniqueness of the substance.

²⁶ Wild, p. 102, E1, Prop. 9.

²⁷ Wild, p. 94, E1, Def. 4.

²⁸ Gebhardt, II, 45. Emphasis added.

²⁹ Haserot, "Attribute," p. 501. Haserot argues that the "intellect" referred to here is the infinite intellect which knows the infinite number of attributes adequately.

³⁰ Haserot, "Attribute," p. 512.

³¹ *Ibid.*

³² Wild, p. 97, E1, Prop. 4, Dem; Gebhardt, II, 47-48: "Nihil ergo extra intellectum datur, per quod plures res distingui inter se possunt praeter *substantias, sive quod idem est (per defin. 4) earum attributa,* earumque affectiones." Emphasis added.

³³ Wild, p. 102, E1, Prop. 9.

³⁴ Gebhardt, II, 51. Emphasis added.

³⁵ R. H. M. Elwes, *Philosophy of Spinoza* (New York: Tudor Publishing Company, 1933), p. 45.

³⁶ J. R. V. Marshant and J. F. Charles, *Cassell's Latin Dictionary* (New York: Funk and Wagnalls, 1952), p. 113.

³⁷ Thomas Thomas, *Dictionarium Linguae Latinae et Anglicanae, 1587* (Menston, England: The Scolar Press, 1972), n. pag.; hereafter cited as *Dictionarium.*

³⁸ A. Souter, *A Glossary of Later Latin to 600 A.D.* (Oxford: The Clarendon Press, 1964), p. 65.

³⁹ I shall argue in the following pages that the Aristotelian view does not provide a consistent interpretation of Spinoza.

⁴⁰ Wild, p. 102, E1, Prop. 10, Schol.; Gebhardt, II, 52: "... non possumus tamen inde concludere, ipsa duo entia, sive duas diversas substantias constituere ...." Note that it is clear that attributes *constitute* the substance and do not "belong to" the substance.

⁴¹ Wild, p. 102, E1, Prop. 10, Schol; Gebhardt, II, 52: "Longe ergo abest, ut absurdum sit, uni substantiae plura attributa tribuere: quin nihil in natura clarius, quam quod unumquodque ens sub aliquo attributo debeat concipi, &, quo plus realitatis, aut esse habeat, eo plura attributa, quae & necessitatem, sive aeternitatem, & infinitatem exprimunt, habeat ...." Emphasis added.

⁴² Wild, p. 94, E1, Def. 6; Gebhardt, II, 45: "Per Deum intelligo *ens* absolute infinitum, hoc est, *substantiam constantem* infinitis attributis, quorum unumquodque aeternam, & infinitam essentiam exprimit." It should be noted that *ens* is not capitalized in the Latin. Emphasis added.

⁴³ Wild, p. 95, E1, Def. 6, Explanation; Gebhardt, II, 46: "... quod autem absolute infinitum est, ad ejus essentiam pertinet, quicquid essentiam exprimit, & negationem nullum involvit."

⁴⁴ Wild, p. 103, E1, Prop. 11, Dem; Gebhardt, II, 52: "Cujuscunque rei assignari debet causa, seu ratio, tam cur existit, quam cur non existit." "For any thing, a cause or a reason must be assigned either why it exists or why it does not exist."

⁴⁵ Wild, p. 104, E1, Prop. 11, Proof; Gebhardt, II, 53: "... posse existere potentia est (ut per se notum)." This recalls Plato's hypothesis that "a mark of existence is power" in *Sophist,* 247e.

⁴⁶ Wild, p. 104, E1, Prop. 11, Schol.

⁴⁷ Wild, p. 95, E1, Axiom 1; Gebhardt, II, 46: "Omnia, quae sunt, vel in se, vel in alio sunt."

⁴⁸ Wild, p. 105, E1, Prop. 11, Schol.

⁴⁹ Wild, p. 146, E2, Prop. 2.

⁵⁰ Wild, p. 193, E2, Prop. 47.

⁵¹ Cf. Wild, pp. 108-109, E1, Prop. 15, Schol.; pp. 140-143, Appendix to Part I.

⁵² Part II of this paper contains an analysis of imagination in *Ethics*, Part II.

⁵³ Wolf, "To Mr. Jarig Jelles," 2 June 1674, Letter 50, in *Correspondence*, p. 269.

⁵⁴ Wolf, "To Mr. John Hudde," about June 1666, Letter 36, in *Correspondence*, pp. 224-225.

⁵⁵ See Curley, *Spinoza*, pp. 50-81.

⁵⁶ Wild, p. 117, E1, Prop. 18.

⁵⁷ Wolf, "To Mr. Henry Oldenburg," November or December 1675, Letter 73, in *Correspondence*, p. 343.

⁵⁸ Wolf, *Correspondence*, pp. 460-461.

⁵⁹ Wolfson, I, 74.

⁶⁰ Wolfson, I, 75.

⁶¹ L. C. Rice, "Methodology and Modality in the First Part of Spinoza's Ethics," in *Spinoza On Knowing, Being and Freedom*, ed. J. G. van der Bend, p. 146.

⁶² Curley, *Spinoza*, p. 49.

⁶³ Curley, *Spinoza*, p. 33.

⁶⁴ Wild, pp. 94-95, E1, Def. 6.

⁶⁵ F. M. Cornford, *Plato's Theory of Knowledge* (New York: The Liberal Arts Press, 1957), p. 183; hereafter cited as Cornford.

⁶⁶ Cornford, p. 183.

⁶⁷ I shall argue in the second part of this book that the method of division is similar to Spinoza's reason. I am not, here, concerned with Plato's epistemology but rather with his metaphysics. In Plato, as in Spinoza, the two are intertwined, but I shall follow Spinoza's lead in first discussing the metaphysics, then the epistemology.

⁶⁸ Cornford, p. 261. Emphasis added.

⁶⁹ Wolf, Letter 9, in *Correspondence*, pp. 106-107.

⁷⁰ Cornford, p. 261. Cornford uses "kinds," "forms" and "ideas" as synonyms.

⁷¹ Cornford, pp. 261-262.

⁷² Cornford, p. 270.

⁷³ Cornford, p. 269.

⁷⁴ Cornford, pp. 262-263.

⁷⁵ Cornford, p. 265.

⁷⁶ Cornford, p. 268.

⁷⁷ Cornford, p. 272.

⁷⁸ Cornford, p. 276.

⁷⁹ *Ibid.*

⁸⁰ Cornford, p. 275.

⁸¹ Cornford, p. 278.

⁸² Wild, p. 94, E1, Def. 6; Gebhardt, II, 45.

⁸³ Wild, p. 149, E2, Prop. 7.

⁸⁴ Wild, p. 103, E1, Prop. 10, Schol.; Gebhardt, II, 52: "... quae ostendunt in rerum natura non, nisi unicam substantiam...." A more fitting translation would be "a unique substance."

⁸⁵ Wild, p. 106, E1, Prop. 12. Emphasis added.

⁸⁶ Wild, p. 106, E1, Prop. 13.

⁸⁷ Wild, p. 106, E1, Prop. 12, Dem.

⁸⁸ *Ibid.*

⁸⁹ Gebhardt, II, 55: "... unaquaeque pars debebit esse infinita, ... constare debebit ex diverso attributo, adeoque ex una substantia plures constitui poterunt...." The Latin again clearly states that attributes constitute substance.

⁹⁰ Wild, p. 107, E1, Prop. 13, Corol. Emphasis added.

⁹¹ Gebhardt, II, 55: "... nullam substantiam corpoream, quatenus substantia est, esse divisibilem." Emphasis added.

⁹² Cf. H. R., I, 229-230, *Principles of Philosophy*, Part I, Principles 26 and 27.

⁹³ H. R., I, 141, Preface to the *Meditations*.

⁹⁴ H. R., I, 240, *Principles of Philosophy*, Part I, Principle 53.

[95] H. R., I, 228, *Principles of Philosophy*, Part I, Principle 23; Alquie, III, 105: "... ainsi, parce que l'extension constitue la nature du corps, et que ce qui est etendu peut etre divise en plusieurs parties, et que cela marque du defaut, nous concluons que Dieu n'est point un corps." A translation more accurate than that of Haldane and Ross might be: "...thus, since extension constitutes the nature of body, and that which is extensive can be divided into several parts, and this is a sign of deficiency, we conclude that God does not have a body."

[96] Wild, p. 107, E1, Prop. 14, Dem.

[97] Wild, p. 109, E1, Prop. 15, Schol.

[98] Wild, p. 106, E1, Prop. 13.

[99] Wild, p. 110, E1, Prop. 15, Schol.

[100] Wild, p. 112, E1, Prop. 15, Schol.; "To Ludovicus Meyer, P.M.Q.D.," 20 April 1663, Letter 12, p. 413.

[101] Wild, p. 112, E1, Prop. 15, Schol.

[102] *Ibid.*

[103] Wild, Letter 12, p. 413.

[104] Wild, p. 111, E1, Prop. 15, Schol.

[105] This distinction between the different types of thought and the different objects thereof is more fully discussed in Part II of this book. It parallels distinctions found in Plato's later dialogues.

[106] Wild, p. 108, E1, Prop. 15.

[107] Wild, p. 112, E1, Prop. 15, Schol.; Gebhardt, II, 60: "Omnia, inquam, in Deo sunt, & omnia, quae fiunt, per solas leges infinitae Dei naturae fiunt...." "Everything, I say, is in God, and everything which becomes (occurs), becomes solely through the laws of the infinite nature of God...."

[108] Wild, p. 113, E1, Prop. 16; Gebhardt, II, 60: "Ex necessitate divinae naturae, infinita infinitis modis (hoc est, omnia, quae sub intellectum cadere possunt), sequi debent." "From the necessity of divine nature, an infinity of infinite modes (that is, everything which can come under the infinite intellect), follows necessarily."

[109] Wild, pp. 113-114, E1, Prop. 16, Corol. 2.

[110] Wild, p. 114, E1, Prop. 17.

[111] Wild, p. 115, E1, Prop. 17, Schol. Parenthetical remark added. Gebhardt, II, 62: "... a summa Dei potentia, sive infinita natura infinita infinitis modis, hoc est, omnia necessario effluxisse, vel semper eadem necessitate sequi...."

[112] Cf. H. R., II, 226: "... I do not think that the essence of things, and those mathematical truths which may be known about them, are independent of God; yet I think that because God so wished it and brought it to pass, they are immutable and eternal."

[113] Wild, p. 116, E1, Prop. 17, Schol.

[114] *Ibid.*

[115] Wild, p. 115, E1, Prop. 17, Schol.

[116] Wild, pp. 116-117, E1, Prop. 17, Schol.

[117] Cf. Wild, p. 95, E1, Axiom 5.

[118] Wild, p. 117, E1, Prop. 17, Schol.

[119] Wild, p. 117, E1, Prop. 17, Schol.; Gebhardt, II, 63: "... est enim haec aeterna veritas...."

[120] Wild, p. 116, E1, Prop. 17, Schol.

[121] Wolfson, I, 369. He likens eternal truths, which are known by intuition, to the innate ideas of Descartes.

[122] Wolfson, I, 367.

[123] Wolfson, II, 37.

[124] Wild, p. 117, E1, Prop. 17, Schol.; Gebhardt, II, 63: "... & ideo secundum essentiam prorsus convenire possunt...."

[125] Wild, p. 117, E1, Prop. 17, Schol.; Gebhardt, II, 63: "... sed, si unius essentia destrui posset, & fieri falsa, destrueretur etiam alterius essentia."

[126] Wild, p. 101, E1, Prop. 8, Schol. 2; Gebhardt, II, 51: "... naturae humanae in genere...."

[127] Wild, p. 101, E1, Prop. 8, Schol. 2; Gebhardt, II, 51: "... ipsa natura humana...." A further discussion of the essence of man and the existence of man may be found on pp. 46-49.

[128] Wild, p. 119, E1, Prop. 21.

[129] Wild, "To Mr. G. H. Schuller," 29 July 1675, Letter 64, p. 464n. Wild says in a footnote to the letter that the face of the whole universe is a mode "consisting of finite Modes." But finite modes are not eternal and infinite. I should think that the face of the universe is, in the attribute of thought, eternal truths, essences of finite ideas, common axioms. Spinoza says that the mode varies in infinite modes, so I should think it is specific to each of the attributes. In Extension it would be the specific laws of motion and rest, essences of bodies. A more complete discussion of the issue will be found in the commentary to this section.

[130] Wild, p. 95, E1, Def. 7; Gebhardt, II, 46: "... quae ex sola suae naturae necessitate existit, & a se sola ad agendum determinatur...."

[131] Cf. Wild, p. 95, E1, Def. 7; Gebhardt, II, 46: "Necessaria autem, vel potius coacta, quae ab alio determinatur ad existendum, & operandum certa, ac determinata ratione."

[132] Wild, p. 95, E1, Def. 8.

[133] Wild, p. 95, E1, Def. 8, Explanation.

[134] Wild, p. 122, E1, Prop. 24, Corol.

[135] Wild, p. 95, E1, Def. 8.

[136] Wild, p. 122, E1, Prop. 24.

[137] Wild, p. 121, E1, Props. 22 and 23.

[138] Cf. Wild, pp. 116-117, E1, Prop. 17, Schol.

[139] Wild, p. 123, E1, Prop. 25, Corol.; Gebhardt, II, 68: "Res particulares nihil sunt, nisi Dei attributorum affectiones, sive modi, quibus Dei attributa certo, determinato modo exprimuntur." It is interesting that Spinoza uses the term particular, finite (Prop. 28), individual and singular (Prop. 28) to represent finite things. Plato, too, refers to finite existences as "particulars."

[140] Cf. Wild, p. 123, E1, Prop. 28; Gebhardt, II, 69: "Quodcunque singulare, sive quaevis res, quae finita est...." Emphasis added.

[141] Wild, p. 104, E1, Prop. 11.

[142] Wild, p. 117, E1, Prop. 17, Schol.

[143] *Ibid.*

[144] Cf. Wild, pp. 100-101, E1, Prop. 8, Schol.

[145] This seems to be quite Platonic. The essential causation seems analogous to the relation between Plato's Forms and particulars; the existential causation seems analogous to that of the relations between particulars which cause one to "come into being." As Being pervades all other Forms and all particulars, so God or Nature pervades all modes in Spinoza.

[146] Wild, p. 138, E1, Appendix.

[147] Wild, p. 126, E1, Prop. 30.

[148] Wild, p. 126, E1, Prop. 30, Dem.

[149] Wild, p. 127, E1, Prop. 31.

[150] Cf. Wild, p. 127, E1, Prop. 31, Schol.

[151] Wild, p. 127, E1, Prop. 31, Corol.

[152] This is discussed in Part II of this book. T. C. Mark, *Spinoza's Theory of Truth*, has an excellent discussion of this view.

[153] Wild, p. 128, E1, Prop. 32, Corol. 1.

[154] Wild, p. 104, E1, Prop. 11, Proof 2.

[155] Wild, pp. 114-117, E1, Prop. 17, Schol.

[156] Wild, p. 128, E1, Prop. 32, Corol. 2; Gebhardt, II, 73: "... voluntatem, & intellectum ad Dei naturam ita sese habere, ut motus, & quies, & absolute, ut omnia naturalia. ..." A better translation might be: "will and intellect are related to the nature of God as motion, and rest, and fully, as is everything natural which must be determined to existence and action in a certain manner." All natural things, everything in Nature is caused or determined.

157 Wild, Letter 64, p. 463.
158 Wild, p. 129, E1, Prop. 33, Schol. 1; Gebhardt, II, 74: "Res aliqua necessaria dicitur, vel ratione suae essentia, vel ratione causae." Something is called necessary either by reason of its essence or by reason of a cause.
159 Wild, pp. 129-130, E1, Prop. 33, Schol. 1.
160 Wild, p. 130, E1, Prop. 33, Schol. 1.
161 Wild, p. 130, E1, Prop. 33, Schol. 2.
162 Wild, p. 131, E1, Prop. 33, Schol. 2.
163 Wild, p. 132, E1, Prop. 33, Schol. 2.
164 Wild, p. 134, E1, Prop. 36, Dem.
165 Haserot, "Attribute," pp. 499-513.
166 Curley, Spinoza, p. 16.
167 Wild, p. 94, E1, Def. 4.
168 Haserot, "Attribute," p. 507.
169 Curley, Spinoza, p. 150.
170 Wild, p. 149, E2, Prop. 7, Schol.; Gebhardt, II, 90: "... quod quicquid ad infinito intellectu percipi potest, tanquam substantia essentiam constituens, id omne ad unicam tantum substantiam pertinet...."
171 Curley, Spinoza, p. 150. Emphasis added.
172 W. Kessler, "A Note on Spinoza's Concept of Attribute," Monist, 55 (1971), 636-639; hereafter cited as Kessler.
173 Kessler, p. 637.
174 Wild, p. 106, E2, Prop. 40, Schol. 2.
175 Wild, p. 193, E2, Prop. 47.
176 Wild, p. 95, E1, Def. 6.
177 Wild, pp. 193-194, E2, Prop. 47, Schol. Emphasis and parentheses added.
178 Wolf, Letter 9, in Correspondence, p. 107. Emphasis added.
179 Kessler, pp. 638-639; quotations from Short Treatise I, Ch. I, p. 19, 1.25ff.
180 Kessler, p. 639.
181 E. Brehier, Histoire de la Philosophie: Tome II. La Philosophie Moderne, 1. Le XVII Siècle. (Paris: Presses Universitaires de France, 1968), p. 151.
182 Brehier, p. 168.
183 Brehier, pp. 168-169.
184 Cornford, p. 257.
185 Cornford, p. 267.
186 Cornford, p. 285.
187 Cornford, p. 270.
188 Cornford, p. 290.
189 Cornford, p. 186.
190 Plato, Timaeus, in The Collected Dialogues of Plato, ed. E. Hamilton and H. Cairns (New York: Pantheon Books, 1964), Cf. 30a-c (pp. 1162-1163). Hereafter cited as Plato.
191 Cf. Plato, Phaedo, 98a-99d (pp. 79-80).
192 Cf. Wild, p. 117, E1, Prop. 18.
193 Cf. Wild, p. 122, E1, Prop. 25.
194 Cf. Wild, p. 122, E1, Prop. 24.
195 Wild, p. 116, Prop. 17, Schol.; Gebhardt, II, 63: "... sed contra veritas, & formalis rerum essentia ideo talis est, quia talis in Dei intellectu existit objective."
196 Wild, p. 117, E1, Prop. 17, Schol. Emphasis added. Gebhardt, II, 63: "Ex. gr. homo est causa existentiae, non vero essentiae alterius hominis; est enim haec aeterna veritas: & ideo secundum essentiam prorsus convenire possunt; in existendo autem differre debent; & propterea, si unius existentia pereat, non ideo alterius peribit; sed, si unius essentia destrui posset, & fieri falsa, destrueretur etiam alterius essentia. Quapropter res, quae & essentiae, & existentiae, alicujus effectus est causa, a tali effectu differre debet, tam ratione essentiae, quam ratione existentiae." Emphasis added.
197 Wild, p. 123, E1, Prop. 25, Corol.
198 Wild, p. 123, E1, Prop. 28.

[199] G. Vlastos, *Platonic Studies* (Princeton University Press, 1973), pp. 76-110; hereafter cited as Vlastos.

[200] Vlastos, p. 100.

[201] Vlastos, p. 110.

[202] Plato, *Parmenides*, 131a (p. 925). Emphasis added.

[203] *Ibid.*

[204] *Ibid.*

[205] *Ibid.* Emphasis added.

[206] Plato, *Parmenides*, 131e (p. 926).

[207] *Ibid.*

[208] R. E. Allen, "Participation and Predication in Plato's Middle Dialogues," in *Plato: A Collection of Critical Essays*, II, ed. G. Vlastos (Garden City, N.Y.: Anchor Books, 1971), p. 176; hereafter cited as Allen.

[209] Allen, p. 179.

[210] Wild, Letter 64, p. 463.

[211] Wild, p. 464n.

[212] R. L. Saw, "The Task of Metaphysics for Spinoza," in *Spinoza: Essays in Interpretation*, ed. M. Mandelbaum and E. Freeman (La Salle: Open Court, 1975), p. 240; hereafter cited as Saw.

[213] L. C. Rice, "Spinoza on Individuation," *Monist*, 55 (1971), 650.

[214] Wild, p. 163, E2, Lem. 7, Schol.

[215] Saw, p. 240.

[216] Wolfson, I, 246-247.

[217] Wolfson, I, 247.

[218] Curley, *Spinoza*, p. 61; Cf. pp. 61-63, 66-68.

[219] Joachim, *TdIE*, p. 209. Emphasis added.

[220] *Ibid.* Parentheses and emphasis added.

[221] Curley, *Spinoza*, p. 74.

[222] Allen, p. 183.

[223] Cf. Plato, *Timaeus*, 49a-51c (pp. 1176-1178).

[224] Curley, *Spinoza*, p. 74.

[225] Wild, *On the Improvement of the Understanding*, pp. 36-37.

[226] Cf. Wolfson, I, 394-395.

CHAPTER TWO

ETHICS: PART II

EPISTEMOLOGY

In the past, there have been many excellent attempts to clarify Spinoza's epistemology. Here, too, recent innovations and stratagems have been ingenious but have added to the confusion.[1]

Problems arise in Spinoza because of his unusual use of terms such as "idea," "image," "imagination," and "object." Because one is liable to impose current definitions, or his own definitions, on these terms instead of adhering to Spinoza's rather clear definitions, one may find himself confused in his attempt to understand Spinoza's use of "truth," "adequacy," and "error."

IDEA—FINITE MODE OF THOUGHT

In Part 2 of the *Ethics*, Spinoza defines an idea: "By idea I understand a conception of the mind which the mind forms because it is a thinking thing."[2] In the explanation to this definition, Spinoza is careful to emphasize the activity included in the idea: "I use the word 'conception' rather than 'perception' because the name perception seems to indicate that the mind is passive in its relation to the object. But the word conception seems to express the action of the mind."[3] Ideas, then, contain or express some sort of activity. Some commentators stress the active aspect of the idea as being the affirmation or denial, the volition, of the idea; others find it in the representational or intentional aspect of the idea and in the *conatus* of the mind.[4] Mark stresses the activity of ideas and indicates that Spinoza thinks of ideas both as the "result of mental activity" and as "a kind of mental activity."[5] He also notes that "the *essentia objectiva* is what is *posited* by the idea; it is like Husserl's 'intended meaning' of a concept."[6] I shall be emphasizing the activity embodied in Spinoza's concept of the idea.

MIND

The human mind is defined as a particular sort of idea. Spinoza says the mind is "the idea of an individual thing already existing."[7] The "individual thing already existing" which is the object of the idea constituting the human mind is the human body.[8] Spinoza refers to the relation between the mind and the body as the body being the 'object' of the idea,[9] and he asserts that modifications of the body are perceived by the mind. Indeed, seen *sub specie aeternitatis*, the mind and the body are identical.

In so far as one thinks of the human mind as being active, one must also think of at least this sort of complex idea as being active, too. So, the mind is an idea, and ideas are active; but it is not the case that all ideas are equally active or active in the same sense as the sort of complex idea which constitutes the mind. Spinoza notes "Man thinks."[10] Man's mind is aware of its thoughts, and this sort of reasoning has led commentators such as Joachim to note that, for Spinoza, knowledge is self-reflective.[11] At any rate, it is true that the mind of man, or this particular sort of idea, is conscious, or aware that it knows, or perceives. There is a dispute between Mark and Radner concerning *what* the mind perceives which shall be examined later.[12] Contrary to Descartes' view, Spinoza states that the mind is an idea and *not* a substance.[13] Mark points out that Spinoza asserts "The human mind is the idea itself or the knowledge of the human body."[14] Although, on occasion, Spinoza lapses into common speech and maintains that the mind *has* ideas or there are ideas *in* the mind,[15] it cannot be that Spinoza is referring to the mind and its ideas in the same sense as Descartes. That is to say, Spinoza cannot have ideas as accidents of a mental substance, because he has expressly denied the substantial nature of the mind and affirmed that the mind itself is an idea. There cannot be a substratum constituting the mind which owns, or has, ideas or in which the ideas inhere. The Aristotelian, Cartesian, Lockean notion of an underlying substratum or support for one's ideas is absent from Spinoza.

How can one "have," "know," "perceive," "be aware of" an idea or any object of knowledge, for Spinoza? We recall that the mind is itself a complex idea which is self-conscious[16] and that a complex idea is constituted by other ideas. Rather than saying that the mind "has" an idea, we *should* say, more precisely, that the core idea constituting mind has added other ideas. To gain an idea, or to acquire knowledge, is simply to add another idea to the complex idea constituting the human mind. When one acquires a "new" idea, it may be by adding a new constituent to the complex idea "mind." One may also acquire "new ideas" by the activity of the idea itself which constitutes the mind; by its deduction, analysis, or rearrangement of ideas of which it is composed. We must recollect that the complex idea—mind—is itself active. If the idea itself is active, or conscious, or thinks, there is no need for an active substance which differs essentially from ideas.

Not only are ideas more active in Spinoza than in Descartes, one also finds Spinoza's extension is more active than Descartes'. Thus, in Spinoza, thought and extension are more akin than in Descartes. The need for mind as an active *substance* occurs, I believe, because of a view of extension as a dead, passive, inert substance which acquires its activity (motion) from an external source. For Spinoza, however, extension has as its immediate infinite mode—its own primary characteristic—motion or rest. The view of ideas as objects of knowledge—as passive things—requires an active substance. The view of an idea as a picture, as a mark on a *tabula rasa*, requires some activity on the part of a substance in order for the mark to be apprehended. But Spinoza is at great pains to indicate the activity of ideas themselves, and to distinguish ideas from dumb, inert marks or pictures. Indeed, the picture-theory of ideas which, at times, Descartes adopts, is replaced by a more definite distinction between ideas and images in Spinoza.[17] One must keep in mind the active aspects of modes of thought.

The active aspect of ideas may be found in the view that all ideas refer, or point toward, or intend something or other. In Mark's terminology, all ideas have objective essences.[18]

IMAGE

In the *Principles of the Philosophy of Descartes*, Spinoza, quoting from Descartes, says:

> Thus, images depicted in the fancy are not the only things I call ideas. In fact, so far as such images exist only in corporeal fancy—that is, when such images are only depicted in some part of the brain—I do not call them ideas at all; rather, only in so far as they inform the mind itself when it is turned toward that part of the brain do I call such images ideas.[19]

In this work Spinoza is explaining Descartes, and this is one of the few examples when Descartes himself is clear about the distinction between ideas, images, and ideas of images. This confusion between these three different terms in Descartes is one of the causes for the subsequent similar confusion in reading Spinoza himself.

Spinoza himself elucidates the difference between an image and an idea of that image. He says, "But in order that we may retain the customary phraseology, we will give to those *affections of the human body*, the ideas of which represent to us external bodies as if they were present, *the name of images of things*, although they do not actually reproduce the forms of the things. When the mind contemplates bodies in this way, we will say that it imagines."[20] This is a most important passage for clarifying the terms: ideas, images, and ideas of images.

In the introduction to this important passage, Spinoza says that he is going "to retain the usual *words*," but he actually clarifies the Cartesian usage by distinguishing between ideas of images and images. Mark says, "Sometimes Spinoza's use of 'idea' for 'image' may be a case of his using the word according to the ordinary usage of the day, when he did not think that his meaning would be obscured."[21] Yet, in the above passage, Spinoza clearly distinguishes between an idea of an image and the image itself.

The translation of "*verba usitata retineamus*" as "retain the customary phraseology,"[22] may be misleading since Spinoza is not here using his terms in the customary manner. As many commentators point out, there is a confusion between idea and image in the seventeenth century, and one example occurs in *Meditation III* of Descartes.[23] Spinoza is retaining the customary or usual *words*—idea and image, but he is *using* those terms more clearly to indicate the difference between ideas and images.

It is clear that the "modifications" (*affectiones*) of the body are images. An image is a mode of extension, and it is not to be included in the attribute of thought and its modes. Mark notes that images are physical and physiological products which "can provide some information about other bodies, but they must be carefully distinguished from ideas formed by the mind, and the information they provide must be distinguished from genuine knowledge."[24] Yet, if images are strictly modifications or changes in the body, they can provide no knowledge or information. Knowledge and information are results or qualities of ideas, not images; of thought, not extension. It is clear from the passage that the *ideas* of the images represent the external objects, *not* the images themselves. Images themselves are joint products of the motion of the external body and the human body itself, but it is the *idea* of the modification which "represent(s) to us external bodies as if they were present"[25] and *not* the image or modification of the body itself. The image itself is dumb, inert, physical—a picture painted on a hidden canvas.

"Those who think that ideas consist of images which are formed in us by meeting with external bodies persuade themselves that those ideas of things of which we can form no similar image are not ideas.... They look upon ideas, therefore, as dumb pictures on a tablet and, being possessed with this prejudice, they do not see that an idea, in so far as it is an idea, involves affirmation or negation."[26] The image defined here is more akin to an optical image and *not* an observed or perceived image. That which is perceived, or observed, or known is an idea and not a physical image itself.

Spinoza stresses the fact that images are modifications of the body in numerous places throughout the *Ethics*.[27] It is striking that he retains the strict Cartesian sense of images in the *Ethics*. He says, "For by 'ideas' I do not understand the images which are formed at the back of the eye, or, if you please, in the middle of the brain, but rather the conceptions of thought."[28] "For the essence of words and images is formed of bodily motions alone, which involves in no way whatever the conception of thought."[29]

IMAGINATION

When the mind forms ideas of these images, we say that the mind imagines. Thus, imagining is *not* the formation of images; that is the result of the interaction of the human body and external bodies. Imagining is an activity of the human mind. "When the mind contemplates bodies in this way (when it forms ideas of images), we will say that it imagines."[30] So, *to* imagine is to form an idea of an image. An idea of an image is *an* imagination. "When the human mind through the ideas of the affections of its body ((through ideas of images)) contemplates external bodies, we say that it then imagines (note, Prop. 17, pt. 2), nor can the mind (Prop. 26, pt. 2) in any other way imagine external bodies as actually existing."[31] The mind imagines when it actively forms an idea of an image. The referent of that idea, its formal essence or ideatum, properly should be the image. The intent of the idea of the image is the *image*.[32]

It should be noted that imagination is a mode of thinking, an activity of the mind, the forming of an idea of an image. Unfortunately, we often call the result of that activity by the same name—an imagination. The term "imagination" is ambiguous in a way similar to that of the term "idea." That is to say, an idea is both the activity of the mind and the resulting object of that activity; an imagination is the object of the mind when it is imagining—when it forms an idea of an image.

In Descartes' *Meditation II*, imagination is defined as the mind turning toward the body "for imagination consists in contemplating the figure or image of a corporeal thing,"[33] and *Meditation VI*: "I always employ the aid of imagination when I think of corporeal things."[34] In *Replies to Objections II*,[35] and in Spinoza's *Principles of the Philosophy of Descartes*[36] ideas and images are mentioned and appear to correspond to E 2, Prop. 17, Note. An imagination is the idea of an image, and it is formed when the mind contemplates, or thinks about, or perceives, a modification of the body caused by an external body or bodies affecting us. When we imagine, we form an idea of an image and that idea represents to us an external object. We often intend that idea to refer to the external body.

Spinoza says E 2, Prop. 40, "... the human body, inasmuch as it is limited, can form distinctly in itself a certain number only of images at once ... in proportion to the number of images which can be formed at the same time in the body will be the number of bodies which the human mind can imagine at the same time."[37] The number of distinct imaginations—ideas of images—which the mind can form is limited to the number of distinct images formed in the body. E 2, Prop. 49: "I warn my readers carefully to distinguish between an idea or conception of the mind and the images of things formed by our imagination."[38] Here, "images" should more properly be "ideas of images." Later in that proposition, Spinoza is more precise in distinguishing the active ideas from the "dumb pictures," or images; and he says that images "involve in no way whatever the conception of thought."[39] E 5, Prop. 11 states that "the greater the number of objects to which an image is related ... the more does it occupy the mind."[40]

I believe that one can take E 2, Proposition 17, Note, for the proper sense of imagination as the formation of an idea of an image. This belief is further buttressed by E 3, Proposition 52, Note, wherein Spinoza says, "This affection of the mind, or imagination of a particular thing, insofar as it alone occupies the mind...."[41] Note that a *mental* modification is an *imagination*, whereas a *physical* modification is an *image*. Further, E 4, Proposition I, Note, states:

> For an imagination is an *idea* which indicates the present constitution of the human body, rather than the nature of an external body, not indeed distinctly but confusedly, so that the mind is said to err. ... So with the other imaginations by which the mind is deceived; whether they indicate the natural constitution of the body or an increase or diminution in its power of action, they are not opposed to truth, nor do they disappear with the presence of truth.[42]

Note that imaginations are not necessarily false, nor are they necessarily the cause of error. Ideas of images *may* lead to error, but they are not essentially or intrinsically deceptive.

I should argue, then, that there is indeed an important distinction between an image and an imagination, an *imago* and an *imaginatio*, and that Spinoza intends us to be aware of this difference. An image is a figure, a physical affect of an external body on the human body, a defective likeness of the external body, whereas an imagination is a conception, or idea, formed by the mind *of* that image.[43] *The* imagination is that activity of the mind whereby it forms an idea of an image or *an* imagination. If we retain these distinctions, perhaps we shall succeed in explicating some puzzles in Spinoza.

OBJECT OF KNOWLEDGE

In order to discuss the meanings of the terms "truth," "adequacy," and "error" in Spinoza, we should first clearly identify the object of knowledge. Radner says, "Spinoza agrees with Descartes that the mental and the material are totally distinct realms; that we are directly aware only of things in the mental realm; and that we can have knowledge of material things by means of the ideas which represent them."[44] The object of knowledge, for Radner, is an idea. This plays a key role in her explication of Spinoza's theory of truth because it is in terms of the relation of the idea to *its object* and to that which it *represents* that she examines tru h, adequacy, and error in Spinoza. The key to Spinoza's theory of the nature of representation is his distinction between the object of the idea and that which the idea represents. Radner has an interesting interpretation of Spinoza's view. She says:

> The term 'the object of the idea' is not synonymous with the term 'that which is represented by the idea,' although in some cases the two terms have the same reference. The object and the thing represented stand in two different relations to the idea. The relation between the idea and its object is explicated in terms of the distinction between objective and formal reality. The relation between the idea and what it represents is explicated in terms of the resemblance of the thing represented to the object of the idea. The object of the idea and the idea are related as formal reality to objective reality.[45]

So, every idea has some formal reality as its object. But, an idea may resemble more or less accurately what it represents. For both Radner and Mark, ideas have objective essence and formal essence—and they agree as to the meaning of the terms. Mark says that the "*essentia objectiva* refer(s) to the being of a thing as it is stated or contained in an idea, and *essentia formalis* refer(s) to the thing in itself—that is, its status in relation to other things of the same kind."[46] This is, for Mark, the same as the relation between the *idea* and the *ideatum*. If idea and ideatum "agree," then we say the idea is true, for Spinoza, Mark, *and* Radner. However, Radner says the mind knows only ideas, whereas Mark says the mind can know ideata because the idea and its ideatum are identical. For Radner, ideas *represent* things whereas for Mark ideas are the things known. The objective essence of the idea "points out" or "refers to" its formal essence or its ideatum for Mark. But, for Radner the idea can represent something other than its ideatum, and this is the cause of error.

Radner's fruitful interpretation depends upon representationalism, but Mark says this is too Cartesian a view and is erroneous. Mark says that the Cartesian picture is one in which "the relation between mind and its ideas is one of direct awareness or apprehension, the relation between the idea or objective reality and the world or formal reality is one of representation, and between the mind and the world there is no relation at all.''[47] Mark says that ''Daisie Radner writes that Spinoza agrees with Descartes 'that we are directly aware only of things in the mental realm,' although she offers neither argument nor textual support for this assertion.''[48] He counters Radner's view with a claim that ''Spinoza ... invokes ... a two-level analysis in which there is no intermediate entity between the mind and what is known and in which what is apprehended is not the representation of something else which is inaccessible.''[49] He says:

> If the objects of ideas are occasionally not mental, then the same may be true of the objects of the mind. But it is patent that ideas *do*, sometimes, have physical things for their objects, and this *is* the case with the idea which is identified with the mind: 'The object of the idea constituting the human mind is a body, or a certain mode of extension actually existing' (E II, 13).... Again, 'the body is the object of the mind.' (E II, 21, Dem.) If the mind were aware only of objects which were also mental, how account (sic) for E II, 22: 'the human mind not only perceives the modification of the body, but also the ideas of these modifications of the body'? Is Spinoza speaking with uncharacteristic imprecision, intending to say that 'the human mind not only perceives the ideas of modifications of the body, but also the ideas of the ideas of these modifications'? Surely that is absurd. Spinoza has the vocabulary (ideas of ideas) to speak of the apprehension of mental contents if he wishes, and he uses that vocabulary with some care in the portion of Part II which we are considering, so there is no reason not to take him literally where he talks of the mind perceiving bodily modifications or of the mind having body as its object.[50]

The issue between Mark and Radner, then, is whether or not ideas intervene or represent something to the mind which is inaccessible directly by the mind itself. If one says the formal essence of the idea is an ideatum which can be either extended or idea, and if one identifies the objective essence of the idea with the referential aspect of the idea, then, according to Mark, the idea and its object are one. Radner would argue that the idea differs from its formal reality and also from that which it represents; that the objective, formal essences, and representations coalesce only *sub specie aeternitatis*.

MIND AND KNOWLEDGE OF BODY

The issue assumes further importance where one is concerned with knowledge of the human body itself. Mark says we know our body directly and Radner would argue that we know it only *via* an idea. Both Mark and Radner agree that images—which are modifications of the body—represent external objects, but Mark says representation ''has to

do only with those ideas which represent to us external objects (i.e., finite
physical objects) other than our own bodies.''[51] Representation has to do
only with ideas of images and not with other ideas. Radner says representation is an aspect of *all* ideas, whether they are ideas of our bodies,
external bodies, or other ideas.

There is no doubt that the mind and its body are one and the same
thing for Spinoza. That is to say, *sub specie aeternitatis* this mode of thought
and this mode of extension are identical in so far as they are both finite
modes of the one and only substance. The mind and body are ''united''
by means of identity. Metaphysically, the mind and its object—the
human body—are identical. However, this is not to say that the mind
and *the object of knowledge* are one and the same, or are identical. The mind
does not become the object of knowledge. When Spinoza is defining the
mind, he says that it is the idea of the body, or the body is the object of
the mind. But, when he is speaking of knowing he is careful, generally, to
indicate that the object of knowledge is an idea and *not* the object itself. In
short, I am suggesting that there is an equivocation on the term ''object''
in Spinoza. That is to say, the object of the mind is identical to the body
in a metaphysical sense or as a definition of the relation between the finite
modes. On the other hand, the object of knowledge—what the mind conceives or perceives—is an idea which may or may not be adequately
known. This sort of analysis of the metaphysical or substantial sense of
''object'' would agree with E 2, Proposition 13[52] and E 2, Proposition 21,
Dem.[53] And, in E 2, Proposition 17, Scholia, Spinoza himself makes
clear the difference between an object which constitutes the essense of the
mind—the metaphysical sense of ''object''—and the object which is
known by mind:

> ... we clearly see what is the difference between the idea, for example, of
> Peter, which constitutes the essence of the mind itself of Peter (Gebhardt,
> II, p. 105: ''quae essentiam Mentis ipsius Petri constituit'') and the idea
> of Peter himself which is in another man; for example, in Paul. For the
> former directly manifests the essence of the body of Peter himself, (*Ibidem*:
> ''Illa enim essentiam Corporis ipsius Petri directe explicat....'') nor does
> it involve existence unless so long as Peter exists; the latter, on the other
> hand, indicates rather the constitution of the body of Paul than the nature
> of Peter; and therefore so long as Paul's body exists with that constitution,
> so long will Paul's mind contemplate Peter as present, although he does not
> exist.[54]

It is to be noted that the idea which *constitutes* the human mind is the idea
of the human body. But, the idea which the human mind knows is different from that which constitutes the essence of the mind. The mind is
not identical to the objects of its knowledge; it is identical to its body seen
sub specie aeternitatis. This is a most important distinction between the con-

stituents or essence of the mind and what it knows. So, the mind is different from *its* ideas. The mind is a complex idea which is itself active and is a sub-set of its acquired ideas. The acquired ideas are objects of the mind's *knowledge*. The *object* of the mind, the formal essence of the mind in the attribute of extension, is the human body.

Mark claims that the mind has immediate knowledge of the body's modifications. However, there are counter-instances where Spinoza indicates that the object of knowledge or perception of the mind is an idea. In E 2, Proposition 12, Spinoza says, "Whatever happens in the object of the idea constituting the human mind, must be *perceived* by the human mind; or, in other words, an *idea* of that thing will necessarily exist in the human mind."[55] This is a rather clear statement that the human mind must have an idea of any modification which occurs in its body. In the demonstration to this proposition, Spinoza says that "the knowledge of this thing will necessarily be in the mind, or the mind perceives it."[56] The idea, then, of the change in the body is known or perceived by the mind. Apparently, there is an intervention of an idea between the mind and the modification of the body which Mark denies.

Again, in E 2, Proposition 13 which Mark had used to support his claim of immediate knowledge of the body by the mind, Spinoza says, "But (Ax. 4, pt. 2) we have ideas of the affections of the body, therefore, the *object* of the idea constituting the human mind is a *body*...."[57] Axiom 4, states that "We perceive that a certain body is affected in many ways."[58] Thus, to perceive that the body is affected, is to perceive that there are modifications of the body, is to have an *idea* of the modification. Further, a modification or an affection of the body is an image, and, if one knows or perceives the image, one has an *idea* of it. One knows his body, then, by means of ideas of the changes which occur in the body and not directly. Ideas *do* intervene in one's knowledge of his body, at least according to Propositions 12 and 13.

E 2, Proposition 19 states, "The human mind does not know the human body itself, nor does it know that the body exists except through ideas of affections by which the body is affected."[59] This proposition apparently contradicts E 2, Proposition 22: "The human mind not only perceives the affections of the body, but also the ideas of these affections."[60] Mark takes note of E 2, Proposition 19 and its difference from E 2, Proposition 22—which Mark argues constitutes evidence for his assertion that the mind perceives the modifications (affections) of the body directly. He says that Spinoza's

> assertion in E II, 19 that the mind does not know 'the body itself' does not have the consequence that what it *does* know must be mental. In this and subsequent propositions Spinoza is determining which objects are

epistemologically primitive in such knowledge as we can have of the
'external world' and considering whether this knowledge can be adequate.
He is not saying that the mind cannot perceive the physical.[61]

On the contrary, we have seen that the mind knows or perceives the body
by means of ideas of affections (modifications) of the body in E 2,
Propositions 12 and 13 and this is supported by E 2, Proposition 19.
Apparently Spinoza is concerned with the mind's knowledge of *its* body
and not of external bodies in Proposition 22. It seems that the only
evidence that Mark can produce for the mind directly knowing its body is
E 2, Proposition 22. I have argued that when Spinoza uses the phrase
"perceives the affections (modifications) of the body" this can be
translated as "has ideas of images." Mark would translate this as "has
an image." But Mark has noted elsewhere[62] that images are physical,
and he claims that the mind knows the images directly without any
intervening ideas. However, causation is intra-attribute, so extended
modes can affect only extended modes, and if an image is extended, then
how can the mind be affected by it? It would seem that mind can be
affected by, or know, or perceive only ideas; some ideas are ideas of
images, some are ideas of ideas. Mark says that the substitution of
"perceives the modifications (affections) of the body" as "perceives the
ideas of the modifications (affections) of the body" is "absurd."[63] But we
have seen above that all references to knowledge or perception of these
modifications incorporate ideas of images. Mark's only evidence for his
thesis, Proposition 22 itself, contains the phraseology of "ideas of affections" and "ideas of ideas" in the Demonstration:

> The ideas of the ideas of affections follow in God and are related to God in
> the same way as the ideas themselves of affections. ... But the ideas of the
> affections of the body are in the human mind (Prop. 12, pt. 2), that is to
> say, in God (Corol. Prop. 11, pt. 2) in so far as He constitutes the essence
> of the human mind; therefore, the ideas of these ideas will be in God in so
> far as He has the knowledge or idea of the human mind; that is to say
> (Prop. 21, pt. 2), they will be in the human mind itself, which, therefore
> not only perceives the affections of the body....[64]

Contrary to Mark, I should read Proposition 22 as meaning: "The
human mind not only perceives the ideas of affections (modifications) of
the body, but also ideas of ideas of these affections (modifications)." This
would then be in accord with the language of the demonstration itself as
well as that of E 2, Propositions 12 and 13, wherein Spinoza speaks of
knowledge of ideas, and also with subsequent Proposition 23: "The mind
does not know itself except insofar as it perceives the ideas of the affections of the body."[65] Furthermore, E 2, Proposition 29, Corollary states:

... for the mind does not know itself unless in so far as it perceives the ideas of the affections of the body. Moreover, *it does not perceive its body unless through those same ideas of the affections by means of which alone it perceives external bodies.*[66]

Spinoza here states that the mind requires ideas of images to know its body *and* to know external bodies. There is, then, apparently some justification for my argument that E 2, Proposition 22 is uncharacteristically imprecise for Spinoza, unless one keeps in mind that "to perceive" is "to have an idea of an image." Evidently, the intervention of ideas is required in order for one to have knowledge of one's own body as well as other bodies.

PERCEPTION

There is some evidence that Spinoza uses the term "perception" as he uses the term "imagination." E 2, Proposition 26 states: "The human mind perceives no external body as actually existing unless through the ideas of the affections of the body."[67] The demonstration reads:

When the human mind through the ideas of the affections of its body contemplates external bodies, we say that it then imagines ..., nor can the mind in any other way imagine external bodies as actually existing.[68]

Evidently, the formation of the idea of any image, or affection (modification) of the body, is termed "imagination" by Spinoza. The formation of ideas of present images is perception; ideas of past images is memory, ideas of past, future, or non-present images is imagination in the sense of fantasy.[69]

I have argued that Spinoza uses "object" in two different ways when he speaks of the object of the human mind and the object of knowledge. If one notices the numerous mentions of *ideas* of affections (modifications) of the body, or ideas of images, one can find at least some basis for the claim that the objects of knowledge are ideas—a claim which is not, on the face of it, as absurd as Mark claims.[70] There is some basis for Radner's assertion that ideas are objects of knowledge which further represent either other ideas, or external bodies, or the body itself. If one accepts Radner's account of the representational aspect of ideas and combines it with Mark's and Brandom's active aspect of ideas, I believe that one can clarify Spinoza's account of truth, adequacy, and error.

I agree with Radner's account of the representational role of ideas. This is contrary to Mark's restriction of representation "to ... only those ideas which represent to us external objects (i.e., finite physical objects other than our own bodies)" and his subsequent restriction of representation to "the first kind of knowledge, which is *necessarily* false."[71] On the

other hand, I should agree with Mark's claim that ideas have objective
and formal essences, and that "the Spinozistic objective essence retains
what we might call a 'referential' dimension: to call an idea an objective
essence is to emphasize the content of the idea, to think of it as the idea of
some particular thing."[72] Later, Mark emphasizes the active aspect of an
idea when he notes that the "referential" dimension retains "an element, we might say, of 'pointing outward,' and it is this element which is
singled out when Spinoza describes an idea as objective essence."[73] Mark
also notes the intentional aspect of the idea when he says, "The essentia
objectiva is what is posited by the idea; it is like Husserl's intended
meaning of a concept...."[74] I should like to stress the intentional aspect of
ideas and of the mind itself—the *"taking* of this idea to represent
something" which is important, I believe, to the analysis of truth and
adequacy. For an idea to refer, or intend, or represent is for the idea to
point to that which it represents, and I shall argue that this may or may
not be the proper formal reality of the idea itself.

Brandom says:

> In particular, there must be some causal analogue of intentionality of
> ideas—the fact that ideas can represent things, by ideas of things ... some
> of these ideas are 'taken as images' of external bodies by a particular mind
> ... what a particular mind takes an idea to represent depends on what
> mind is considered, as well as what idea is considered.[75]

Brandom also states here that "All ideas in the human mind have as their
objects affections of the human body."[76]

TRUTH

Spinoza defines truth in *Ethics*, Part I, Axiom 6: "A true idea must
agree with that of which it is the idea."[77] This definition has led to some
disputation. Some claim that Spinoza is committed to a correspondence
theory of truth, and they argue that this produces later inconsistencies.
Mark has convincingly argued that a correspondence theory does *not*
necessarily entail that with which the idea corresponds must be an
extended object, and that the attribution of a correspondence theory to
Spinoza is an anachronism.[78] The basis of this "correspondence theory"
seems to be found in the claim that the true idea "agrees" with its
ideatum. The term "agree" is, in Latin, *convenire*, which is the root
word for "convention," and means etymologically "to come together or
to collect." The secondary meaning is "to visit or meet," and thirdly "to
agree with, to harmonize, or be fitting."[79]

Thomas defines *convenio* as "to come together, to assemble, to
resorte to a place; to come or talk with, to be meete, fit or commonsent,

to beseeme, to accorde or agree..."[80] I think the translation of
convenire as "agree" has misled philosophers to attribute a correspondence theory of truth to Spinoza. The meaning of *convenire*
seems to include an active coming together, fitting together, or harmoniz-
ing of the idea with its ideatum; and this is lost in accepting a correspondence theory which entails that the idea is an inert object of
thought which must be matched with an extended object. I believe that
the activity of the idea itself and the mind is more fully expressed when
we think of the idea itself fitting with its ideatum, or when we "take" the
idea to refer to an ideatum. The idea coalesces with its ideatum, and this
enables us to more fully appreciate the ultimate identity of idea and
ideatum *sub specie aeternitatis*.

The definition of truth as a "coming together" of an idea and its
ideatum seems to be opposed to the attempt to interpret Spinoza's theory
of truth along propositional lines. A proposition states a relation between
two terms or two classes. This Aristotelian interpretation does not
provide for any activity between ideas and their objects.

In Letter 4 to Oldenburg, Spinoza says "every definition, or clear and
distinct idea, is true."[81] He later says that there are two different sorts of
definitions, one "which serves to explain a thing whose essence only is
sought, and concerning whose essence alone there is doubt, and a definition which is put forward only to be examined."[82] The latter requires
only that it should be conceivable, that is, that none of its constituents
should be contradictory. This sort of definition need not be true.
However, the former ought to be true. Spinoza says, "Therefore, a
definition either explains a thing as it exists outside of the understanding,
and then it ought to be true, and it does not differ from a proposition, or
an axiom...."[83] So, a clear and distinct idea is true, a definition of some
real thing is true and does not differ from a proposition. We know by
definition that an idea is true if it fits with its ideatum, and a proposition
is true if it "explains a thing as it exists outside of the understanding."[84]

A clear and distinct idea and a true proposition are both true insofar as
they correctly fit with some ideatum or some formal reality as it actually
exists outside the understanding. It is not necessary that the ideatum
should be an extended mode; "outside the understanding" does not
necessarily refer to an extended mode. It can also refer to an idea of God.
Ideata can be ideas, ideas of ideas, the attribute of Thought, or God. It is
only important that the objective reality—the idea—fits with its proper
ideatum—formal reality—for the idea to be true. Ideas and propositions
are true insofar as they describe reality, insofar as the idea "points out,"
or "matches," or "fits with" its proper ideatum. A definition explains its
ideatum (definiendum), and a proposition describes an actual state of

affairs. Thus, it appears feasible that the terms in a proposition refer to ideas which, in turn, refer to, or fit with, ideata. The ideas are true if the terms refer to their appropriate ideata and if, in fact, the ideata are related as the terms indicate the ideas are related. This view is similar to that which Mark calls an "ontological theory of truth."[85]

Mark says, "Correspondence—saying that that which is is—is recognized as the form that truth takes in connection with statements or sentences; here we are dealing with 'truth of statement.' But on the most general level, truth is identified with being: things are 'true' insofar as they *are*."[86] Mark goes on to note that "Theories of this kind can be found in ancient philosophy—in Plato and Aristotle—and neo-Platonist philosophers like Plotinus."[87] He concludes: "The point I wish to make is simply that Spinoza's view of truth ... can be understood as a natural development of a very old tradition, with which Spinoza was incontestably acquainted, and it seems to me that his theory of truth is better seen as a version of ontological truth than as a version of the coherence theory of truth of nineteenth-century idealism."[88] I agree whole-heartedly with Mark's claim that truth and being are related for Spinoza, and with the general outlines of the ontological theory of truth.[89]

ADEQUACY

Spinoza defines an adequate idea as "an idea which, insofar as it is considered in itself, without reference to the object, has all the properties or internal signs (*denominationes intrinsecas*) of a true idea."[90] Here, Spinoza is concerned with the intrinsic relations of the idea itself, without regard to the extrinsic relation of the idea to its own ideatum. This notion of adequacy is generally considered to be the correlate of clarity and distinctness in Descartes' epistemology. Mark says that "possession of an adequate idea is awareness of a content which exhibits the logical feature of self-completeness."[91] He goes on to state, "An adequate idea thus is the apprehension of a content which is self-contained and self-explanatory; from the two-term analysis of knowledge it follows that the content of the idea and the object of the idea are not distinct, and so an adequate idea amounts to a direct grasp of what is."[92] To have an adequate idea is to apprehend all the causes of that idea and when one has accomplished this task, one understands the existence and the essence of the idea itself. So, the idea is self-complete, is understood as it is in itself. It is self-evident, and it can be seen to contain no contradictory elements. It can be analyzed into the causes from which it developed.

Spinoza equates clarity and distinctness with adequacy in E 2, Proposition 28[93] and further adds that inadequate ideas are confused ideas; that is to say, they are not clear and distinct. Furthermore, confused ideas "are like conclusions without premisses."[94] A clear and distinct idea would be one which was like a conclusion which *did* follow from its premisses. Now, premisses in a valid deductive argument are really identical to the conclusion, and one often refers to the premisses as the reasons or causes of the conclusion. Thus, an adequate idea is one which expresses its causes, or contains its own reasons or causes, as a valid argument is one wherein the conclusion is contained within the premisses. A valid argument is self-complete, self-contained and is one which has all of its evidence present—it is, in short, a self-evident argument. An adequate idea, then, would be one which is self-evident, contains its own causes, is self-complete.

Spinoza also says that adequate knowledge of anything adequately "expresses its nature."[95] Thus, an adequate idea expresses the nature of that of which it is the idea. That which expresses the nature of a thing is its definition.[96] Ltr. 60 to Tschirnhaus states: "I observe one thing only, that the idea or definition of the thing should express its efficient cause."[97] So, an adequate idea is also a definition of the object of the idea such that one could know that the formal reality of the idea must exist. Spinoza says that "the word adequate refers to the nature of the idea itself."[98] From the intrinsic signs of the idea itself, one knows that the object of the idea exists. We have seen that a definition is a clear and distinct idea,[99] that a clear and distinct idea is adequate, and an adequate knowledge of anything expresses its nature and its efficient causes. Thus, the self-completeness of an adequate idea is the same as the self-completeness of a deductive argument. Adequate ideas are those which are internally self-evident, which do not refer to the ideatum of the idea but which are complete within themselves. Adequate ideas are definitions—they contain their own justifications, reasons, causes and do not depend upon anything else. Further, adequate ideas are certain guides to the existence of the object of the ideas.

Simple ideas would be adequate ideas for Spinoza. Complex ideas which are reducible to their simple components also would be adequate if the simple ideas were non-contradictory, for Spinoza. For example, the essence "human nature" is compossible; and, as an idea in the intellect of God, it must exist. The existence of any individual person would depend upon knowledge of the cause of that existence. An idea which could be analyzed into its simple components by complete enumeration would be adequate.

The idea of a self-caused being would be adequate, and those ideas which were immediately or mediately deducible from it or caused by it would be adequate. For Spinoza, the idea of God, Nature, or Substance is self-evident, self-complete, and adequate; the ideas of the attributes are adequate, as are the ideas of the immediate and mediate infinite modes. Thus, the ideas which constitute the second type of knowledge—Ratio— are adequate, because, as Spinoza says, ideas which follow from ade- quate ideas are adequate. What of ideas which represent bodies, can these be adequate?

Ideas of images cannot be adequate, for Spinoza. The mind does not even have an adequate idea of its body because it knows its body only "through ideas of affections by which the body is affected."[100] That is to say, the human mind doesn't have adequate knowledge of its body by means of perception or imagination.[101] This is because the human body is complex and composed of innumerable complex parts. The complex parts are themselves composed of "simplest bodies which are distin- guished from one another by motion and rest, speed and slowness alone."[102] But, these simplest parts can be replaced by other simplest bodies, and the complex human body will retain its relative identity (though, not its numerical identity) so long as *its* particular ratio of motion and rest is retained. However, if the constituent simplest bodies are not retained, then the ideas of these simplest bodies would not be retained either. Thus, one cannot identify or re-identify the body or the mind in terms of its components from instant to instant. One cannot reduce the complex bodies to their simplest parts, nor can one reduce the idea of the body to its simplest parts. The human mind does not know itself adequately by means of perception—because it cannot reduce the body or its idea of the body to its component simplest parts. Because of this irreducibility of the body and the concomitant irreducibility of the idea of the body—the mind—to its simplest ideas, there can be no ade- quate knowledge of the nature, existence, or essence of any particular body or mind itself—no knowledge of its complete definition—by means of perception or imagination.[103] Furthermore, it is impossible to ascertain the infinite number of finite modes which constitute the efficient, or proximate, cause of this body so as to be able to deduce its existence. So, neither by reduction nor by causation can one gain an adequate knowledge of the mind or the body utilizing only the first sort of knowledge—perception or imagination.

If knowledge of one's own body is inadequate, then knowledge of the effects of external bodies gained by means of images—modifications of my own body—is also inadequate. So, knowledge of bodies acquired by perception or imagination is inadequate. Spinoza states, "I say expressly that the mind has no adequate knowledge of itself, nor of its body, nor of external bodies, but has only a confused knowledge, as often as it perceives things in the common order of nature, that is to say, as often as it is determined to the contemplation of this or that externally—namely, by a chance coincidence...."[104] Some argue that because all ideas derived from the first sort of knowledge are inadequate, and because all false knowledge is due to mutilated and confused ideas of the first sort of knowledge, than all knowledge derived from "the common order of Nature" is false. This may be true in fact, but it is not necessary that inadequate ideas cause falsehood.

FALSITY

Mark says that all representative ideas, "ideas which represent to us external objects (i.e., finite physical objects other than our own bodies)" are "images of things" and are "necessarily inadequate."[105] This is quite true, but then he proceeds to say, "Thus, knowing by means of representative entities is confined to what Spinoza calls the first kind of knowledge, which is necessarily false. (E II, 41)"[106] I have argued that all ideas are representative (p. 99 ff.), but the reference appealed to by Mark does not support his contention that the first sort of knowledge is necessarily false. E 2, Proposition 41 states:

> Knowledge of the first kind alone is the cause of falsity; knowledge of the second and third orders is necessarily true.... To knowledge of the first kind we have said ... that all those ideas belong which are inadequate and confused, and therefore (Prop. 35, Part 2) this knowledge alone is the *cause* of falsity.[107]

E 2, Proposition 35 says, "Falsity consists in the privation of knowledge, which inadequate, that is to say, mutilated and confused ideas involve."[108] It is true that all ideas of images are inadequate[109] and *cause* falsity, but it does not necessarily follow that all inadequate knowledge is *false*.

Mark is concerned to show that falsity lurks in the representational aspect of ideas found only in the first sort of knowledge which is composed of inadequate ideas. But, Radner, and Brandom, and I have argued that *all* ideas are representational and that *adequacy* is concerned with representation, whereas truth is concerned with the relation of the idea's objective essence to its formal essence. Mark wishes to collapse truth and adequacy; since ideas of images are inadequate, they must be false. However, Spinoza does not say that all inadequate knowledge is due to or involves false ideas. It may involve true ideas which are inadequate. Some inadequate ideas cause falsity, but all inadequate ideas are *true*. Insofar as truth is the fitting of an idea with its ideatum, and insofar as every idea has an ideatum, all ideas are true. Every objective essence has some formal reality or other to which it refers. Even ideas which are

representative must be true, although they need not be adequate. For
God, all ideas are true and adequate, but it is not necessarily the case that
for *man* all ideas are adequate.[110] Men have inadequate ideas, but these
do not lead necessarily to false knowledge. One must be careful in relying
on the first sort of knowledge, but it is not always false.[111] Falsehood is a
function of adequacy, but all inadequate ideas are true. So, the usual
contrast between false and true does not hold for Spinoza.

INADEQUATE IDEAS AND ERROR

Inadequate ideas, or mutilated and confused ideas, cause falsity and
error. Falsity is due to a privation which ideas of images involve and the
mind errs "in so far as it is considered as wanting in an idea which
excludes the existence of those things which it imagines as present."[112]
Inadequate ideas do not include in their intrinsic nature the necessary
existence of the formal natures which they represent. This is due to the
fact that inadequate ideas are not reducible to simple ideas nor are they
deducible from adequate ideas. It should be noted that there is nothing
erroneous about the idea of the image itself. Rather, when one *takes* that
idea to represent *not* the image—the affection (modification) of the body
alone—but when one takes the idea of the image to refer to, represent, or
resemble the present existence of the external body as it is in itself, then
one errs. In addition, if one takes his idea to refer not to *his* image as the
affection (modification) of his body, but to the actual interaction of the
external body and his body as known by God, then one errs. God has no
images; He apprehends the real interactions. Images are reserved for
humans in their knowledge of their own bodies and external bodies.

Thus, the idea of the image—the imagination or the perception
itself—is not the cause of error, although it is an inadequate idea of the
human body and of the external body. The objective reality of the idea of
the image matches the formal reality of the image itself. So, the idea of
the image is true. The cause of error is the lack of restraint involved when
the mind takes the idea to represent the external object or the interaction
of that object with the human body and not just the affection (modification) of its body. It is an error due to intention and not an error due to the
nature of the idea because it is an idea of an image. The idea fits with my
image and not with the external object, and my mis-taking or mis-fitting
of the idea with its proper object is the cause of error. False knowledge,
then, is not due to perception or imagination *per se*, but rather it is due to
the intention involved when the idea is taken to refer to something
beyond its proper object—beyond *its* ideatum. It would be a true
idea—though inadequate—if it was taken to refer to the affection

(modification) of the body. It becomes a cause for error when one's intention is not restrained, when the idea does fit with its own proper object, but the mind attempts to fit that idea with an improper object. The idea of the image is true insofar as it refers to the image; it is false insofar as it refers to the cause of the image or the actual interaction of bodies.

Imagination leads to false knowledge if it fails to exclude the existence of the cause of the image—the external body itself. As Spinoza says in discussing the error involved in our knowledge of the distance of the sun:

> ... the error not consisting solely in the imagination, but arising from our not knowing what the true distance is when we imagine, and what are the causes of our imagination. ... We still imagine it near us, since we imagine it to be so near, not because we are ignorant of its true distance, but because an affection of our body (the image) involves the essence of the sun in so far as our body itself is affected by it.[113]

So, error is due to a lack of knowledge of the cause of the image and to the nature of the image itself as being a composite effect of the human body—itself inadequately known—and the external body. Only human beings have inadequate ideas, only human beings err—and it is due to the first sort of knowledge that we err.[114] Error is due to inadequate ideas derived from the body and from the affections (modifications) of the body—but knowledge of these sorts of ideas is not necessarily false *if* it can be held within its proper limits.

Therefore, if a true idea is one which fits with its ideatum, and all ideas have ideata with which they coalesce, falsity or error can result if one mistakes the ideata which are the proper objects of the ideas and if one asserts that these mis-taken ideata exist. That is to say, if all ideas represent, refer, point out, can be "taken for" something else, then intention is wherein the error lies. *What* the ideas *stand for* is the difficulty which leads to error—not *what* the ideas *are* or what are the formal essences to which they refer. The mis-representation is due to mis-taking the ideatum of the idea; and *that* mis-intention is the cause of error. Insofar as the idea has an ideatum with which it fits, it is true; if we mis-fit the idea to an ideatum, we do so intentionally by not restricting the idea to its proper formal reality.

Falsity or error, then, is a function of the adequacy or inadequacy of an idea. It is a failure of reference, representation, or resemblance. It is *not* a failure of the relation of the objective to formal reality. Error is not the negation of a *true* idea. All ideas are true. Error is caused by a mis-representation due to the intention of the human mind. That is to say, the *relation* of idea to its ideatum *per se*, as it is in God or Nature, is always true and adequate. But as a human mind forms a definition, deduces a conclusion, takes the idea to refer, resemble, or represent some ideatum or other, it forms a judgment which can be erroneous. The very human activity of judging based upon inadequate ideas is the cause of error.

The errors of mis-representation, or mis-intention, or mis-taking occur in the area of ideas of images—perception or imagination. Errors have three sources, I believe. The first which I have discussed above, is in the formation of any image whatsoever. The difficulty is due to the inadequacy of our knowledge of the human body and its constituents, and this leads to the inadequacy of all ideas which have as their ideata the human body or its affections. In this instance, it is caused by mis-taking the idea of the image to represent the body itself or the external body and by the assertion that the external body exists as it is so represented. The second difficulty arises from the nature and limitation of the body itself. The body "inasmuch as it is limited, can form distinctly in itself only a certain number of images at once. If this number be exceeded, the images will become confused, and if the number of images which the body is able to form distinctly be greatly exceeded, they will all run one into another."[115] If this happens, the mind will not be able to form a distinct idea of these images and will "distinctly imagine that only in which all of them agree insofar as the body is affected by them."[116] The mind forms universal notions from the excessive number of ideas of images. There is no clear ideatum to which the idea can refer, and the possibility of mis-taking the ideatum is great. The third sort of error occurs when we mis-take the object of a word or sign. A word can be a cause for recollecting an image. We have ideas of those past images (memory) which we take to refer to the things themselves—to the external objects—and not just to the image. Thus, the word—a physical thing—causes an image to be recollected—another physical thing. We have an idea of that image (memory) and mis-take the object of that idea. The third cause of error is similar to the first.

Spinoza says, "The first kind of knowledge alone is the cause of falsity."[117] He defines the first kind of knowledge as:

1. From individual things represented by the senses to us in a mutilated and confused manner and without order to the intellect. These perceptions I have therefore been in the habit of calling knowledge from vague experience.
2. From signs; as, for example, when we hear or read certain words, we recollect things and form certain ideas of them similar to them, through which ideas we imagine things. These two ways of looking at things I shall hereafter call knowledge of the first kind, opinion, or imagination.[118]

I have argued that these causes of error are really due to the intention of the idea—its referential aspect—and the activity of the mind insofar as the mind mis-takes the idea and mis-fits it to some improper ideatum.

I believe that Radner is correct when she observes that the relation between the idea and its ideatum (object) is not the same as the relation between the idea and what it represents. She says:

> The key to Spinoza's theory of the nature of representation is his distinction between the object of the idea and that which the idea represents. The term 'the object of the idea' is not synonymous with the term 'that which is represented by the idea,' although in some cases the two terms have the same reference. The object and the thing represented stand in two different relations to the idea. The relation between the idea and its object is explicated in terms of the distinction between objective reality and formal reality (truth). The relation between the idea and what it represents is explicated in terms of *the resemblance of the thing represented to the object of the idea*[119] (adequacy and falsehood).

I should agree with Radner's view of the dual relations of ideas, but I should stress that the representational relation is not simply a relation of the idea itself but is a relation of what the human mind *takes* the idea to represent. That is to say, the human mind is one factor responsible for the representational aspect of the idea insofar as it is the human mind which takes the idea to refer, resemble, represent, or fit with something which may or may not be the formal reality of that idea. (This is, I believe, the arena of belief and disbelief, or assent and dissent, which leads to error.) The human intention supervenes the adequacy or inadequacy of the idea itself, and the affirmation or denial of the idea itself, by taking ideas to represent that which is other than the formal reality of the idea itself. Every idea *per se* has an ideatum, or object, or formal reality (every idea is true), and some ideas do represent their ideata (adequacy). Some ideas do not represent any existent formal reality (such as classes, abstractions), and humans err insofar as they take them to represent something in fact.

Ideas of images are inadequate and can lead to error. Radner says:

> An idea is adequate or inadequate, not with respect to its object, but with respect to what it represents.... Since ideas are adequate or inadequate with respect to that which they represent, the existence of inadequate ideas does not conflict with the exact correspondence of ideas and their objects. An idea may be inadequate with respect to that which it represents and yet agree with its object.[120]

So, an idea can be true and yet be the cause of falsity on two accounts. First, the idea properly represents X and is mistakenly taken to represent Y. In this case, both X and Y exist as formal realities (ideata) of some idea. Second, the idea does not represent anything existent, and humans take it to represent something. In the second case, the ideatum of the idea is non-existent—an abstraction, or a fiction. (This case raises some difficulties for the ontological theory of truth; but I believe these problems can be overcome.) So, the source of error is, indeed, inadequate or confused and mutilated ideas and human intentions.

EXISTENT IDEATA AND ERROR

An adequate idea is one which is clear and distinct, one which has all of the "intrinsic relations" of a true idea. Radner says:

> We have an adequate idea of X if the idea which represents X to us is the idea which represents X to God, that is, if the idea by which God knows X is in God in so far as he forms the nature of the human mind (E II, 34, Dem.).[121]

Brandom assimilates adequate knowledge to adequate causation, as does Spinoza, by asserting that we know X adequately only by knowing the proximate causes of X and being able to deduce X from those prior causes.[122] If my idea represents what God's idea represents, it is an adequate idea. Furthermore, an adequate idea follows necessarily—is caused by—other ideas in God and can be deduced from them. Ideas in God represent or resemble their ideata; so, in God or Nature, the representation of an idea and its proper ideatum are identical. This is simply to assert that in God all ideas are true and adequate.[123] Furthermore, the ideata of God's ideas exist necessarily, either because they are ideas which follow (are deducible) from adequate ideas, or because they are bodies caused by other bodies in accord with causal laws of extension.

In God, the object of the idea coalesces with what the idea represents, but not in man. If an idea in my mind represents what an idea in God represents, then it is a true and adequate idea for me. If an idea represents to me what is not represented to God, then the idea may be true (because it does have *some* ideatum) but not adequate. This could be the case because my idea represents something different in God than what I take the idea to represent, or it could result because the ideatum of my idea in this latter case would represent something which is *not* in God, does not exist, or is not real. That is to say, there can be ideas in humans which have ideata not found in God or Nature—non-existent ideata. If I have an idea which represents an ideatum in God, then I may have an adequate and true idea.

Ideas which have images for their ideata are inadequate because we intend them to represent or resemble something that is not represented by God's ideas. God has adequate ideas because they are ideas of ideas, but he does not have images as *we* know them. Images are results of external objects affecting the human body, and God has knowledge of these insofar as He knows the human body and external bodies as they are in themselves and not passively by means of their interaction. God has the ideas of images—affections (modifications) of the human body—because they are ideas which do have real ideata—but God has adequate ideas of these affections (modifications). The "ideas of the affections of the body are in God in so far as He forms the nature of the human mind."[124] These ideas are known adequately by God because He can analyze the image into its causes and constituents. Spinoza says:

> ... the knowledge of each part composing the human body exists in God in so far as He is affected by a number of ideas of things, and not in so far as He has the idea of the human body only, that is to say (Prop. 13, pt. 2), the idea which constitutes the nature of the human mind....[125]

We know external bodies and our own bodies only insofar as we have, or as we are, the idea of the human body alone; thus the passivity of our perceptions is the cause of the inadequacy of our ideas of images. So, if an image is defined simply as the effect of an external object on the human body alone, then God does not have an idea of an image in the sense of an idea which is incomplete and limited by the passivity or affection of the body. Humans know the external bodies only by their effects on the human body, and they know the human body only inadequately because they know neither its constituents as they are in themselves nor their causes. Therefore, the ideas of images in humans are inadequate because they do not represent the image—the affection (modification) of the body—as it is in God. However, the idea of the image does have a real existent ideatum—the image itself. If an idea in a human being represents what that idea represents in God, then, that idea in God is reducible to its simple constituents and deducible from its prior ideas or causes, and the idea is adequately known by a human being. An idea of an image in man cannot represent anything like it in God and is, therefore, inadequate. For God, the ideatum and the idea are identical; they can be reduced to their simple components, and they can be deduced from their prior causes.

"No ideas, therefore, are inadequate or confused unless in so far as they are related to the individual mind of some person."[126] Insofar as we know external bodies only by their effects on the human body, we have inadequate ideas of images. Humans alone have inadequate ideas—those which cannot be deduced from other ideas or reduced to their simplest components. When one recalls that all ideas in God are true, adequate, caused, and resemble or are identical to their ideata, then one sees that the failure to have only adequate ideas is a failure to be certain that what one's ideas represent or resemble exist. So, for humans, the representation of some ideas is not necessarily existent, while for God that which an idea represents does necessarily exist.

When one takes an idea to represent X (his image—the effect of an external body on one's own body), and that idea in God represents Y (the real interaction of the external body and the human body *per se*), then one mis-takes the idea's representation and errs. It should be noted that the ideatum exists—the image as it is in man and the interaction of the human body and the external body as it is in Nature or God. My idea which represents X does not in fact represent what it represents in God (Y) or in reality and so is inadequate. My intention, or mis-taking, may lead me to assert that what my idea resembles does exist in actuality as I know it, and this can be erroneous. If I claim that my idea of the image represents, or resembles the actual interaction of the bodies *per se*, I err. If I cannot define an idea, know its essential nature by enumeration of its constituents or by deducing its existence from its prior causes, then I cannot be certain that what is represented by my idea exists as so represented. This occurs most frequently—although not exclusively—in my ideas of images. Thus, because of my failure, I may attribute existence to that which my idea resembles, my idea of the image, and this leads to falsity. Furthermore, if I take my idea of an image to represent the external body, because I don't know my body or the external body itself by means of deduction or reduction, I erroneously attribute existence to the external body *as if* it resembled the *image*.

So, ideas of images cause falsity in two ways: (1) my idea of an image does not resemble the image—the interaction of bodies *per se*—as it is in God; (2) my idea of an image does not resemble the external object itself. The object of my idea is the image, and if I restrict myself to noting that my idea fits my image but does not represent anything real—or anything represented by that idea in God, then I shall not err. My knowledge of particular things, of individual finite extended modes, is inadequate because it does not represent *their* particular essence in God. So, *my* intention, *my* taking what the idea represents, *does* play an important role in Spinoza's account of adequacy, truth, and error. Error and the inadequacy of the idea result from my taking the idea to represent or resemble something which it cannot represent or resemble in God. If my idea represents an *image* of a particular thing, then it represents only the *effect* of other bodies on my body as known *via* perception. My idea of the image has the image as its ideatum and is, therefore, true. It is inadequate because my idea of the image does not resemble or represent the actual interaction of the external bodies on my body. God has an adequate knowledge of the idea of the image, because His idea does resemble the interaction of the bodies. All of my ideas of images of particular things are inadequate and lead to error if I attribute existence to that which my idea of an image resembles—the inadequately known affection (modification) of my body. Error is due to inadequate but true ideas. These ideas are inadequate because they do not represent or resemble the actual interaction of bodies as represented by the idea in God. So, inadequacy is the result of perception, of limiting one's knowledge exclusively to the effects of external bodies on the human body.[127] The ideata of perceived ideas exist but not as we perceive them.

What is represented by an idea in God is real and is identical to the idea—it exists just as represented by the idea in God. What is represented by an idea in man may not exist as so represented or may not exist at all. The test for ascertaining existence or non-existence of ideata is that of reduction or deduction. What is reducible to compossible simples can exist, and what is deducible from adequate ideas—ideas which are in God—must exist. Ideas of images cannot be thus reduced or deduced, so they are inadequate. They represent or resemble nothing as it is in God, so they resemble non-existent objects. Still, the object of the idea—its ideatum—does fit with the idea, so the idea is true. The ideatum exists as *my* image but not as an external body. My idea adequately resembles nothing; it inadequately resembles my image. Thus, the ideatum exists but not as it is represented by my idea. My idea is true and fits with an ideatum which exists, but the ideatum does not resemble my idea. If I take the idea to resemble the ideatum—the affection (modification) of my body as it actually exists—I err. If my idea of the image was adequate, then I would know the affection (modification) of my body as God knows it, or as it occurs in Nature. This would entail having adequate knowledge of both my own body and the external body. My idea is inadequate, because I cannot fathom its resemblance to the ideatum as it actually exists, but it is a true idea insofar as there is an ideatum with which it fits.

NON-EXISTENT IDEATA AND TRUTH

Humans form ideas of universals because of the limitation in the number of distinct images which the human body can produce.[128] Universals are "ideas in the highest degree confused." Transcendental terms refer to confused images, too.[129] Still, my ideas of universals are true insofar as the ideata of such ideas are the very confused images. I can make true statements about "man, horse, dog, and triangle", but I cannot assert that these universals exist or are real. The ideas of universals do not represent anything in God, because God does not form confused ideas of images and is not limited to the number of images or ideas which He can have. So, ideas in humans which represent universals represent and resemble nothing in God; therefore their representations do not exist, and they are inadequate ideas. However, there can be true ideas of universals—in man—insofar as there is an ideatum for those ideas in the human mind. Nowhere does Spinoza state that the ideata of all of man's ideas must exist in God or Nature.

Ideas of memories have ideata and are true, although the representations of the memory do not exist. So, there is true but inadequate knowledge of ideas of past images. Ideas of expectations have those expectations as ideata and are true, but the expectations do not exist, so the knowledge is inadequate. Even ideas of fictions, such as Mr. Pickwick, have as their ideata the fictions and are true, although the representations of the fictions do not exist in reality. So, ideas of memory (past), expectations (future), and fictions are inadequate because they represent nothing in man which can be represented in God. In particular, God cannot have ideas which involve duration.

TRUTH, ADEQUACY AND EXISTENCE

As God is constituted by the attributes of Thought and Extension and their modes, then one might view God as the coalescence of the representation of the idea and the object of the idea. Thus, he cannot have inadequate ideas. Thus, one's inadequate ideas cannot represent what God's ideas represent. Only humans can have ideas of images which are confused and mutilated; only they can have ideas involved with temporality; and only they can have ideas of non-existent entities. Only humans can have inadequate ideas which lead to falsity or error. In Spinoza, the ideata of all of God's ideas must exist because God's ideas represent something to God Himself. Thus, adequacy, representation, and existence coalesce in Spinoza's epistemology, for God.

The relation of truth to necessary existence holds only in God, because all of Gods' true ideas are also adequate. For humans, a true idea is one which has some ideatum, but this does not necessarily entail that the ideatum exists in Nature; because not all of our ideas are adequate.

All ideas are in God, agree with the ideata of which they are ideas, and are true.[130] Falsity is due to ''privation of knowledge'' which is involved in ''inadequate, that is to say, mutilated and confused ideas.''[131] The ''privation'' invoked here is the human inability to exclude existence from the ideatum of an idea; that is, the inability to restrain from attributing existence to the cause of the image or modification of the body. The human mind errs when it has an idea of an image and that ''idea does not exclude the existence or presence of the nature of the external body, but posits it.''[132] Thus, a ''false idea'' is an idea of a thing or ideatum which does not exist. Falsity, then, is a function of adequacy.

And adequacy is a function of intention—*taking* an idea as being a representation of some ideatum. So, falsehood, adequacy and intentionality are all interwoven. Furthermore, since adequately known ideas must exist, and their ideata must exist, adequacy and necessity are interwoven. Contingency and possibility are due to inadequately known ideas, and these may have non-existent ideata.

Spinoza says, "For with regard to the difference between a true idea and a false idea, it is evident from Prop. 35, pt. 2, that the former is related to the latter as being is to non-being."[133] This statement has led some to assert that the *truth* of an idea—the fitting together of the idea and ideatum—is also a guarantee of the existence of the ideatum. It has been argued here that not truth but *adequacy*—the representation, or resemblance, or reference of the idea to its object—is the test of existence. Failure in adequacy can lead to error. It is believed that a closer inspection of Proposition 43 seems to bolster this view and to counter the true idea—existence contention.

The first sentence of the demonstration to Proposition 43 says, "A *true* idea in us is that which in God is adequate, in so far as He is manifested by the nature of the human mind."[134] The demonstration itself concludes with the statement that he "who has an adequate idea, that is to say (Prop. 34, pt. 2), he who knows a thing truly, must at the same time have an *adequate* idea or a true knowledge of his knowledge...."[135] Finally, the Scholium to this proposition concludes "that our mind, in so far as it truly perceives things, is a part of the infinite intellect of God (Corol. Prop. 11, pt. 2), and therefore it must be that the *clear and distinct ideas* of the mind are as true as those of God."[136] Again, a clear and distinct idea is an adequate idea. Both Propositions 34 and 35 are primarily concerned with the issue of adequacy and its relation to truth and falsity. There is no question but that adequacy *and* truth preclude falsity and error; and, there is no question that inadequacy brings in its train the possibility of error. I have argued that adequacy is concerned with representation or resemblance of an idea to its ideatum and with the existence of the ideatum. Adequacy can be determined by an inspection of the idea itself—its intrinsic denominations—by means of reduction to simples or deduction from other adequate ideas. The determination of the existence of an ideatum, then, is a function of the adequacy of an idea not of its truth.

Some indication of the necessity of adequacy for certitude and for the attribution of existence to an ideatum is to be found in E 2, Proposition 42. Here, Spinoza says that knowledge of the second and third kind—that sort of knowledge concerned only with adequate ideas—is what "teaches us to distinguish the true from the false."[137] He says that to mark this distinction one "must have an *adequate idea* of the true and false."[138] So, I suggest that the relation of truth and falsity to being and non-being is really better expressed and more in keeping with the preceding propositions which include references to adequacy, by interpreting the phrase thusly: a true *and adequate* idea and a true and *inadequate* idea are related as being and non-being. That is to say, *adequacy* alone is the test for the existence of ideata; truth is simply the relation of the idea to its ideatum. The statement that "truth is its own standard"[139] should really be read as an expression of the need for adequacy: a true and adequate idea is one which agrees with its ideatum and whose ideatum necessarily exists. One can determine this sort of standard by an inspection of the intrinsic properties of the idea and can conclude from reduction or deduction that the ideatum exists as represented by the idea. Furthermore, one may be assured by the adequacy of the idea that one's idea resembles God's idea. The adequate ideas of the human mind represent what God's ideas represent. This interpretation of adequacy, truth, and existence is advantageous in that it permits true ideas of non-existent things—triangles, man, etc. and it still adheres to Spinoza's ideas of truth and adequacy.

CONATUS

One of the major causes for error is to be found not only in the inadequacy of the idea itself but also in the *conatus* which constitutes the mind of man. As noted before, all ideas point out, or have intentional aspects, themselves. That is to say, all ideas *per se* are representative, although what they represent may not exist. The ideatum which is the human body has as its idea the human mind. This idea, the mind, is peculiar because "man thinks"; that is to say, this idea is aware of other ideas, or is constituted of ideas of which it is aware. Insofar as a person's mind is an idea, it has a "pointing out," or "referring," or "striving" aspect. It, too, has an intentional aspect which is a *conatus* and may be interpreted epistemologically as "taking an idea to represent, resemble, or refer to something." This intentionality is a function of the adequacy of an idea. The *conatus* in man, then, is related to the adequacy of an idea. A person's *conatus*, one's taking an idea to resemble something, can lead one to err when he mis-takes the representation of the idea, or when he attributes existence or presence to the ideatum of the idea. This "taking" the idea to refer or resemble something is a function of the particular *conatus* of each mind and can lead to error. The activity of the mind, or its *conatus*, is responsible for the intention of an idea which causes error when one mis-takes an inadequate idea to resemble some ideatum. Error occurs when the ideas which are mis-taken, or mis-represent something, are ideas which have as their ideata affections (modifications) of particular, differing bodies. That is to say, ideas of images or ideas of ideas of images are the singular results of a particular extended object on a particular, individual, human body.

Ideas of images are all subjective—peculiar to a particular individual—, and the ideas of particular images constitute subjective knowledge that is the source of error. One can have true knowledge—idea and ideatum agree—even if true ideata are subjective. There can be no commonality of knowledge insofar as the ideas have images as ideata and insofar as those images differ for each individual. Humans can achieve a commonality of knowledge of ideas which have images as ideata only insofar as they overlook the differences amongst such ideas and stress the common aspects of those ideas. Ideas of common properties of images can constitute knowledge because they are inter-subjective. Reality, existence, and adequate knowledge require inter-subjectivity which is one guarantee that one's idea represents something in Nature itself. We *can* also have common knowledge of ideas of universals because their representation in humans' minds are ambiguous, indistinct, and indistinguishable from one mind to another. So, all humans can agree that triangles include 180°, because the universal ''triangle'' is an ambiguous representation in human minds. However, as soon as we seek to make the representation of that idea distinct, then the commonality disappears and disagreement results. When the ideas of images become distinct, then, awareness becomes too individualized to constitute common knowledge, for humans. But God can and does have knowledge of singular things because, for God, the idea of the particular is identical to the particular itself (ideatum) in any attribute and because that idea does in reality represent that mode. A person can know at least one particular, singular thing in this way, too—God Himself. One can apprehend the existence of a necessary being; he can reduce it to its compossible attributes; and he can know that it is self-caused.

If one cannot acquire adequate knowledge from those ideas related to images, and if one needs to obtain *distinct* knowledge which would be common to all rational beings, then one must turn to ideas known independently from perception and imagination.

Ideas whose ideata are images are inadequate for us because those ideas cannot represent what they represent in God. Ideas in God are adequate, or clear and distinct, and necessarily existent. Humans can ascertain the properties of an adequate idea by the reduction of a complex idea to its compossible simples (as in a definition) and by deduction either from an adequate idea or from a self-caused cause—or a necessary Being, or God Himself. If ideas whose ideata are images cannot be adequate because of their failure in reducibility or deducibility, then we must find ideas whose ideata are not images, ideas whose ideata are other ideas or God.

ADEQUACY AND IDEAS OF IDEAS

Mark says:

> An adequate idea thus is the apprehension of a content which is self-contained and self-explanatory; from the two-term analysis of knowledge it follows that the content of the idea and the object of the idea are not distinct, and so an adequate idea amounts to a direct grasp of what is. Since its object must exist as apprehended, we can say that the idea agrees with its object, or that the idea is true.[140]

What Mark here terms "self-contained and self-explanatory," I have called reducible to simples and deducible from God—both intrinsic properties of adequate ideas alone which in no way refer to their ideata. When Mark says the content of the idea and the object of the idea are not distinct, I have stated that the representations of the idea and the ideata are identical. God's ideas are adequate, self-complete, self-explanatory.

If the ideatum of a person's idea is an idea, then that idea may be the representation of an idea in God. Ideas in God are causally related and are deducible from one another. If one's idea is itself reducible and deducible, then it is adequate and true. If one's idea has an idea as its ideatum, then it is possible that it is adequate, too. The relation between an idea and the idea of that idea is that of formal and objective essences of the idea alone—without reference to the object of the idea as being an image. Spinoza says:

> For, indeed, the idea of the mind, that is to say, the idea of the idea, is nothing but the form of the idea in so far as this is considered as a mode of thought and without relation to the object, just as a person who knows anything, by that very fact knows that he knows, and knows that he knows that he knows, and so *ad infinitum*. But more on this subject afterwards.[141]

So, ideas of ideas are related intrinsically to one another, as they are within the same attribute and as one is the form of the other. These ideas are adequate because they represent, resemble, or refer to other ideas. Indeed, it should be noted that the relation between ideas of ideas is discussed in the same terms, and is referred to, in note to E 2, Proposition 43, wherein Spinoza is discussing a true idea as being its own standard. Thus, if I have an adequate idea, then God has an adequate idea; but the only ideas that both God and I can have adequately or in common are ideas of God Himself or ideas of ideas. God's ideas of extended modes differ from my ideas of extended modes because my ideas have images as their objects, and God can have no images as I have them. In order for me to have an adequate idea of a finite extended mode, I should have to have an idea whose object was an idea and which represented an idea in God. Now, ideas in God *can* have as their objects and their representations the finite extended modes because, in God, the idea and the ideatum are identical; there is a coalescing of ideatum and representation. This is so because, in God, the ideas are clear and distinct and follow necessarily, causally from one another. Ultimately, of course, they follow from God Himself because of His Nature as a self-caused cause. So, if my idea represents God's idea and has as its ideatum an idea, then that idea can be adequate. Mark and I agree on the adequacy of knowledge of ideas of ideas.

Radner says, "The idea representing A is an *adequate idea*, just in case it has the internal characteristics of a true idea—namely, that which it represents is or includes its object."[142] An idea of an idea does represent its object (namely, itself), or it includes its object (a constituent of a complex idea is included in the complex idea). So, the idea of an idea—an idea whose ideatum is an idea and which represents an idea in God—is an adequate idea.

Radner, Mark, and I agree that ideas of ideas are adequate ideas and constitute adequate knowledge.

ADEQUATE IDEAS AND ADEQUATE CAUSES

Radner goes on to distinguish between adequate ideas and adequate causes:

> On the other hand, the cause of the idea representing A is an *adequate cause*, just in case the idea follows from the nature of this cause alone, without the concurrent influence of anything else. Spinoza confuses these two notions of adequacy.... In *Ethics* III Spinoza proves that if an idea is adequate in the human mind, then the mind is adequate cause of what follows from the idea (E III, I, Dem.). But he nowhere proves that if an idea is adequate in the human mind, the mind is the adequate cause of the idea itself. On the contrary, from what has been said of the adequacy of ideas and of causes, it seems perfectly possible that the mind may have an adequate idea and yet not be the adequate cause of this idea.[143]

Brandom disagrees with Radner on the notions of adequate ideas and adequate causes insofar as Brandom says that the two are identical. That is, if the mind has an adequate idea, the mind is the adequate cause of the idea. He says:

> Our definition of the thing an idea represents is the 'object of the adequate cause of the subsequent ideas' (those ideas of which the representing idea

is a proximate cause). ... We could take ideas as representing other ideas
on the basis of the definition of representation only if it is possible for one
idea to be the object of another. But this is just the doctrine which Spinoza
put forth in Eth. II, 21-29....[144]

Brandom shows that ideas of ideas are identical to their objects, that the
mind is the adequate cause of such ideas, that the mind has adequate
knowledge of these ideas, the mind has adequate knowledge of itself. He
further states that this is related to the *conatus* of the individual because
"the adequate idea involves activity on the part of the mind."[145] As I am
the cause of the ideas of ideas and I have knowledge of their object, the
idea of an idea is identical to its ideatum. Here Brandom notes that the
"human mind (and its modifications) is the only finite individual
Spinoza ever instances as the object of intuitive knowledge (by an idea
ideae 'of' the mind ...)."[146] I think that Brandom's analysis of ideas of
ideas is convincing and serves to demonstrate that adequate knowledge as
well as adequate causation can be acquired only by means of "idea
ideae."

THE SECOND SORT OF KNOWLEDGE
(COMMON PROPERTIES AND NOTIONS)

"Common properties" are common to all finite modes and are the
properties of God Himself. That is to say, God expresses Himself
through the range of modes from immediate infinite modes to finite
modes, and the properties of God or Nature run through all of these expressions. In the realm of *ideas*, these properties are common; the mind is
an idea, and *its* ideas have properties in common not only with the mind
(the cause of its ideas) but also with all of the ideas which form the nexus
of finite modes of thought. The mind is the adequate cause of its ideas
and not of images. Moreover, the ideas which are represented by my
ideas are also represented by ideas in God, since God is their adequate
cause, too. So, ideas of ideas—ideas which represent ideas in me, also
represent those ideas in God and are common properties, then, of all
ideas insofar as they are expressions of God *via* the attribute of Thought.
Furthermore, the causal relation or deduction of such ideas constitutes
natural laws in the attribute of Thought and are the "common notions"
which tie together those ideas. We know the causal relations, or laws of
deduction, which run through *all* ideas, and we can have adequate
knowledge of them. This is the second sort of knowledge, or reason, for
Spinoza.

However, reason is not only confined to knowledge of ideas of ideas
but also includes common notions and common properties of bodies.

This knowledge is *not* derived from particular ideas of images of the body, because such ideas are not known adequately by human beings. Humans cannot acquire such ideas from the "common order of Nature."[147] However, one's ideas of the common properties and natural laws of bodies are ideas which represent God's ideas of the human body as well as external bodies. God's ideas of the human body and all extended bodies are adequate ideas. Of course, God's idea of each finite mode is an adequate idea, but my knowledge of *particular* extended modes is derived from modifications of *my* body—*my* images—and is inadequate for me. However, if I note not the particularity of each idea of my image, but rather those properties which all ideas of my images have in common, I can gain adequate knowledge, because that which is represented by my idea of the common properties is represented by God's idea. Ideas of the common properties and natural laws of extension are derived *not* from the peculiar and individual ideas of my images which are bound to my knowledge of my body but from ideas which are common to all bodies. So, I can "rise above" my individuality and subjectivity—my ideas of my images—to grasp the commonality (God's adequate ideas of my body and all bodies) of all bodies, just as I can grasp the commonality of all ideas.

> Let it be supposed that the human body is affected by an external body through that which it has in common with the external body, that is to say, by A. The idea of this affection will involve the property of A (Prop. 16, pt. 2), and therefore (Corol. Prop. 7, pt. 2) the idea of this affection, in so far as it involves the property of A, will exist adequately in God in so far as He is affected by the idea of the human body, that is to say (Prop. 13, pt. 2), in so far as He constitutes the nature of the human mind.[148]

What is common to the human body and all bodies is, of course, motion and rest. We *can* know motion and rest adequately because our idea of motion and rest—although derived from imagination—is not particular and individual but is common to all ideas of images, and it represents in me what the idea represents in other humans and in God.

In God, ideas and bodies are identical, so God's knowledge of bodies is adequate. One can know bodies adequately insofar as one knows their common properties. One cannot know them insofar as one knows them only by their particular effects on a particular body but only insofar as one's idea of their effects represents God's idea. One can know adequately only ideas of what all images have in common and what all bodies have in common—their causal relations and common properties. The inadequate ideas of my images cannot exist in God, because God has *no* inadequate ideas. The only adequate ideas of images which humans can have are ideas which are *not* due to their individuality. Only ideas which represent common properties and laws of all bodies represent what God's ideas represent. So, there is no adequate knowledge of individual finite extended modes *via* perception or imagination because the representation of ideas of images is inadequate and cannot be a representation of God's ideas. There is adequate knowledge based upon perception or imagination only of common axioms and common properties. This sort of knowledge of common notions is reason, but it depends upon the apprehension of common properties of objects presented by perception or imagination.

Thus, we can account for Spinoza's observation that we can have adequate as well as inadequate knowledge of ideas of images. Adequate ideas of images are those which are concerned with—or represent—common properties or axioms. Spinoza says:

> There is no affection of the body of which we cannot form *some* clear and distinct conception.
>   Those things which are common to all cannot be otherwise than adequately conceived (Prop. 38, pt. 2), and therefore (Prop. 12 and Lem. 2, following Note, Prop. 13, pt. 2), there is no affection of the body of which we cannot form *some* clear and distinct conception.[149]

The difference between the adequacy or inadequacy of knowledge derived from ideas of images (or of the ideas of images themselves) is due to the *conatus* or intention of the human mind. If the mind takes the idea of the image to "refer to," "represent," or resemble a particular thing, the idea or knowledge is inadequate. If it takes the idea to represent a common axiom or property, it is adequate. Again, it is important to observe the role of intention in Spinoza's epistemology. If the idea of the image is intended to represent the common properties or axioms, then the idea is related to God insofar as it represents in man what it represents in God.[150]

THE THIRD SORT OF KNOWLEDGE (INTUITION)

To acquire adequate knowledge of individuals, one must rely upon intuition. It is conceivable that one might have an adequate idea representing a particular idea or even a particular body, if one's idea represented an idea of God's which represented another particular idea or a finite extended mode. An idea which represents another idea is, of course, an adequate idea, and anything which is deducible from an adequate idea (in Brandom's terms, anything which an adequate idea represents or causes, or in Mark's terms any self-complete idea) is adequate. So long as the object of an idea is another idea which is not related to or does not represent an image, then the idea is adequate; or, in other words, it would constitute adequate knowledge. If the ideatum of my idea is God's idea, I can know the idea adequately, in short. And, if that idea of God has as *its* ideatum a finite body, I could have adequate knowledge of that body because in God the idea and its ideatum are identical. This sort of knowledge of individuals is, I believe, what Spinoza terms "intuitive science."

Intuitive science is defined as knowledge which "advances from an adequate idea of the formal essence of certain attributes of God to the adequate knowledge of the essence of things."[151]

While some commentators have interpreted this sort of knowledge as providing knowledge of only God or Nature itself, Curley says, "(intuition) includes adequate knowledge of the essences of singular things, i.e. finite modes, but it does not include adequate knowledge of the essences of the divine attributes."[152] Adequate knowledge of the essences of divine attributes—those common notions and properties to which Spinoza refers—is acquired by reason for Curley. The essences of the attributes are the definitions of the attributes. If one does not distinguish the nature of God from that of His attributes, it could be argued that reason suffices for knowledge of God Himself—or Nature itself. However, if one should argue that the attributes of God differ from God Himself, insofar as God is a unitary, singular Being and there are many attributes, one might contend that the apprehension of the coalescence of unity of Nature is different from the apprehension of the nature of the infinite number of attributes and their particular essences. I should conclude that the grasp of the unity and singularity of God or Nature, too, is a function of intuition.[153]

Spinoza says that the human mind knows itself adequately by means of the third sort of knowledge and states that it is clear that

> our mind, with regard both to essence and existence follows from the divine nature and continually depends upon God. ... I might show, by this example, what that knowledge of *individual objects* which I have called intuitive or of the third kind (Schol. 2, Prop. 40, pt. 2) is able to do, and how much more potent it is than the *universal* knowledge which I have called knowledge of the second kind.[154]

There is, then, no question that intuitive knowledge is knowledge of singular, or individual things. The human mind knows itself adequately—as an idea of an idea, which in God represents what the idea in man represents—by intuition. Curley says:

> As I understand Spinoza, he believed that this kind of knowledge of the "intimate nature" of a finite singular thing—which in the *Ethics* appears to be the only kind of intuitive knowledge—had to wait upon our having attained an adequate knowledge of the laws of nature and in particular on our having attained a knowledge of the way in which our senses work.[155]

Now, knowledge of the laws of nature is acquired by reason, and knowledge of our sense-perception is due, I should believe, to a combination of perception and reason. Curley, Brandom and I agree that adequate knowledge of the laws of nature (common notions) and common properties is acquired by the second sort of knowledge.

I should agree that adequate knowledge of singular things is attained by intuition. But I should note, contrary to Curley, that God or Nature is itself a singular thing insofar as it differs in essence and existence from any other thing and is distinguishable from any other thing. It is clear that we have adequate knowledge of God and the idea of God is one or unique.[156] It is true that Spinoza says that God can only improperly be called one or single:

> ... a thing can only be said to be one or single in respect of its existence and not of its essence: for we do not conceive things under numbers until they have been subsumed under a common class. ... Hence it seems clear that nothing can be called one or single unless some other thing has first been conceived which (as has been said) agrees with it. But since the existence of God is His essence itself, and since we can form no general idea of His essence, it is certain that he who calls God one or single has no true idea of God, or is speaking of Him inappropriately.[157]

God is a unique Being insofar as both His existence *and* His essence are different from that of any other Being. Thus, the term "one" or "singular" applies to God or Nature in a way different from those things which are one only in respect to their existence and not their essence—finite modes. Still, God and each finite mode are singular in respect to existence. So, one may say, however inappropriately, that God is the most unique, different, and singular of any existent and cannot be compared to any other thing in terms of essence or existence.

One cannot know God by means of common notions or common properties, since there is no general idea of His essence. And, one cannot form an idea of God by perception. It is true that Proposition 47, Part 2 proceeds from the common essences of ideas and bodies to God, but the unity of these common essences as one Being or as unitary Nature is not a universal, general, or common sort of knowledge. As argued above, the grasp of the singularity and "unique-ness" of Nature is different from the apprehension of commonality afforded by the second sort of knowledge and is not acquired by means of ideas of images. It must be concluded, however inappropriately, that if we know God or Nature as unique at all—and we do—this knowledge must be an instance of intuition, too. Thus, *all* knowledge of the existence of singular things—be they finite modes or Nature itself—is acquired by intuition.

Brandom notes that one can ascend by reason—from ever more inclusive common essences which can be known adequately—to a knowledge of God.

> From the point of view of Spinoza's total project, the prime positive result of the investigation of common properties by Ratio is an adequate idea of God. ... Ratio provides an adequate idea of God's essence, and hence sets the stage for intuition to reverse the direction of inquiry beginning with God and proceeding down to finite essences.[158]

I should agree that Ratio proceeds up the ladder from common essences to ever more inclusive common essences, but the most inclusive common essences provide only knowledge of the immediate infinite modes of Thought and Extension. In Spinoza's view, God is *not* a common essence, as we have seen in Letter 50, which can be known by inclusion in other common essences. The end of the ladder of commonality is the infinite mode. To apprehend the identity of each of the attributes and their unification with one another requires knowledge of that "unique" God or Nature, and this can be accomplished only by intuition. Having grasped that unique existence and essence, then one can descend to the knowledge of finite essences.

The notion of the ascent and descent of knowledge involved in Spinoza's second and third sorts of knowledge which has been remarked on by Brandom and other commentators is most illuminating, I believe, if one recalls Plato's method of collection and division in the *Sophist*. The second type of knowledge is one of collecting common essences until one reaches the most common essences of the attributes of Thought and Extension. Then, by means of an intuition of Being, Nature, or God, or the attributes, one can proceed by division to reach the finite essences and, in some instances (the human mind itself) one can grasp a finite existence itself. It is true that Plato did not foresee this final step of intuition since he stopped at the apprehension of the least (finite) common essences. It should prove interesting to note the similarities between Plato and Spinoza in their accounts of knowledge.

NOTES

[1] Daisy Radner, "Spinoza's Theory of Ideas," *The Philosophical Review*, 80 (1971), 338-359; hereafter cited as Radner; Robert Brandom, "Adequacy and the Individuation of Ideas in Spinoza's Ethics," *Journal of the History of Philosophy*, 14 (1976), 147-162; hereafter cited as Brandom; Thomas C. Mark, "Truth and Adequacy in Spinozistic Idea," *Southwestern Journal of Philosophy*, 8 (1977), 11-34; hereafter cited as Mark, "Truth." The papers of Mark, Radner, and Brandom are primarily concerned with Spinoza's epistemology rather than with his metaphysics. They deal more with issues raised in *Ethics, Part II* than do most papers on Spinoza. Consequently, they shall be referred to in large measure in this part of my work which deals with Spinoza's epistemology.

² Wild, p. 144, E2, Def. 3, Explanation.

³ *Ibid.*

⁴ Brandom, p. 156.

⁵ Thomas C. Mark, *Spinoza's Theory of Truth* (New York: Columbia University Press, 1972), p. 25; hereafter cited as *Theory*. It is interesting to note that Descartes has the same sort of duality of idea—as an object and as an activity, not only in his account of ideas but in his account of innate ideas.

⁶ Mark, *Theory*, p. 22.

⁷ Wild, p. 155, E2, Prop. 11.

⁸ Wild, p. 157, E2, Prop. 13.

⁹ Wild, pp. 156-157, E2, Props. 12 and 13.

¹⁰ Wild, p. 145, E2, Axiom 2; Gebhardt, II, 85: "Homo cogitat < : of anders, sy weten dat wy denken > ": Man thinks (in other words, we know that we think).

¹¹ Joachim, *TdIE*, p. 170.

¹² Cf. pp. 94-102.

¹³ Wild, pp. 153-156, E2, Props. 10 and 11.

¹⁴ Mark, "Truth," p. 15; Wild, p. 170, E2, Prop. 19, Dem.; Gebhardt, II, 108: "Mens enim humana est ipsa idea, sive cognito Corporis humani."

¹⁵ Wild, p. 157, E2, Prop. 13, Dem.; "... we have ideas ..."; Gebhardt, II, 96; Gutman, p. 101, E2, Prop. 22, Dem.: "Ideas ... are *in* the human mind"; Cf. Gebhardt, II, 109: "At ideae affectionum Corporis in Mente humana sunt...."

¹⁶ Wild, p. 165, E2, Prop. 15; p. 145, E2, Axiom 2.

¹⁷ Mark has an excellent passage on Spinozistic distinction between ideas and images. Mark, *Theory*, pp. 23-26.

¹⁸ Mark, *Theory*, pp. 19-23; Mark, "Truth," p. 23.

¹⁹ B. Spinoza, *Earlier Philosophical Writings*, trans. F. A. Hayes (Indianapolis: Library of Liberal Arts, Bobbs-Merrill Co., Inc., 1963), pp. 21-22, hereafter cited as Hayes.

²⁰ Wild, pp. 167-168, E2, Prop. 17, Schol. Emphasis supplied; Gebhardt, II, 106: "Porro, ut verba usitata retineamus, *Corporis humani affectiones*, quarum ideae Corpora externa, velut nobis praesentia repraesentant, rerum imagines vocabimus, tametsi rerum figuras non referunt. Et cum Mens hac ratione contemplatur corpora, eandem imaginari dicemus." Emphasis supplied.

²¹ Mark, *Theory*, p. 26.

²² Wild, p. 167, E2, Prop. 17, Schol.

²³ H. R., I, p. 159.

²⁴ Mark, *Theory*, p. 23.

²⁵ Wild, pp. 167-168, E2, Prop. 17, Schol.; p. 231, E3, Prop. 27.

²⁶ Wild, p. 198, E2, Prop. 49.

²⁷ Wild, pp. 184-185, E2, Prop. 40, Schol. 1; pp. 197-198, E2, Prop. 49; p. 231, E3, Prop. 27; p. 237, E3, Prop. 32.

²⁸ Wild, p. 156, E2, Prop. 48, Schol.; Gebhardt, II, 130: "Non enim per ideas imagines, quales in fundo oculi, &, si placet, in medio cerebro formantur, sed Cogitationis conceptus intelligo <, of het voorwerpelijk wezen/Esse objectivum/van een zaak, voor zo veel't alleenlijk in denking bestat > ."

²⁹ Wild, p. 198, E2, Prop. 49, Schol.; Gebhardt, II, 132: "Verborum namque, & imaginum essentia a solis motibus corporeis constituitur, qui cogitationis conceptum minime involvunt."

³⁰ Wild, p. 168, E2, Prop. 17, Schol. 1; p. 231, E3, Prop. 27, Dem.

³¹ Wild, p. 175, E2, Prop. 26, Dem. of Cor. Interpolation added; Gebhardt, II, 112: "Cum Mens humana per ideas affectionum sui Corporis corpora externa contemplatur, eandem tum imaginari dicimus; nec Mens alia ratione corpora externa, ut actu existentia, imaginari potest."

³² It is this point which helps explain the problem of error in the first sort of knowledge for Spinoza, as will be shown later. See E2, Props. 26, 27, 40.

³³ H. R., I, 152.

³⁴ H. R., I, 186.

[35] H. R., II, 52.

[36] Hayes, pp. 21-22.

[37] Wild, p. 184, E2, Prop. 40, Schol. 1; Gebhardt, II, 120-121: "… quod scilicet humanum Corpus, quandoquidem limitatum est, tantum est capax certi imaginum numeri … in se distincte simul formandi … quod Mens humana tot corpora distincte simul imaginari poterit, quot in ipsius corpore imagines possunt simul formari."

[38] Wild, pp. 197-198, E2, Prop. 49, Schol.; Gebhardt, II, 131: "… moneo, ut accurate distinguant inter ideam, sive Mentis conceptum, & inter images rerum, quas imaginamur."

[39] Wild, p. 198, E2, Prop. 49, Schol.

[40] Wild, p. 377, E5, Prop. 11; Gebhardt, II, 289: "Quo imago aliqua ad plures res refertur. … Mentis imagis occupat."

[41] Wild, p. 255, E3, Prop. 52, Schol.; Gebhardt, II, 180: "Haec Mentis affectio, sive rei singularis imaginatio, quatenus sola in Mente versatur.…"

[42] Wild, p. 289, E4, Prop. 1, Schol. Emphasis added; Gebhardt, II, 211-212: "Nam imaginatio idea est, quae magis Corporus humani praesente(m) constitutionem, quam corporis externi naturam indicat, non quidem distincte, sed confuse; unde fit, ut Mens errare dicatur. … sic reliquae imaginationes, quibus Mens fallitur, sive eae naturalem Corporis constitutionem, sive, quod ejusdem agendi potentiam augeri, vel minui indicant, vero non sunt contrariae, nec ejusdem praesentia evanescunt."

[43] Cf. Thomas, *Dictionarium.*

[44] Radner, p. 346.

[45] *Ibid.*

[46] Mark, *Theory*, p. 20.

[47] Mark, "Truth," p. 12.

[48] Mark, "Truth," p. 31, n. 10.

[49] Mark, "Truth," p. 16.

[50] Mark, "Truth," p. 15.

[51] Mark, "Truth," p. 16.

[52] Wild, p. 157, E2, Prop. 13.

[53] Wild, p. 171, E2, Prop. 21, Dem.

[54] Wild, p. 167, E2, Prop. 17, Schol. Interpolations added.

[55] Wild, p. 156, E2, Prop. 12. Emphasis added.

[56] *Ibid.*

[57] Wild, p. 157, E2, Prop. 13. Emphasis added.

[58] Wild, p. 145, E2, Axiom 4.

[59] Wild, p. 170, E2, Prop. 19.

[60] Wild, p. 172, E2, Prop. 22; Gebhardt, II, 109: "Mens humana non tantum Corporis affectiones, sed etiam harum affectionum ideas percipit."

[61] Mark, "Truth," p. 31, n. 11. Parenthetical remarks added.

[62] Mark, *Theory*, p. 23.

[63] Mark, *Theory*, p. 8. Parentheses added.

[64] Wild, p. 172, E2, Prop. 22, Dem.

[65] Wild, p. 172, E2, Prop. 23.

[66] Wild, p. 177, E2, Prop. 29, Cor. Emphasis supplied; Gebhardt, II, 114: "Nam Mens se ipsam non cognoscit, nisi quatenus ideas affectionum corporis percipit. Corpus autem suum non percipit, nisi per ipsas affectionum ideas, per quas etiam tantum corpora externa percipit.…"

[67] Wild, p. 175, E2, Prop. 26.

[68] Wild, p. 175, E2, Prop. 26, Dem.; Gebhardt, II, 112: "Cum Mens humana per ideas affectionum sui Corporis corpora externa contemplatur, eandem tum imaginari dicimus, nec Mens alia ratione corpora externa, ut actu existentia, imaginari potest."

[69] Cf. Wild, pp. 168-169, E2, Prop. 18, Schol.

[70] Mark, "Truth," p. 15.

[71] Mark, "Truth," p. 16. Emphasis added. I shall argue that representation is required for both the first and the second sorts of knowledge, and that the first sort of knowledge is *not* necessarily false.

128   ETHICS: PART II

72 Mark, "Truth," p. 18.
73 Mark, "Truth," p. 23.
74 Mark, *Theory*, p. 22.
75 Brandom, p. 156.
76 *Ibid.*
77 Wild, p. 96, E1, Axiom 6; Gebhardt, II, 47: "Idea vera debet cum suo ideato convenire."
78 Mark, *Theory*, pp. 51-56, 85.
79 J. R. V. Marshant and J. F. Charles, *Cassell's Latin Dictionary*, pp. 155-156.
80 Thomas, *Dictionarium*.
81 Wolf, Letter 4, in *Correspondence*, p. 81.
82 Wolf, Letter 9, in *Correspondence*, p. 106.
83 *Ibid.* Parentheses added.
84 *Ibid.*
85 Mark, *Theory*, p. 85.
86 Mark, *Theory*, p. 86.
87 Mark, *Theory*, p. 87.
88 Mark, *Theory*, p. 88-89.
89 I shall stress the Platonistic aspects of the theory, their application to Spinoza, and show how an added emphasis on the intentionality of ideas clarifies Spinoza's view of truth and error.
90 Wild, p. 144, E2, Def. 4; Gebhardt, II, 85: "Per ideam adaequatam intelligo ideam, quae, quatenum in se sine relatione ad objectum consideratur, omnes verae ideae proprietates, sive denominationes intrinsecas habet."
91 Mark, "Truth," pp. 19-20.
92 Mark, "Truth," p. 20.
93 Wild, p. 176, E2, Prop. 28.
94 *Ibid.*
95 Wild, p. 177, E2, Prop. 29.
96 Cf. Wolf, Letter 9, in *Correspondence*, p. 106.
97 Wolf, "To Mr. Ehrenfried Walter Von Tschirnhaus," January 1675, Letter 60, in *Correspondence*, p. 301.
98 Wolf, Letter 60, in *Correspondence*, p. 300.
99 Wolf, Letter 4, in *Correspondence*, p. 81.
100 Wild, p. 170, E2, Prop. 19.
101 Wild, p. 175, E2, Prop. 27.
102 Wild, p. 161, E2, Axiom 2, Lemma 3, Cor.
103 Wild, pp. 173-174, E2, Prop. 24. It is interesting that Spinoza's account of the identity of a body is similar to that of Hume.
104 Wild, p. 177, E2, Prop. 29, Schol.
105 Mark, "Truth," p. 16.
106 *Ibid.*
107 Wild, p. 187, E2, Prop. 41. Emphasis supplied.
108 Wild, p. 180, E2, Prop. 35.
109 Wild, p. 175, E2, Prop. 26, Cor.
110 Wild, p. 179, E2, Prop. 32.
111 I hope to show that the distinction between truth and adequacy and the application of the representational aspect of an idea will account for true knowledge even where ideas are inadequately known.
112 Wild, p. 168, E2, Prop. 17, Schol.; Gebhardt, II, 106: "... quatenus consideratur, carere idea, quae existentiam illarum rerum, quas sibi praesentes imaginatur, secludat."
113 Wild, p. 181, E2, Prop. 35, Schol.
114 Wild, p. 181, E2, Prop. 36.
115 Wild, p. 184, E2, Prop. 40, Schol. 1.
116 *Ibid.*
117 Wild, p. 187, E2, Prop. 41.

118 Wild, p. 186, E2, Prop. 40, Schol. 2; Gebhardt, II, 112.
119 Radner, p. 346. Parenthetical remarks added.
120 Radner, p. 352.
121 Radner, pp. 352-353.
122 Brandom, p. 162.
123 Wild, p. 179, E2, Prop. 32; p. 188, E2, Prop. 43, Dem.
124 Wild, p. 170, E2, Prop. 19.
125 Wild, p. 174, E2, Prop. 24, Dem.
126 Wild, p. 181, E2, Prop. 36, Dem.; Gebhardt, II, 118.
127 Wild, p. 176, E2, Prop. 28.
128 Wild, p. 185, E2, Prop. 40, Schol. 1.
129 *Ibid.*
130 Wild, p. 113, E1, Prop. 16; p. 149, E2, Prop. 7; p. 181, E2, Prop. 36.
131 Wild, p. 180, E2, Prop. 35.
132 Wild, p. 166, E2, Prop. 17, Dem.; Gebhardt, II, 104.
133 Wild, p. 189, E2, Prop. 43.
134 Wild, p. 188, E2, Prop. 43, Dem. Emphasis added.
135 *Ibid.* Emphasis added. Spinoza is speaking here of "knowing truly" and "true knowledge" and this may indicate that true *knowledge* or certain knowledge is a function not only of the *ideas* but also of *adequate* ideas.
136 Wild, p. 190, E2, Prop. 43, Schol. Emphasis added.
137 Wild, p. 187, E2, Prop. 42.
138 Wild, p. 188, E2, Prop. 42, Dem. Emphasis added.
139 Wild, p. 189, E2, Prop. 43, Schol.
140 Mark, "Truth," p. 20.
141 Wild, p. 172, E2, Prop. 21, Schol.
142 Radner, p. 357.
143 *Ibid.*
144 Brandom, p. 161.
145 *Ibid.*
146 Brandom, p. 160.
147 Wild, p. 177, E2, Prop. 29, Cor.
148 Wild, p. 183, E2, Prop. 39, Dem.
149 Wild, p. 369, E5, Prop. 4, Dem.
150 Cf. Wild, pp. 378-379, E5, Prop. 14.
151 Wild, p. 186, E2, Prop. 40, Schol. 2. Brandom argues, and I agree, that knowledge of the formal essence of attributes is derived from ratio or reason.
152 E. M. Curley, "Experience in Spinoza's Theory of Knowledge," in *Spinoza: A Collection of Critical Essays*, ed. M. Grene (Garden City, N.Y.: Anchor Books, 1973), p. 57; hereafter cited as "Experience."
153 Each attribute is also a singular thing which can be known only by intuition.
154 Wild, p. 393, E5, Prop. 36, Schol. Emphasis added; Gebhardt, II, 303: "... ut hoc exemplo ostenderem, quantum *rerum singularium* cognitio, quam intuitivam, sive tertii generis appellavi (*vide* 2, Schol., Prop. 40, pt. 2), polleat, potioque sit *cognitione universali*, quam secundi generis esse dixi." Emphasis added.
155 Curley, "Experience," p. 59.
156 Wild, p. 193, E2, Prop. 47; p. 147, E2, Prop. 4.
157 Wolf, Letter 50, in *Correspondence*, pp. 269-270.
158 Brandom, p. 152.

COMMENTARY

PLATO AND SPINOZA: EPISTEMOLOGY

INTRODUCTION

It is always dangerous to compare the works of two philosophers of different times, cultures and viewpoints. Still, the danger should be weighed against the possibility of aiding the understanding of the philosophers in question. If one takes the position that philosophers do not ''write only for their times,'' or for their situations, but rather that philosophers write for all time, then one may hope to compare their works. It is, perhaps, true that no contemporary philosopher would aspire to write eternal truths, but I believe it is indisputable that both Plato and Spinoza wrote philosophies which they intended to be eternally true. Plato was concerned with BEING *per se* and with knowledge of the eternal Forms; Spinoza was concerned with God, Substance, or Nature as it could be known *sub specie aeternitatis*. So, with some hope to avoid anachronistic judgments about Plato's views in the *Sophist*, I shall indicate some of the affinities between Plato's *Sophist*, as interpreted by Cornford, and Spinoza's *Ethics*, Part II.[1] The comparison may illuminate Spinoza's epistemology and may enable one to resolve some of the problems inherent in an Aristotelian interpretation of Spinoza.

If one is not inclined to accept the Platonism of Spinoza, then perhaps one could accept this account as an interpretation of Spinoza's epistemology intended to clarify his work without entailing the further claim that Spinoza either read or consciously adopted Plato's account as it appears in the *Sophist*. It would be a mistake, I believe, to argue that Spinoza was merely a Platonist and simply applied Plato's doctrines to problems in modern philosophy. Spinoza was an original thinker, without a doubt. Still, it is conceivable that he applied a methodology similar to that of Plato, although he himself came to employ that methodology independently of a study of Plato. In any event, this account is only intended to clarify Spinoza's epistemology by noting analogies and disanalogies between Plato and Spinoza without necessarily implying that Spinoza was simply a Platonist.[2]

PHILOSOPHY AND DEFINITION

One of the main thrusts of the early philosophers was to gain a clear definition of philosophical terms. This is apparent in the early, or Socratic, dialogues of Plato as well as in the middle dialogues. The

Cratylus is primarily concerned with the problem of language and its uses, but the theme of the importance of definitions runs through Plato's works. Plato says that the concern of the *Sophist* is to gain a definition of the Sophist, to

> try to bring his nature to light in a clear formula. ... it is always desirable to have reached an agreement about the thing itself by means of explicit statements, rather than be content to use the same word without formulating what it means.[3]

Spinoza, too, is concerned with acquiring clear definitions of the nature or essence of the thing under discussion. He says:

> ... a definition either explains a thing as it exists outside of the understanding, and then it ought to be true, and does not differ from a proposition, or an axiom, except in so far as it deals with the essences of things or of states, whereas an axiom is wider....[4]

He also says:

> The true definition of each thing includes nothing but the simple nature of the thing defined.[5]

For both Plato and Spinoza definitions capture the nature or essence of the thing defined. For Spinoza "the idea or definition of the thing should express its efficient cause," and the emphasis on causation is lacking in Plato.[6] Still, when Spinoza defines God as Being which exists necessarily, he does not seem to differ from Plato's use of Existence or Being in the *Sophist*. For Plato, the Forms exist necessarily and eternally just as God, Nature, or Substance exists necessarily for Spinoza. The efficient cause of the attributes and God or Nature is to be found in their essence or nature, and all other modes of existence are to be defined by means of their efficient causes. For Plato, Existence, Same, Different, Motion and Rest exist necessarily, and all the subordinate forms are included under the genera of these five important Forms. Both Plato and Spinoza accept the position that there are real definitions which provide knowledge of the essential nature of things.

COLLECTION AND DIVISION

It is also interesting to note that the Forms are the only things capable of being defined by the dialectical science of Collection and Division employed in the *Sophist*. Individual objects of knowledge—the Forms themselves—are definable for Plato, but individual objects of perception are not definable. For Spinoza, finite modes—individual things which are generally held to be objects of perception—are indefinable, too. He says:

... We only need Experience in the case of whatever cannot be deduced from the definition of a thing, as, for instance, the existence of Modes: for this cannot be deduced from the definition of a thing. But we do not need experience in the case of those things whose existence is not distinguished from their essence and therefore follow from their definition. Indeed, no experience will ever be able to teach us this: for experience does not teach us the essence of things; the utmost that it can effect is to determine our mind so that it only thinks of certain essences of things. Therefore, since the existence of attributes does not differ from their essence, we shall not be able to apprehend it by any kind of experience.[7]

God or Nature and the attributes are not known by experience; they are definable.

Common notions are also definable for Spinoza. E. M. Curley says that Ratio, or reason, for Spinoza is inferential and includes "not only cases where our knowledge of something presupposes knowledge of the common notions, but also our knowledge of the common notions themselves."[8] For Spinoza, reason is concerned with adequate ideas and cannot be the cause of error. Similarly, for Plato, properly conducted dialectical reasoning from a Collection to Divisions according to natural kinds cannot be erroneous. Knowledge which deals with Forms alone cannot be erroneous for Plato. If one should argue that Forms are common characters of things, one might discern an analogy between Spinoza's reasoning from common notions and Plato's later dialectic. As Forms and their relations constitute the objects of dialectic and are objects of certain knowledge for Plato, so "common notions and adequate ideas of things" constitute the objects of reason and are objects of certain knowledge for Spinoza.[9]

INTUITION

A proper collection is required for the initiation of the dialectical procedure. Cornford says, "The preliminary Collection is to fix upon the genus to be divided."[10] At 253D, the Eleatic Stranger says, "And the man who çan do that discerns clearly *one* Form everywhere extended through the many...."[11] Cornford says that this

> refers specially to the preliminary process of Collection, described in the *Phaedrus* as 'taking a synoptic survey of widely scattered Forms (species) and bringing them into a single (generic) Form.' ... The dialectician surveys the collection and 'clearly discerns' *by intuition* the common (generic) character 'extended throughout' them all. So he *divines* the generic Form that he will take for division.[12]

The words "intuition" and "divines" are Cornford's terms for Plato's "clearly discerns," but they do seem to capture that form of immediate awareness as opposed to discursive reasoning, termed ''intuition'' in the seventeenth century.

Intuitive science, or intuition, is defined by Spinoza as a ''kind of knowing (which) advances from an adequate idea of the formal essence of certain attributes of God to the adequate knowledge of the essence of things.''[13] According to this definition, intuition seems to be discursive and more akin to reasoning than immediate awareness. However, in his mathematical explanation, Spinoza eschews the rules of mathematics and demonstration to say ''because from the ratio in which we see *by one intuition* that the first stands to the second we conclude the fourth.''[14] Immediate awareness seems to be implied by ''one intuition,'' but there may be still an argument for demonstrative reasoning based on the phrase ''we conclude.'' Later, Spinoza argues that one can know that the mind's essence and existence depends on God. He says, ''I thought it worth while for me to notice this here, in order that I might show ... what the knowledge of individual objects[15] which I have called intuitive or of the third kind (Schol. 2, Prop. 40, pt. 2) is able to do, and how much more potent it is than the universal knowledge[16] which I have called knowledge of the second kind.''[17]

Curley notes that in the *Treatise*, ''there appear to be two species of intuition: (i) knowing a thing through its essence, and (ii) knowing it through its proximate cause.''[18] Curley suggests that the first species of intuition is concerned with knowledge of uncreated, necessarily existing things, such as God and the attributes, whereas the second species is concerned with knowledge of the modes. To know God or the attributes by means of their essence alone is to know them by definition and adequately. This sort of knowledge—clear and distinct, and consistent—would be apprehended immediately and not discursively. This may be akin to the apprehension of the genus by Collection for Plato. On the other hand, knowledge of a thing by means of its proximate cause *could* be inferential and could be akin to the Division which follows from the Collection in Plato's dialectic. This second sort of intuition is similar to reason.

Curley goes on to say:

> In the *Ethics*, intuition seems to be conceived more narrowly. It *includes* adequate knowledge of the essence of *singular things, i.e. finite modes*, but it does not include adequate knowledge of the essences of divine attributes. Knowledge of the nature of an *attribute*, such as extension, is knowledge of something *universal*, of something *common* to all bodies.[19]

I should agree that knowledge of singular things is knowledge of finite modes, as Curley says and as Spinoza indicates in *Ethics* V, Proposition 36.[20]

I should disagree with Curley's assertion that intuition does not include knowledge of the attributes and with his assertion that knowledge of the attributes is knowledge of "something universal, of something common to all bodies." First, Spinoza says that intuition begins with the adequate idea of the formal essence of certain attributes of God. That is to say, it proceeds from the definition of God's attributes and these definitions must be known in order to provide the basis for the knowledge of finite modes. Spinoza's account of the first species of intuition in the *Treatise* would account for this knowledge of the essence of attributes. Additionally, knowledge of the attributes also constitutes knowledge of God or Nature. We know that we have adequate knowledge of God and of the attributes, and we must account for that sort of knowledge. It appears, on the basis of Spinoza's arguments for the existence of God, which are primarily ontological and *a priori*, that this knowledge is based upon an adequate idea of the essence of God. This cannot be knowledge of the first sort, since it is not from vague experience nor is it from signs. It cannot be knowledge acquired through reason, because it is not knowledge of a "common notion" or "adequate ideas of the properties of things." "Common notions" are also axioms, and these are not Thought or Extension, but rather the laws or relations which operate within the realm of minds and bodies. Neither are the attributes the common properties of things, since we know that motion and rest, and understanding are common properties of bodies and minds and are infinite *modes*.

I should argue that these infinite modes, and perhaps even the infinite mediate mode, are the universal common properties rather than attributes, contrary to Curley's view. I suggest that knowledge of the attributes is acquired by intuition in the first sense of the term—by definition and by the immediate apprehension of their necessary existence. Furthermore, it could be argued that each of the attributes and also God, or Nature, is in itself a singular thing. Each attribute is a thing which cannot be defined or deduced from anything else but God or Nature. Each attribute is itself unique and individual. God or Nature is also a singular thing, unique and alone.

I suggest that the phrase "singular thing" is ambiguous. It can, and does, refer to finite modes; but it also refers to Nature and to each of the attributes, none of which has anything "mutually in common" with any other attribute and is "in itself."[21] So each attribute and Nature itself is a singular thing; and has as its proximate cause itself, whereas finite modes have proximate causes other than themselves and can be understood through other finite modes. The attributes and Nature are infinite singular things, apprehended by intuition of their essences. Spinoza says:

> ... a thing can only be said to be one or single in respect of its existence and not of its essence; for we do not conceive things under numbers until they have been subsumed under a common class. ... But since the existence of God is His essence itself, and since we can form *no general idea of His essence*, it is certain that he who calls God one or single has no true idea of God, or is speaking of him inappropriately.[22]

It should be noted that Spinoza claims that no general or universal idea of God's essence can be formed. But an attribute is defined as that "which the intellect perceives of substance as if constituting its essence,"[23] and we know that substance is God or Nature. So, contrary to Curley's claim that the attributes are universal or common properties is Spinoza's statement that one cannot have a universal or general idea of an attribute, or in Spinoza's terms one cannot have a general idea of God's essence or His attributes.

Spinoza himself does say "that God is one, that is to say (Def. 6), in Nature there is but one substance, and it is absolutely infinite...."[24] Spinoza says here that God is *one*, although in Letter 50 he denies the possibility of assigning a number to God. Spinoza also says that each attribute is one and independent of any other attribute.

> ... This is the nature of substance that each of its attributes is conceived through itself, since all the attributes which substance possesses were always in it together, nor could one be produced by another; but each expresses the reality or being of substance. ... Being ... consists of infinite attributes, each one of which expresses a certain essence, eternal and infinite.[25]

It appears that Spinoza is denying the attribution of number to God or Nature, or even the attributes, because numbers are distinctions of reason which apply to things of the same essential nature. Since God and each of the attributes has its own particular essential nature and has no common genus with anything else but itself, strictly speaking, it is improper to assign it the *number one*. On the other hand, God and the attributes are *unique* generically.[26] So in terms of *genus* or *essence*, they are singular or unique although no *number* can be properly assigned to them.

This appears quite similar to Plato's claim that each Form is one, unique, singular thing and is also many things. It is one genus which includes many species. So, substance is one and includes or pervades many attributes, and each attribute is one and pervades many modes. The attribute is one, unique thing or essence which, if it is apprehended at all, must be known by intuition as God or Nature is known. It is also many insofar as it pervades its infinite and finite modes; so it is similar to the Collection—the genus—of Plato which, according to Cornford, is known by intuition.

Thus, contrary to Curley, I have argued that an attribute is *not* only something universal or common to all bodies, but it is to be considered as a unique, singular thing. Only intuition can account for our knowledge of God and the attributes as unique things which can then serve as the basis for our adequate knowledge of finite singular things. The collection, the genus, or the attribute is apprehended by intuition. One may know common notions or properties by reason.

Brandom notes:

> ... the prime positive result of the investigation of common properties by Ratio is an adequate idea of God. We have seen how an adequate idea of the immediate infinite mode of extension is possible in the second kind of knowledge. But by the definition of a mode, any mode can only be conceived through substance, which must accordingly be conceived adequately if any mode, infinite or not, is so conceived. We can restate this argument: since motion-and-rest are caused immediately by God, and knowledge of the effect depends upon and involves knowledge of the cause, the adequate knowledge of motion-and-rest Ratio assures us of involves adequate knowledge of God. This is essentially the argument of Eth. ii, 45-47. Ratio provides an adequate idea of God's essence, and hence sets the stage for intuition to reverse the direction of inquiry, beginning with God and proceeding down to finite individual essences.[27]

Brandom's and Curley's claim that Ratio provides knowledge of God's essence—his attributes—does not coincide with Spinoza's definition of reason as being concerned with common notions and common properties of things. To make this point, Brandom must rely on the argument that anything which is known adequately must involve knowledge of God. For Brandom, the distinction between reason and intuition is simply one of direction: reason proceeds from common properties to attributes of God; intuition proceeds from God to finite individuals. Knowledge of God as a whole, as a genus, or as a unique substance cannot be acquired from knowledge of common properties or notions. The apprehension of a unique entity as singular differs from the apprehension of common properties or notions. The difference between reason and intuition for Brandom is simply one of starting point in the procedure: reason starts with common notions and ascends to God; intuition starts with God and descends to finite modes.

I should argue, on the basis of Spinoza's definition of reason in E II, Prop. 40, Schol. 2 that the ascent of reason stops at infinite modes.[28] Later, Brandom himself argues that intuition must "proceed down from an *adequate knowledge of the infinite modes*, to an adequate knowledge of some finite, relative wholes."[29] Spinoza differs from Brandom's account of intuition in *Ethics* II, Prop. 40, Scholium 2, wherein Spinoza specifically asserts that intuition proceeds "from an adequate idea of the formal essence of certain attributes of God.''[30] The ''formal essence'' of an attribute is its definition, not its infinite immediate mode. Brandom thus collapses the end result of reason and the starting point of intuition, contrary to Spinoza. For Brandom, reason is concerned with an ascent from the mediate infinite mode, to the immediate infinite mode and to the attribute itself. Brandom thus agrees with Curley, who says that knowledge of the attribute is ''knowledge of something universal, of something common to all bodies. In the *Ethics* ... this kind of knowledge is classified under the heading of reason.''[31] But, it has been argued that Spinoza views attributes as singular and unique not simply as common or universal properties. If one accepts my account of reason as ascending to the infinite immediate modes from an apprehension of the laws and common properties of the ordered experience of finite modes, and intuition as being both the apprehension of Nature and the attributes and a descent from them to an adequate idea of the essence of finite modes, then this would be consistent with Spinoza's definitions and would clearly differentiate between reason and intuition on the basis of both their initial and final points.

I disagree with Curley and Brandom insofar as I argue that knowledge of the essential nature of God—the attributes—is acquired by the same method as knowledge of God or Nature itself, that is, by intuition. However, I agree with Curley and Brandom that intuition, in the second sense of the term, proceeds from the attributes to the finite modes. Brandom says:

> The descent of intuition from the essence of God to the essences of particular things must be different in kind from the step-by-step analysis by which Ratio proceeds, for there is no next smaller whole after the 'face of the whole universe.' There would thus be an infinite number of 'steps' for reason to go through to get to any particular individual. But Spinoza's sole non-metaphysical example of the different kinds of knowledge contrasts the step-by-step figuring of a proportion by Ratio to 'just seeing it' by immediate intuition, so this is an expected difference.[32]

One meaning of intuition is that of ''immediate awareness.'' This accounts both for our knowledge of God and the attributes *and* our adequate knowledge of finite modes. But, the downward process from the attributes to immediate awareness of the essence of a finite mode is also an aspect of intuition according to Spinoza's definition.

PLATO AND SPINOZA: REASON AND INTUITION

An analogy to the processes of reason and intuition can be found in the dual processes of Collection and Division as found in Plato's *Phaedrus*,

Sophist, *Statesman*, and *Philebus*. The apprehension of the common nature of specific Forms and their collection into a "synoptic genus" is a correlate for Spinoza's reason or second sort of knowledge. The apprehension of the immediate and mediate infinite modes by means of reason is knowledge of a less pervasive genus, or lesser whole, than the apprehension of an attribute or God. Apprehension of attributes and God is accomplished by intuition, as the apprehension of the five important kinds is by means of intuition for Plato. It can be noted that Being is a most pervasive kind for Plato and, similarly, God or Nature is termed Being by Spinoza. Indeed, of the five most important kinds, only motion and rest could not qualify as being as pervasive as the others for Spinoza, perhaps because Plato can be interpreted as accepting a sort of change or motion in the soul when it acquires or forgets knowledge, while Spinoza restricts motion and rest to the world of extension, or bodies. Reason would be concerned with the "upward path" from finite to infinite modes; and perhaps, with the interrelations among the immediate and mediate infinite modes.

If the awareness of Being, for both Plato and Spinoza, is accomplished by intuition, then the division which follows from that point would be akin to Spinoza's "downward path" of intuition. The great difference between Plato and Spinoza in the descent by division is to be found in the entities which constitute the conclusion of the descent and in the degree of knowledge which results from it. For Plato, the end point of division is the *infimae species*. This enables him to describe knowledge as from Forms, to Forms, by means of Forms, to limit the objects of knowledge to Forms, and to retain the stability and eternity of truth. For Spinoza, the end point of the descent of intuition is the finite mode—a temporal thing. One may account for this difference if one recalls that, for Plato, the objects of perception are shadowy entities, somewhat less real than the objects of knowledge, whereas nowhere in Spinoza does one find a claim that finite modes are not real. Spinoza, then, argues that one can achieve adequate knowledge of particulars or individuals, but this cannot be done by means of opinion or imagination. Plato would deny the possibility of attaining knowledge, in the strict sense, of particulars but would relegate them to the world of belief, opinion, *doxa*. It is interesting that for both Spinoza and Plato, intuition and reason (or dialectic) which deal with eternal entities result in certain or adequate knowledge. The "knowledge" which is concerned with temporal things and which is fallible is termed imagination or opinion.

PLATO AND SPINOZA: PERCEPTION AND IMAGINATION

The epistemological difficulties faced by Plato and Spinoza are similar insofar as they both claim that the use of reason and intuition results in certainty. Plato claims that to know the Forms or Ideas is to have certain knowledge. Spinoza argues that all ideas are true. How, then, can they account for error?

It is clear that there must be some "bogus" sort of knowledge, concerned with some different sorts of entities than those apprehended by knowledge in the proper sense of the term. For Plato, these entities of opinion in some sense "share in non-being" or are, to some extent, less real than the Forms. For Spinoza, however, the problem is more complicated, because he argues that all ideas, even those ideas of finite modes, are true. Spinoza terms God, Nature, or Substance "Being absolutely infinite"[33] and says that finite modes "follow from" God. One may readily note his similarity to Plato for whom the particulars participate in Being, but are of a different order of reality than Being itself. So, while Spinoza does not say that finite modes are not real, he does note that being finite entails having less power. So they would have less power to exist than an infinite substance. He says:

> inability to exist is impotence, and, on the other hand, ability to exist is power, as is self-evident. ... For since ability to exist is power, it follows that the more reality belongs to the nature of anything, the greater is the power for existence it derives from itself....[34]

This is strikingly close to Plato's statement in the *Sophist*, 247E:

> Stranger: I suggest that anything has real being, that is so constituted as to possess any sort of power either to affect anything else or to be affected, in however small a degree, by the most insignificant agent, though it be only once. I am proposing as a *mark* to distinguish real things, that they are nothing but power.[35]

For Plato, these "lesser beings" are images; for Spinoza, they are finite modes.

Plato's account of perception, in the *Theaetetus*, is similar to Spinoza's account. Cornford says, "The quality I perceive (my sense-object) becomes or arises at the moment when it is perceived and only *for* a single percipient; it has no enduring independent existence in the physical objects at other times."[36] Socrates says, at *Theaetetus* 154, "What we say 'is' this or that colour will be neither the eye which encounters the motion nor the motion which is encountered, but something which has arisen between the two and is peculiar to each several percipient."[37] Cornford goes on to say that the colour perceived has no permanent being anywhere; it arises between the sense-organ and the physical object when they encounter. Also, it is peculiar to the individual percipient in two ways: my sense-object is private to me in that no one else can see just what I see, and *peculiar* in that no two people, looking at the same thing, will see precisely similar colours; nor will even the same person at different moments, because the condition of his sense organ will be always varying.[38]

Spinoza says that an image is an affection of the human body by an external body.[39] Images are the result of the interaction of the body of the perceiver and some external object. Our *idea* of the image "indicates the constitution of our own body rather than the nature of external bodies."[40] So, for Plato and Spinoza, objects of perception do not represent the external object itself, but rather its effect on the percipient.

Because the body itself is constantly changing, the idea of the image is private and peculiar to the individual at that particular time, just as is Plato's object of perception. What Plato terms a perceived object, an appearance, an image, an *eidola*, is very similar, then, to Spinoza's external body itself. Plato does not clearly distinguish between the *eidola*, the image, and the knowledge or idea of the image as does Spinoza. Apparently this distinction, or the intervention of the idea between the mind and the object represented by the idea, is a development which occurred later in the history of philosophy. Consequently, it is necessary to keep in mind that the problem of the *knowledge* of images is the *primary* problem in *Sophist*, rather than the metaphysical problem of the existence of images.[41]

Still, Plato must prove that there are things other than Forms, if he is to explain falsity. These *eidola*, or images, are the key to his explanation. Images are copies of reality but have the same name as the Form itself, although they have a "lower grade of reality."[42] Images partake of non-Being; they are something different from the Forms. Appearances or images are always changing, so they cannot have formal or real definitions which express their essences. For Plato, Forms can be defined; for Spinoza, God or Nature, attributes, infinite modes can be defined. But one cannot define a particular or an image for Plato, nor can one define a particular finite mode, known by the first sort of knowledge, for Spinoza. Images and ideas of images are the primary cause of error in Plato and Spinoza.

PLATO AND SPINOZA: PERCEPTION AND ERROR

There is an analogy to this account of error to be found in Plato. It has generally been agreed that Plato's *Theaetetus* is concerned with that sort of knowledge derived from perception. Since this is the area where

Spinoza's problems of truth and falsehood arise, in the "first sort of knowledge," let us concern ourselves with the relation between perception, or imagination, and error. If perception is simply the formation of an idea of a present image, then we can see how it is possible for Spinoza to say that "these imaginations of the mind, regarded by themselves, contain no error, and that the mind is not in error because it imagines...."[43] Cornford says that perception is "in a sense, infallible ... but it cannot apprehend existence and truth."[44] Subsequently, Plato distinguishes between perception and judgment, and notes that judgments may be true or false. For Spinoza, the mind can relate an idea to an ideatum in terms of referring, representing, or resembling; so one can assimilate his view of error with that of Plato in *Theaetetus*. The bare idea *by itself* is not true or false; it "points towards" its formal reality. As we take it *for* some ideatum, as we refer it to something "outside the understanding," it can be the cause of error. Knowledge, or forming a judgment, requires an activity of taking the idea or intending the idea to refer to some ideatum; insofar as we merely perceive or are acquainted with the idea without asserting that its ideatum exists, there is no error or truth involved.

A true judgment involved in the first sort of knowledge occurs when one matches the idea of the image to the image—that is, the idea is taken for the image alone. A false judgment is one wherein the idea is taken for the external object which causes the modification of the body (image), or it asserts that my image exists as I know it. Error occurs when we literally mis-take the idea to stand for the cause of my image and/or when we take my image to be the real interaction of an external body and my body. The Platonic analogue for this explanation is to be found in *Theaetetus* 194 A-B:

> Socrates: But there was left over the case I have been describing in which we say false judgment does occur: the possibility that you may both know and see or otherwise perceive both, but not get the two imprints to correspond each with its proper perception. Like a bad archer, you may shoot to one side and miss the mark—which is indeed another phrase we use for error ... it is precisely in the field of objects both known and perceived that judgment turns and twists about and proves false or true—true when it brings impressions straight to their proper imprints; false when it misdirects them crosswise to the wrong imprint.[45]

Plato's account can be rendered in Spinozistic terms. If one mis-directs the idea to an improper ideatum, then one makes a false judgment. If one takes the idea to refer only to the existence of the image, and not to the existence of the external object which is but one cause of the image, nor to the actual interaction of bodies, one will not err. It is interesting to note that Plato's explanation of error here is concerned with memory and perception, and this corresponds to Spinoza's account of an idea of a past or present image.

Earlier in the dialogue, Plato said a false judgment can occur when one

> hurries to assign the proper imprint to a proper visual perception, like fitting a foot into its own footmark to effect a recognition; and then make the mistake of interchanging them, like a man who thrusts his feet into the wrong shoes and apply the perception of each to the imprint of the other.[46]

The simile of "fitting a foot into the proper shoe" is very close to the "fitting together" translation of *convenio* that I have favored in defining truth for Spinoza.[47] *Convenio* can be translated as "a foot fitting a shoe."[48] This use of the term is found in Cicero in relation to the Stoic's view of happiness as independent of duration. According to Cicero, the Stoics argue that it is erroneous to say that lasting happiness is more desirable than brief happiness "just as supposing the merit of a shoe were to fit the foot, many shoes would not be superior to a few shoes."[49] We know that Spinoza read Cicero, and it is at least conceivable that Spinoza had this meaning of *convenio* in mind when he defined truth in Axiom 4.

Plato says that there are false appearances. An appearance is a "combination of perception and judgment which ... occurs when I see an indistinct figure and, rightly or wrongly, judge it to be someone I know."[50] The Greek word used for "appearing" is φαντασία, *phantasia*, which becomes "imagination."[51] However, this sense of imagination—the combination of perception and judgment is quite different from picturing "an absent or imaginary object not perceived at the moment."[52] In fact, Plato's use of *phantasia* is very similar to Spinoza's use of imagination—the forming of ideas of images, of perceived things. Spinoza, too, is at pains to note that this is not just passive perception or imprinting of pictures on a waxen tablet but contains, as do all ideas, the element of judgment. That is to say, Spinoza maintains that all ideas carry with them their own affirmation and denial, and this seems to coincide with Plato's meaning of judgment. Thus, ideas of images may be correlated with Plato's *phantasia* and, again, in both philosophers we discern agreement in one of the causes of error. "This judgment rightly or wrongly interpreting a present perception is all that 'appearing' means here. It is the one kind of judgment that may be false which the psychological apparatus of the *Theaetetus* was adequate to describe."[53] With the exception that imagination covers not only the formation of present ideas of images but also past and future ideas of images for Spinoza, there is an apparent agreement among the philosophers. Improper words, or signs, together with improper ideas of images—or *phantasia* are the causes of error, and the impropriety is one of mistaking, or mis-representing what the words and ideas of images refer to, represent, or resemble.

PLATO AND SPINOZA: LANGUAGE AND ERROR

Words and their relations to the perceived images are derivative causes of error for both Plato and Spinoza insofar as words or signs which should represent, respectively, Forms or Nature, can cause ideas of the finite particular things or images of things and so lead us to mis-match the word with its proper referent. At 260 E the Stranger says, "That is why we must begin by investigating the nature of discourse and thinking and appearance, in order that we may then make out their combination with not-being and so prove that falsity exists."[54] One notes the twin causes of error—particulars, or appearances, and language. For Plato, as for Spinoza, words refer to things. Terms define or are signs for ideas, for Spinoza, and those ideas may represent images, ideas, substance or attributes. "Plato defines a word, not as a token of mental affection, but as a vocal sign ... used to signify being. This at once implies that every word stands for something or means something; it is not meaningless noise."[55] Spinoza says that words can cause us to "recollect things and form certain ideas of them (things) similar to them (the things themselves), through which ideas we imagine things."[56] Words cause us to form ideas of images, and these ideas may be incorrectly associated with the object itself rather than just its effect on us. A word does stand for some entity in Plato as well as in Spinoza. For Spinoza, the word is a physical thing, and the thought of the word causes us to recollect an idea of an image, and the idea once again intervenes between the mind and the things. This intervention occurs for Spinoza and Plato only in the case of images; the being signified by Forms or Nature is a being where one can know the essential nature of the thing itself by intuition and one can inspect the definition, the term, to see if it does include the essence. But words which refer to images cannot be defined, and, whereas the images are things which exist, their existence is not necessary and is not known by means of non-contradiction. Their existence is known by perception. "Plato's definition of 'word' ... covers two senses (1) A common name *signifies* or '*means*' a 'nature' which is a Form, as well as 'standing for' or *indicating* existing things. (2) A proper name *stands for* or *indicates* an existing thing only."[57]

In a true proposition, for Plato, "each word *stands for* one element in a complex fact. The statement as a whole is complex and its structure *cor-*

responds to the structure of the fact. Truth means this correspondence.''[58]
At least one interpretation of Spinoza argues that his "ideas" are
propositions.[59] Many also claim that Spinoza has a correspondence
theory of truth.[60] If all of Spinoza's ideas are true, if they all have some
ideatum, then all of his ideas "stand for" or "refer" to something. So, for
both Plato and Spinoza, falsehood cannot be exclusively a function of the
statement, or the word, or the idea itself; it must refer to or correspond
with something or other. A false statement, for Plato and for
Spinoza—with the exceptions of statements composed of meaningless
strings of terms or statements composed of contradictory terms, is not
false *per se* but because it represents something different from what is the
fact. The mis-fitting of the statement with its fact is an analogue to the
mis-fitting of an idea of an image to an idea of an idea or an external
object for Spinoza. For both philosophers, the "taking" of the statement
or the idea to represent something which it does not properly represent,
or taking the statement to represent something different or other than its
proper correspondent objects or beings, is one cause of error.

For both philosophers the occurrence of error is explained by the mis-
taking of an idea or a term which has the possibility of dual representation. In the true statement: ''Theaetetus sits,'' there is the correspondence between the existing fact of ''sitting'' and the Form
''Sitting.''

> The word 'sits' has now a double significance: it *stands for* a part of the ex-
> isting facts, and it *means* the Form. To put it differently, the phrase 'thing
> that is in your case' (ὄν περὶ ἐόν) has two senses: (1) an existing element in
> the fact in which you are the other element, (2) the Form of which this ex-
> isting element 'partakes.' This Form is an object of knowledge, not of
> perception, and is permanently real, independently of any existing facts;
> whereas the particular 'sitting' which is part of the existing fact occurs at
> some time and place and ceases to be.[61]

The term which has a dual significance is ''sitting''—it refers to a particular action as well as to the Form.

In Spinoza, *terms* of dual significance have their counterpart, I believe,
in ideas of images. These ideas—and the terms with which they are
associated—properly refer to images and *should* be taken to represent only
the images. Unfortunately, such ideas can be mis-interpreted as
representing the actual interaction of objects on one's body, the idea itself
or the external object itself. When the idea of an image goes beyond its
proper representation (the image itself) and mis-represents the existing
fact, the finite mode itself, error results.

In a false statement, each term has ''a meaning, and so the statement
as a whole has meaning.''[62] This is similar to the interpretation of

Spinoza that each term has an idea which can refer to another ideatum. "What is missing in the case of the false statement is: (1) the relation 'partaking' between the actual 'sitting' and the *different* Form Flying."[63] This is analogous to the mis-fitting of an idea of an image with an idea of an idea. The idea of the image does have a meaning, a referent: the image. *My* idea of the image fits with the image insofar as it involves only the nature of *my* body. The mis-fit of that idea occurs when one takes it to represent the actual interaction of the external body and my body, or the thing itself rather than just my image. All of these ideas are true; my idea of an image represents my *image*; but that is something different from the *idea* of the external object itself and the modification of the body itself by that object as it is in God or Nature. Similarly, Cornford says, "... 'flies' does not stand for this 'sitting,' though it has a meaning of its own which the word calls up to the hearer's mind."[64] The word calls up an idea which does indeed refer to something—for Spinoza, it refers to an image. However, the word is mis-interpreted, and instead of representing the idea of my image, it is mis-taken and mis-represents the idea of the idea, the interaction of bodies, or thing itself. The false statement "Theaetetus flies" is composed of terms which refer to existing things: Theaetetus himself, and the Form "Flying." But the existing fact of "Theaetetus sitting" also refers to an existent Theaetetus and the Form "Sitting." The error occurs when the term "flies" refers properly to its Form, but mis-represents the fact—the sitting. The term "flies" is akin to the idea of an image—it does represent the image not the external object itself. Thus 'flies' does represent "Flying," not "Sitting." All terms refer, as all ideas have ideata; but not all terms refer to existing facts; as not all ideas are taken to represent their ideata.

> ... the conception of false judgment in the *Theaetetus* (is that of), some kind of 'misjudgment'—mistaking one thing for another. ... Hence the notion of 'thinking that one thing is another' or 'mistaking one thing for another' can be reviewed with a new meaning. The 'things' we interchange are not old memory images but eternally real objects of thought.[65]

This is much like the mis-taking of one's ideas of images for ideas of ideas, and this form of mis-judgment is clearly found in both Plato and Spinoza. When one takes a sense-perception or a term to refer to an idea of an image, one does not err; when one takes it to refer to an idea of an idea or an idea in the mind of God, error results. The error is not due to the term itself, because the term *does* refer to something—but something other than the idea in the mind of God or the idea of the external object itself. This mis-taking of images and ideas, of mis-representing the object of one's perceived ideas, is the cause of error and is, I believe, common to Plato and Spinoza.

Spinoza can account for error, even though all ideas are true, by a mis-match of an idea of an image with an idea of the interaction of the external object and the human body, an idea of an idea, or the idea of the external body itself. Cornford says that missing the intended mark is also a definition of ignorance for Plato. "Ignorance (ἄγνοια) is the swerving aside of the soul's impulse toward truth, and (as Socrates had taught) is always 'involuntary'—against the wish for the right end."[66] This improperly directed intention misses the goal and results in error. The cause may be the mis-matching of the term with its defined object or meaning, or the mis-taking of an image for an idea or thing itself.

There is an analogue in the accounts of intuition of Being, God, or Nature for Spinoza and at least the Form Being or Existence for Plato. There is a similarity between Plato's account of Collection and Division, and Spinoza's account of intuition and reason. Finally, there is a correlation between Spinoza's account of imagination and opinion and Plato's account of *phantasia*, perception and belief. Both identify the cause of error with this latter sort of "knowledge," and the causes of error—mis-matching of words and meanings, and of images and reality, are identical. Thus, one may note the coincidence of Plato's epistemology with that of Spinoza.

ARISTOTLE

It is erroneous to attempt to explain Spinoza's epistemology by appealing to Aristotle or Aristotelian logic. The Forms are not classes in the Aristotelian sense of the term. "... Plato, in the *Parmenides* and throughout the *Sophist* uses 'kind' (γένος) and 'Form' (εἶδος) indifferently. Both mean, not 'genus' or 'species' or 'class' but 'Form' or 'Nature.' No one of the Kinds is thought of as a class, either of entities or of predicates."[67] Plato's dialectic was not the symbolic, propositional science that Aristotle calls logic. Plato's dialectic is an ontological science—a "tracing out" of reality and the relations between "Natures" or "Forms." Far from being amenable to a divorce from ontology as occurs in modern logic, Plato's dialectic is intimately connected with metaphysics. Formal logic is not dialectic. "The beginning of Formal Logic is marked precisely by the introduction of symbols. These were, so far as we know, first used by Aristotle."[68]

> Plato does not use symbols or construct propositional forms. The factors he recognizes are these: (1) The immutable structure of Forms or Kinds, eternally combined or disjoined in the system of truth or reality (similar to Spinoza's Nature, attributes, infinite modes and, quite different from Plato, finite modes). (2) Our thoughts about these objects ... (Spinoza's

ideas of Nature, etc., ideas of ideas of images). (3) Statements, the vocal expression of thoughts and judgments, consisting of spoken names and verbs.[69]

Plato's dialectic is not concerned with propositional forms but with reality. The method of Collection and Division is a method for discovering the nature of reality. Similarly, Spinoza's method is a "tracing out" of reality and *its* relations. Spinoza's method is not amenable to symbols, propositional logic, or symbolic logic. It is a method which is a mirror of reality and an investigation of reality itself, not simply a method of dealing with language or mathematics. The following is as true of Spinoza as of Plato: "All through, Plato is speaking of the real nature of the Kinds mentioned and their actual relation in the structure of reality, not about symbolic patterns under which statements can be classified."[70] As Plato's dialectic is not Aristotle's logic, and as Plato's "Forms" or "Natures" are not Aristotle's "classes," similarly, Spinoza's method is not Aristotelian logic, and his realities are not those of Aristotelian logic.[71] And, furthermore, it must be stated that no satisfactory account of Spinoza's metaphysics or method can be given in terms of Aristotelian ontology or logic.

The "Forms" as "Beings" or "Natures" bear a close relation to Spinoza's God, or Nature, or Substance and the attributes. Indeed, the relations between the Forms seem to parallel the relations between Nature, its attributes and infinite modes. As I argued above for the similarity of dialectic with the "downward path" of intuition and reason, I have argued that the metaphysical relation of *Ethics* Part I is similar to the "mingling" and "pervading" of Forms in the *Sophist*. The relation between Forms and particulars is one which is not reflexive, as is the relations amongst Forms themselves. Particulars, or individuals, or images, "partake" of Forms or participate in Forms or are copies of Forms but not *vice versa*. Similarly, finite modes "follow from" infinite modes, which follow from attributes, but not *vice versa*. The relation between attributes is reflexive and, with only the exception of the term "absolutely infinite," the relation between Spinoza's Nature and the attributes is one of identity.

CONCLUSION

The close comparison of the metaphysics and epistemology of Spinoza with those of Plato, as found in his later dialogues, has indicated some striking analogies. To be sure, Spinoza was not simply a seventeenth century Platonist, but it does appear that his philosophy reverberates with Platonic themes. Of course, other philosophers prior to Spinoza carried

forth the doctrines and spirit of Plato, but it has been worthwhile to trace
some of Spinoza's theses to those of Plato. Some have argued that the
seventeenth century philosophers were inventing a new philosophy while
rejecting the prevailing philosophy of Aristotle. It is evident that, among
the rationalists, Descartes initiated the break with Aristotle, and surely
Spinoza and Leibniz continued that schism. I believe that one of the
effects of their "new philosophy" was a return to the mathematical
model of Plato for inspiration. It seems that one can come closer to
understanding some of Spinoza's writings by comparison with Plato.
Certainly, there are differences in their work; this is to be expected since
they were separated by about two thousand years. But surely there are
similarities, too, which are too evident to be summarily dismissed.
Whatever serves to illuminate the work of Spinoza, if only to add a
sparkle to the bright light shining through his lenses, should be valuable
for those of us who seek to understand the nature of Nature and man. It
is my hope that this work provides such a sparkle.

NOTES

[1] Cornford.
[2] It should be the case that the Platonistic interpretation of Spinoza's epistemology correlates with the Platonistic interpretation of Spinoza's metaphysics in Part I of this book.
[3] Cornford, pp. 167-168.
[4] Wolf, Letter 9, in *Correspondence*, p. 106.
[5] Wolf, "To Mr. John Hudde," 7 January 1666, Letter 34, in *Correspondence*, p. 218.
[6] Wolf, Letter 60, in *Correspondence*, p. 301.
[7] Wolf, Letter 10, in *Correspondence*, p. 109.
[8] Curley, "Experience," p. 52.
[9] Wild, p. 186, E2, Prop. 40, Schol. 2.
[10] Cornford, p. 184.
[11] Cornford, p. 262.
[12] Cornford, p. 267. Emphasis added.
[13] Wild, p. 186, E2, Prop. 40, Schol. 2.
[14] Wild, p. 187, E2, Prop. 40, Schol. 2. Emphasis added.
[15] Gebhardt, II, 303: "rerum singularium."
[16] Gebhardt, II, 303: "cognitione universali."
[17] Wild, p. 393, E5, Prop. 36, Schol.
[18] Curley, "Experience," p. 55.
[19] Curley, "Experience," p. 57. Emphasis added.
[20] Wild, pp. 392-393, E5, Prop. 36.
[21] Wild, pp. 95-96, E1, Axioms 1 and 5.
[22] Wolf, Letter 50, in *Correspondence*, pp. 269-270. Emphasis added; Gebhardt, IV, 239-240: "... respondeo, rem solummodo existentiae, non vero essentiae respectu unam, vel unicam dici: res enim sub numeris, nisi postquam ad commune genus redactae fuerunt, non concipimus. ... Quoniam vero Dei existentia ipsius sit essentia, deque ejus essentia universalem non possimus formare ideam, certum est, eum, qui Deum unum, vel unicum nuncupat, nullam de Deo veram habere ideam, vel improprie de eo loqui."
[23] Wild, p. 94, E1, Def. 4.

[24] Wild, pp. 107-108, E1, Prop. 14, Cor. 1; Gebhardt, II, 56: "Hinc clarrisimi sequitur 1°. Deum esse unicum, hoc est (per Defin. 6) in rerum natura non, nisi unam substantiam, dari, eamque absolute infinitam esse...."

[25] Wild, p. 102, E1, Prop. 10, Schol.; Gebhardt, II, 52: "... id enim est de natura substantiae, ut unumquodque ejus attributorum per se concipiatur; quandoquidem omnia, quae habet, attributa simul in ipsa semper fuerunt, nec unum ab alio produci potuit; sed unumquodque realitatem, sive esse substantiae exprimit. ... quam quod ens absolute infinitum necessario sit definiendum ... ens, quod constat infinitis attributis, quorum unumquodque aeternam, & infinitam certam essentiam exprimit."

[26] Cf. E. G. Boscherini, *Lexicon Spinozanum* (The Hague: Martinus Nijhoff, 1970), pp. 1070-1071: "Unicus -a-um."

[27] Brandom, p. 152.

[28] Wild, p. 186, E2, Prop. 20, Schol. 2.

[29] Brandom, p. 155.

[30] Wild, p. 186, E2, Prop. 40, Schol. 2.

[31] Curley, "Experience," p. 57.

[32] Brandom, p. 155.

[33] Wild, pp. 94-95, E1, Def. 6; Gebhardt, II, 45: "Per *Deum* intelligo ens absolute infinitum, hoc est, *substantiam* constantem infinitis attributis ...." Emphasis added.

[34] Wild, pp. 104-105, E1, Prop. 11. Another proof and Schol.; Gebhardt, II, 53-54: "Posse non existere impotentia est, & contra posse existere potentia est (*ut per se notum*). ... Nam, cum posse existere potentia sit, sequitur, quo plus realitatis alicujus rei naturae competit, eo plus virium a se habere, ut existat...."

[35] Cornford, p. 234. Emphasis added.

[36] Cornford, p. 39.

[37] Cornford, p. 40.

[38] *Ibid.*

[39] Wild, p. 167, E2, Prop. 17, Schol.

[40] Wild, p. 165, E2, Prop. 16, Cor. 2.

[41] Cornford, pp. 248, 323.

[42] Cornford, p. 199.

[43] Wild, p. 168, E2, Prop. 17, Schol.

[44] Cornford, p. 108.

[45] Cornford, p. 125.

[46] Cornford, p. 124; *Theaetetus* 193 b-c.

[47] Cf. Part II, pp. 100-102.

[48] C. T. Lewis and C. Short, *Harper's Latin Dictionary* (New York: American Book Company, 1907), p. 463.

[49] Cicero, *De Finibus Bonorum et Malorum*, trans. H. Rackham (Cambridge: Harvard University Press, 1914), p. 264.

[50] Cornford, p. 319.

[51] *Ibid.*

[52] *Ibid.*

[53] Cornford, p. 320.

[54] Cornford, p. 302.

[55] Cornford, p. 306.

[56] Wild, p. 186, E2, Prop. 40, Schol. 2. Interpolations added; Gebhardt, II, 122: "... quibusdam verbis rerum recordemur, & earum quasdam ideas formemus similes iis, per quas res imaginamur."

[57] Cornford, p. 307.

[58] Cornford, p. 311.

[59] Curley, *Spinoza*, p. 123.

[60] Mark has an excellent discussion of this in *Spinoza's Theory of Truth*, pp. 51-54.

[61] Cornford, p. 315.

[62] *Ibid.*

[63] *Ibid.*

[64] *Ibid.*

[65] Cornford, p. 317.

[66] Cornford, p. 179.

[67] Cornford, p. 276.

[68] Cornford, p. 263.

[69] Cornford, p. 265. Parenthetical remarks are added.

[70] Cornford, p. 265.

[71] Cornford, p. 268.

BIBLIOGRAPHY

Alexander, S. *Philosophical and Literary Pieces*. London: MacMillan & Co., 1939.

Allen, R. E. "Participation and Predication in Plato's Middle Dialogues." In *Plato: A Collection of Critical Essays*. Vol. I. Ed. G. Vlastos. Garden City, N.Y.: Anchor Books, 1971, pp. 167-83.

Aristotle. *Introduction to Aristotle*. Ed. R. McKeon. New York: Modern Library, 1947.

Balz, A. G. A. *Cartesian Studies*. New York: Columbia University Press, 1951.

Boscherini, E. G. *Lexicon Spinozanum*. The Hague. Martinus Nijhoff, 1970.

Bowne, L. *Blessed Spinoza*. New York: MacMillan & Co., 1932.

Brandom, Robert. "Adequacy and the Individuation of Ideas in Spinoza's Ethics." *Journal of the History of Philosophy*, 14 (1976), 147-62.

Brehier, E. *The History of Philosophy: The Seventeenth Century*. Trans. W. Baskin. Chicago: University of Chicago Press, 1966.

———. *Histoire de la Philosophie: Vol. II, Part I: Le XVII Siècle*. Paris: Presses Universitaires de France, 1968.

Cicero. *De Finibus Bonorum et Malorum*. Trans. H. Rackham. Cambridge: Harvard University Press, 1914.

Copleston, F. C. "Spinoza as Metaphysician." In *Spinoza: Essays in Interpretation*. Ed. M. Mandelbaum and E. Freeman. La Salle, Illinois: Open Court, 1975, pp. 215-34.

Cornford, F. M. *Plato's Theory of Knowledge*. New York: The Liberal Arts Press, 1957.

Curley, E. M. "Experience in Spinoza's Theory of Knowledge." In *Spinoza: A Collection of Critical Essays*. Ed. M. Grene. Garden City, N.Y.: Anchor Books, 1973, pp. 25-59.

———. "Reply to Williamson." *Australasian Journal of Philosophy*, 51 (1973), 162-64.

———. *Spinoza's Metaphysics: An Essay in Interpretation*. Cambridge: Harvard University Press, 1969.

De Dijn, Herman. "Historical Remarks on Spinoza's Theory of Definitions." In *Spinoza On Knowing, Being and Freedom*. Ed. J. G. van der Bend. Assen: Van Gorcum & Comp. B. V., 1974, pp. 41-50.

Descartes, R. *Œuvres Philosophique*. Ed. F. Alquie. Vols. II and III. Paris: Editions Garnier Freres, 1967 and 1973.

———. *Philosophical Works of Descartes*. Trans. E. S. Haldane and G. R. T. Ross. New York: Dover Publications, Inc., 1955. Vols. I and II.

Elwes, R. H. M. *Philosophy of Spinoza*. New York: Tudor Publishing Company, 1933.

Freudenthal, J. *Die Lebensgeschichte Spinoza's*. In *Quellenschriften, Urkunden und Nichtamtlichen Nachrichten*. Leipzig: 1899, pp. 160-64.

Gebhardt, Carl. "Spinoza und der Platonismus." *Chronicon Spinozanum* [The Hague], 1 (1921), 178-234.

Haserot, F. S. "Spinoza and the Status of Universals." *The Philosophical Review*, 59 (1950), 469-92.

———. "Spinoza's Definition of Attribute." *The Philosophical Review*, 62 (1953), 499-513.

Joachim, H. H. *A Study of the Ethics of Spinoza*. 1901; rpt. New York: Russell & Russell, 1964.

———. *Spinoza's Tractatus de Intellectus Emendatione*. Oxford: Clarendon Press, 1940.

Kessler, W. "A Note on Spinoza's Concept of Attribute." *Monist*, 55 (1971), 636-39.

Lewis, C. T., and C. Short. *Harper's Latin Dictionary*. New York: American Book Company, 1907.

Mark, Thomas C. *Spinoza's Theory of Truth*. New York: Columbia University Press, 1972.

———. "Truth and Adequacy in Spinozistic Idea." *Southwestern Journal of Philosophy*, 8 (1977), 11-34.

Marshant, J. R. V., and J. F. Charles. *Cassell's Latin Dictionary*. New York: Funk and Wagnalls, 1952.

Nelson, J. C. *Renaissance Theory of Love—The Context of Giordano Bruno's Ennoia Furori*. New York: Columbia University Press, 1958.

Plato. *Parmenides, Phaedo* and *Timaeus*. In *The Collected Dialogues of Plato*. Ed. E. Hamilton and H. Cairns. New York: Pantheon Books, 1964.

Radner, Daisie. "Spinoza's Theory of Ideas." *The Philosophical Review*, 80 (1971), 338-59.

Rice, L. C. "Methodology and Modality in the First Part of Spinoza's *Ethics*." In *Spinoza On Knowing, Being and Freedom*. Ed. J. G. van der Bend. Assen: Van Gorcum Comp. B.V., 1974, pp. 144-55.

——. "Spinoza on Individuation." *Monist*, 55 (1971), 640-59.

Saw, R. L. "The Task of Metaphysics for Spinoza." In *Spinoza: Essays in Interpretation*. Ed. M. Mandelbaum and E. Freeman. La Salle: Open Court, 1975, pp. 235-43.

Souter, A. *A Glossary of Later Latin to 600 A.D.* Oxford: The Clarendon Press, 1964.

Spinoza, B. *The Correspondence of Spinoza*. Trans. A. Wolf. New York: Lincoln MacVeagh, Dial Press, 1927.

——. *Earlier Philosophical Writings*. Trans. F. A. Hayes. Indianapolis: Library of Liberal Arts, Bobbs-Merrill Co., Inc., 1963.

——. *Spinoza Opera*. Ed. C. Gebhardt. 1925; rpt. Heidelberg: Carl Winter, 1972. Vols. II and IV.

——. *Ethic*, Part I and II, transl. W. H. White, in *Spinoza: Selections*. Ed. J. Wild. Copyright 1930, 1958 New York: Charles Scribner's Sons.

Thomas, Thomas. *Dictionarium Linguae Latinae et Anglicanae, 1587*. Menston, England: The Scolar Press, 1972.

Vlastos, G. *Platonic Studies*. Princeton University Press, 1973.

Wolf, A. *Spinoza's Short Treatise on God, Man, and His Well-Being*. London: Adam & Charles Black, 1910.

Wolfson, A. *Spinoza—A Life of Reason*. New York: Philosophical Library, 1969.

Wolfson, H. A. *The Philosophy of Spinoza*. Cambridge: Harvard University Press, 1934. Vols. I and II.

ACKNOWLEDGEMENTS

S. Alexander, *Philosophical and Literary Pieces*, Copyright 1939, MacMillan & Co., London, England. Reprinted with permission of MacMillan & Co.

R. E. Allen, "Participation and Predication in Plato's Middle Dialogues," in *Plato: A Collection of Critical Essays*, edited by G. Vlastos, Copyright 1971, University of Notre Dame Press. Originally appeared in *The Philosophical Review*, 69 (1960). Reprinted with the permission of University of Notre Dame Press, *The Philosophical Review* and the author.

R. Brandom, "Adequacy and the Individuation of Ideas in Spinoza's Ethics," *Journal of the History of Philosophy*, 14 (1976). Reprinted with permission of *Journal of the History of Philosophy*.

E. Brehier, *The History of Philosophy*, Volume IV, 17th Century, transl. W. Baskin, Copyright 1966, The University of Chicago Press. Reprinted with the permission of the University of Chicago Press.

F. C. Copleston, "Spinoza as Metaphysician" in *Spinoza: Essays in Interpretation*, edited by M. Mandelbaum and E. Freeman, Copyright 1975, The Open Court Publishing Co. Reprinted by permission of The Open Court Publishing Co., LaSalle, Illinois.

F. M. Cornford, *Plato's Theory of Knowledge*, Copyright 1957. Reprinted with permission of Humanities Press Inc., Atlantic Highlands, N.J. 07716 and with permission of Routledge & Kegan Paul Ltd., London, England.

E. M. Curley, "Experience in Spinoza's Theory of Knowledge" in *Spinoza: A Collection of Critical Essays*, edited by M. Grene, Copyright 1973, University of Notre Dame Press. Reprinted with the permission of University of Notre Dame Press.

H. De Dijn, "Historical Remarks on Spinoza's Theory of Definition" in *Spinoza on Knowing, Being and Freedom*, edited by J. G. van der Bend, Copyright 1974, Van Gorcum & Co. B. V. Reprinted by permission of Van Gorcum & Co. B. V., Assen, The Netherlands.

R. Descartes, *Philosophical Works of Descartes*, transl. E. S. Haldane and G. R. T. Ross, Copyright 1955, Cambridge University Press. Reprinted with the permission of Cambridge University Press.

H. H. Joachim, *Spinoza's Tractatus de Intellectus Emendatione*, Copyright 1940, Oxford University Press. Reprinted with permission of Oxford University Press.

T. C. Mark, *Spinoza's Theory of Truth*, Copyright 1972, Columbia University Press. Reprinted with the permission of Columbia University Press.

D. Radner, "Spinoza's Theory of Ideas" in *The Philosophical Review*, 80 (1971). Reprinted with the permission of *The Philosophical Review* and the author.

L. C. Rice, "Methodology and Modality in the First Part of Spinoza's Ethics" in *Spinoza on Knowing, Being and Freedom*, edited by J. G. van der Bend, Copyright 1974, Van Gorcum and Co. B. V. Reprinted with permission of Van Gorcum and Co. B. V., Assen, The Netherlands.

R. L. Saw, "The Task of Metaphysics for Spinoza" in *Spinoza: Essays in Interpretation*, edited by M. Mandelbaum and E. Freeman, Copyright 1975, The Open Court Publishing Co. Reprinted by permission of The Open Court Publishing Co., LaSalle, Illinois.

A. Souter, *A Glossary of Later Latin to 600 A.D.*, Copyright 1964, Oxford University Press. Reprinted with permission of Oxford University Press.

B. Spinoza, *Ethic*, Part I and II, transl. W. H. White, in *Spinoza: Selections*, edited by John Wild. Copyright 1930, 1958 Charles Scribner's Sons. Reprinted with the permission of Charles Scribner's Sons.

B. Spinoza, *Spinoza Opera*, edited C. Gebhardt. Copyright 1925, reprinted 1972, Carl Winter Universitätsverlag. Reprinted with permission of Carl Winter Universitätsverlag.

B. Spinoza, *Spinoza's Short Treatise on God, Man, and His Well-Being*, transl. A. Wolf. Copyright 1910, Adam and Charles Black Publishers, London, England. Reprinted with permission of Adam and Charles Black Publishers.

B. Spinoza, *The Correspondence of Spinoza*, transl. A. Wolf. Copyright 1927, Lincoln MacVeagh, Dial Press. Reprinted with the permission of Dial Press.

T. Thomas, *Dictionarium Linguae Latinae et Anglicanae, 1587*, Copyright 1972, The Scolar Press, London, England. Reprinted with the permission of The Scolar Press.

G. Vlastos, *Platonic Studies*, Copyright 1973 by Gregory Vlastos. Published by Princeton University Press. Reprinted with the permission of Princeton University Press.

INDEX

Activity, 21, 27-32, 36, 41, 44, 46, 50-61, 65, 67-69, 71, 72, 78, 80, 88, 89, 92, 101; see also Power, Existence

Affection, 19, 53, 56, 72, 90, 92, 93, 95, 97-100, 104, 106, 107, 111-113, 117, 121, 122, 140; see also Modes

Affirmation, 58, 59, 88, 91, 109, 142

Alexander, S., 12n

Allen, R. E., 8, 29-31, 36, 74, 78, 87n

Anselm, 24

Aristotle, 1-3, 9, 10, 11n, 19-21, 25, 32-36, 77, 78, 89, 101, 102, 130, 146-148

Assent, 64, 109

Atomists, 10

Attributes, 2-7, 11, 14, 18-22, 24-26, 47, 50-56, 61-69, 71, 72, 76, 114-118, 120, 123, 125, 131-138, 147; see also Extension, Thought

Balz, A. G. A., 12n

Being (Form of), 30-32, 34, 55, 130, 131, 146

Belief, 59, 138, 146

Body, 6, 89-93, 95-99, 101, 104, 106, 110-113, 117, 120, 121, 138, 141, 143, 145; see also Modes, Finite

Boscherini, E. G., 149n

Bowne, L., 9, 13n

Boxel, H., 10

Bradley, F. H., 8

Brandom, R., 99, 100, 105, 110, 119, 122, 124, 125, 136, 137, 149n

Brehier, E., 2, 3, 11n, 12n, 64, 65, 86n

Brown, M. H., ix

Cause, Adequate, 15, 16, 61, 119, 120

Causation, 6, 16, 17, 23, 45, 52, 56, 59, 65, 68, 72, 98, 110, 121, 131

Causation, Self, 16, 21, 22, 27; see also Freedom

Cause, Proximate, 15, 16, 22, 23, 42, 44, 47, 48, 51, 53-55, 59, 103, 104, 110, 120, 133, 134

Cause, Self-Caused, 15-17, 19, 23, 24, 28, 37, 38, 50, 51, 53, 103, 117, 119

Cause, Sufficient, 15, 22, 23

Charles, J. F., 82n

Cicero, 142, 149n

Coincidentia Oppositorum, 24

Collection, 30, 31, 33-35, 66-69, 71, 73, 76, 80, 125, 131-133, 135-138, 146, 147

Conatus, 88, 116, 120, 122

Copleston, F. C., 5, 11n, 12n

Cornford, F. M., 30-36, 65-68, 83n, 86n, 130, 132, 135, 139, 141, 145, 146, 148n, 149n, 150n

Cratylus, 131

Curley, E. M., ix, 1, 2, 5, 8, 9, 11n, 12n, 13n, 27, 29, 32, 61, 62, 76, 78, 81n, 83n, 86n, 87n, 123, 124, 132-137, 148n, 149n

Cusa, Nicholas of, 18, 24

DeDijn, H., 13n

Deduction, 14-17, 63, 79, 89, 103, 104, 107, 110-113, 115-118, 120, 122, 132

Definition, 6, 7, 14-18, 20-22, 24, 30, 46, 48, 51, 52, 54, 55, 58, 59, 62, 63, 77, 78, 88, 96, 101, 103, 104, 107, 117, 119, 123, 130-134, 140, 143

Demiurge, 36, 49, 64, 69, 70, 79

Democritus, 10

Denial, 59, 88, 91, 109, 142

Descartes, R., 1, 4-7, 9, 10, 12n, 16, 25, 28, 39, 40, 43, 74, 83n, 84n, 89-92, 94, 95, 102, 148

DeVries, S., 14, 63

Dialectic, 30, 32, 33, 36, 73, 132, 133, 138, 146, 147

Dialogues of Love, 3-5

Dissent, 109

Division, 30, 31, 33-35, 66-74, 76, 79, 80, 125, 131-133, 137, 138, 146, 147

Ebreo, Leone, 3-5; see also Dialogues of Love

Elwes, R. H. M., 19, 82n

Emotions, 44

Epicurus, 10

Error, 8, 25, 88, 93, 94, 99, 106-110, 112-117, 132, 140-146; see also Falsity

Essence, 15-18, 21-24, 26, 28, 29, 40-63, 66, 69, 71-74, 76, 78, 79, 96-98, 101-104, 112, 123, 124, 131, 143

Essence, Formal, 14, 19, 30, 49, 57, 72, 92, 94, 95, 97, 100, 101, 103, 105-107, 109, 118, 123, 133-135, 137, 140, 141

Essence, Objective, 49, 60, 88, 90, 94, 95, 100, 101, 105-107, 109, 118

Eternity, 4, 10, 17, 20, 29, 33, 40, 42-44, 46-56, 60, 63, 67, 68, 71-74, 76-79, 80, 135; see also Nature

Evil, 70